Jazz
The Complete Story

This is a **FLAME TREE** book
First published in 2007

Publisher and Creative Director: Nick Wells
Project Editor: Sara Robson
Picture Research: Melinda Révész
Art Director: Mike Spender
Digital Design and Production: Chris Herbert
Layout Design: Ray Barnet

Special thanks to: Chelsea Edwards, Victoria Garrard, Victoria Lyle, Geoffrey Meadon and Claire Walker

07 09 11 10 08

1 3 5 7 9 10 8 6 4 2

Created and produced by
FLAME TREE PUBLISHING
Crabtree Hall, Crabtree Lane
Fulham, London SW6 6TY
United Kingdom

www.flametreepublishing.com

Flame Tree Publishing is part of the Foundry Creative Media Co. Ltd.

ISBN 978-1-84451-566-0

Printed in China

Jazz

The Complete Story

Bob Allen, Lloyd Bradley, Keith Briggs, Leila Cobo, Cliff Douse, James Hale,
Todd Jenkins, Howard Mandel, Kenny Mathieson, John McDonough, Bill Milkowski,
Garry Mulholland, Steve Nallon, Douglas J. Noble, Ed Potton, William Schafer

General Editor: Julia Rolf

Foreword by John Scofield

**FLAME TREE
PUBLISHING**

CONTENTS

INFLUENCES OF JAZZ

HOW TO USE THIS BOOK

The reader is encouraged to use this book in a variety of ways, each of which caters for a range of interests, knowledge and uses.

- The book is organized into three main **categories**: **The Jazz Story**; **Styles of Jazz**; and **Influences of Jazz**.

- Each **category** is divided into the main **eras** of jazz or **styles** of music to enable the reader to quickly locate specific areas of interest. For **The Jazz Story** this list includes The Thirties, The Eighties etc., and for **Styles of Jazz** this list includes Chicago Jazz and Hard Bop.

- Each **era** or **style** has a leading page that introduces the reader to the section. The remaining pages discuss the context within which it was created, the key artists and the development of the style.

- Each **entry** is introduced at the head of the page to enable ease of reference to specific areas of interest.

- Quotes from artists, producers and commentators are used throughout to enable the reader to get to grips with the feel and passion of the music.

- Lists of key artists and key tracks relating to each era or style of music are used throughout to give a flavour of the artists and tracks that defined the music.

- Detailed picture credits give further information on the artists included.

Key Artist: Clarence Williams

Clarence Williams was born in 1898 in Plaquemine, Louisiana, migrating to New Orleans in his teens to play piano and begin a long career as a composer, bandleader and musical promoter. He was manager of two early jazz venues – the Big 25 Club and Pete Lala's Café – hiring the best musicians in the city.

He opened a publishing business with Armand J. Piron, the leader of a popular dance band operating at the Lake Pontchartrain resorts. In 1919 he partnered with the savvy publisher-writer Spencer Williams. They gathered, annotated and copyrighted musical numbers that were floating in the air around the dance halls, bars and brothels of the city publishing such enduring mega-hits as 'Home Of My Jelly Roll' and 'Royal Garden Blues'.

'He was very important in teaching and teaching and working in our artists. He could somehow manage to get the best out of them.'

Frank Walker

Williams left for Chicago around 1917, pursuing publishing and becoming an agent for recording companies. In the 1920s he shifted to New York City as it became a hub for hot music. He assembled bands of friends from New Orleans for Okeh and Columbia Records, including the seminal Blue Five group, which united a young Louis Armstrong and Sidney Bechet. Among important songs he recorded were 'Cakewalking Babies From Home', 'Papa De Da Da' and 'Texas Moaner Blues'.

In his long career, Williams' gift for spotting fresh talent and potential musical hits was renowned. Among the first-rate musicians he assembled were trumpeters such as King Oliver, Jabbo Smith, Henry Allen, Ed Allen, Bubber Miley and Louis Metcalf. He recorded clarinettists such as Buster Bailey, Arville Harris and Albert Nicholas and trombonists Charlie Irvis and Ed Cuffee. He was the session piano player on many recordings but he was most comfortable as a musical director for Okeh Records, and an arranger and composer of jazz and pop tunes. With a fine ear for both novelty jazz material and songs that bridged the gap between pure jazz and pure pop, Williams was an important transmitter of New Orleans traditions to the East Coast musicians he met. In the 1930s, during the squeeze of the Depression, Williams closed his publishing office, turned to radio promotion and went on to run an antique store in Harlem. He died in 1965, having sold his vast catalogue to Decca Records in 1943.

Pianist, composer, arranger and musical director Clarence Williams (back left) with one of his bands

Entry title

Introduction to the entry

Era or style
of music

42

THE TEENS

Key Artist: Clarence Williams

Clarence Williams was born in 1898 in Plaquemine, Louisiana, migrating to New Orleans in the teens to play piano and begin a long career as a composer, bandleader and musical promoter. He was manager of two early jazz venues – the Big 25 Club and Pete Lala's Café – hiring the best musicians in the city.

He opened a publishing business with Armand J. Piron, the leader of a popular dance band operating at the Lake Pontchartrain resorts. In 1919 he partnered with the savvy publisher-writer Spencer Williams. They gathered, annotated and copyrighted musical numbers that were floating in the air around the dance halls, bars and brothels of the city, publishing such enduring mega-hits as 'None Of My Jelly Roll' and 'Royal Garden Blues'.

'He was very important in coaching and teaching and working on our artists. He could somehow manage to get the best out of them....'

Frank Walker

Quotes
from artists,
producers and
commentators

Williams left for Chicago around 1917, pursuing publishing and becoming an agent for recording companies. In the 1920s he shifted to New York City as it became a hub for hot music. He assembled bands of friends from New Orleans for OKeh and Columbia Records, including the seminal Blue Five group, which united a young Louis Armstrong and Sidney Bechet. Among important songs he recorded were 'Cakewalking Babies From Home', 'Papa De Da Da' and 'Texas Moaner Blues'.

Information
about the music

In his long career, Williams' gift for spotting fresh talent and potential musical hits was renowned. Among the first-rate musicians he assembled were trumpeters such as King Oliver, Jabbo Smith, Henry Allen, Ed Allen, Bubber Miley and Louis Metcalf. He recorded clarinettists such as Buster Bailey, Arville Harris and Albert Nicholas and trombonists Charlie Irvis and Ed Cuffee. He was the session piano player on many recordings but he was most comfortable as a musical director for OKeh Records, and an arranger and composer of jazz and pop tunes. With a fine ear for both novelty jazz material and songs that bridged the gap between pure jazz and pure pop, Williams was an important transmitter of New Orleans traditions to the East Coast musicians he met. In the 1930s, during the squeeze of the Depression, Williams closed his publishing office, turned to radio promotion and went on to run an antique store in Harlem. He died in 1965, having sold his vast catalogue to Decca Records in 1943.

Pianist, composer, arranger and musical director Clarence Williams (back left) with one of his bands.

Picture caption

FOREWORD

I think everyone agrees Jazz is one of the most influential, overriding and ultimate musical styles of the twentieth century. Without it, popular music as we know it would not exist. I've always been happy to be part of this hugely important movement. Jazz makes a recognizable and significant contribution to cultures everywhere. I see this in all aspects of my life. Music transcends languages and local culture, ties us together and maintains a powerful thread between the past, present and the future. Who among us does not have a soundtrack to his or her own life?

Believe it or not, I decided to become a professional guitar player before I had ever held one in my hands. After a brief period of begging, my parents (not understanding my sense of true destiny) *rented* me a cheap guitar and I began to practice. I focused on learning to play with a joyful, albeit dogged, enthusiasm that has not waned to this day.

The first music I was interested in was more in the folk tradition. Peter, Paul & Mary and the Kingston Trio were frontline in the American consciousness of the early 1960s. We saw folk music on TV, heard it on the radio and sheet music was readily available. Concurrently, America was experiencing what we called the British Invasion. From my 12-year-old perspective, the Beatles and Stones seemed to be the coolest people on the planet. They played songs by Muddy Waters, Howlin' Wolf and Chuck Berry, so I checked *them* out too.

Folk music and rock'n'roll both forged a link to the blues. Liner notes and word-of-mouth/ common knowledge led me from blues to jazz. More importantly, jazz was the music that truly grabbed me, my first love. I can't recall which came first – seeing Barney Kessel on television or hearing a Django Reinhardt record my father bought for me – but I was quickly and permanently swayed in a jazz direction.

My experience in this field is something that I never take for granted. I'm so fortunate that I get to do this, so fortunate that it worked out. Music has given me an international existence that few ever know. I'm continually surprised that I am able to make a decent living doing what I love to do. The travel, the accolades, the personal validation are all benefits, but those perks pale next to the thrill of playing with other musicians – learning from them and sharing music with them. I still pinch myself when I think of the opportunities I've had to play with so many of my idols. But it's not only the older ones; I've been equally inspired by people half my age.

That being said, my one greatest joy is simply the MUSIC itself. Listening and playing every day of my life, I keep going back to much of the same music that originally inspired me. I still discover performances I have never heard and artists new to me that continue to surface from early eras. Great new music shows up on the scene today too. As much as I've listened to any older piece, if I hear it again after several years away, I usually get something new from it. My own musical development gives me a deeper sense and appreciation of what I hear. Music is never finite!

What you'll find in this book is a history, a celebration of what I love. I am inspired, motivated and intrigued by jazz music every day – and am a better person for it.

John Scofield, 2007

THE JAZZ STORY

Jazz music has travelled a long way over the last 100 years, from its humble beginnings in the shady establishments of New Orleans' notorious Storyville district to the popular dance crazes of the Swing Era, the slick, urban sounds of the 1950s, the explorations and fusions of the 1960s and 1970s, to eventually reach the more elevated position that it enjoys today as a sophisticated, virtuosic – even intellectual – music form.

Along this journey, jazz has seen its musical centre shift across America and even branch out to other continents, all the while absorbing and exerting musical influences to become an integral part of the modern world's ever-changing musical climate.

Throughout its history, the jazz scene has boasted some of the most talented musicans, gifted arrangers, inspirational bandleaders and eccentric characters of the music world, and the profiles of hundreds of these exceptional artists are brought together here to present a fascinating and colourful insight into this most innovative of musical styles.

In this section of the book, we follow the course of jazz music decade by decade, focusing first on the social, historical and cultural context of the era and then discussing in detail the developments in jazz music, and how these were affected by the events and protagonists of the time. Detailed overviews of the key jazz performers of the decade are then followed by an A–Z section of other important artists, composers, producers and other figures prominent in jazz music at the time.

On each text page, an additional information feature provides an evocative quotation, looks at particular tracks that defined their era.

As the centre of jazz music shifted to New York by the end of the 1920s, Duke Ellington's band was leading the way at Harlem's infamous Cotton Club.

Introduction

Like a great river that runs endlessly, forming numerous tributary streams as it flows, jazz continues to evolve over time. And no matter how far the River Jazz may flow from its source – whether through stylistic evolution or technological innovation – the essential spirit of the music remains intact.

Granted, the more academic and esoteric extrapolations of avant-gardists such as Anthony Braxton and Cecil Taylor may, on the surface of it, appear to be light years away from the early innovations and earthy expressions of Louis Armstrong and Sidney Bechet. In essence, however, both widely divergent approaches are imbued with that spirit of spontaneous creativity, risk-taking and discovery that is at the core of all jazz. Regardless of what instruments are being used; whether the general tone is harshly electric or purely acoustic; and whether the form is defined by straight 4/4 time, or more intricate rhythmic variations, or no time at all; jazz is, in all of its manifestations, fundamentally about improvising and the art of playing without premeditation – or, in the parlance of Louis Armstrong, 'taking a scale and making it wail'.

Cool jazz or fusion, swing-era big bands or bebop quintets, Dixieland or the avant-garde: the music thrives on a collective spirit of interplay and the daring chances taken by the participants individually or as a group, and strictly in the moment. Jazz is, as the noted critic Whitney Balliett once called it, 'the sound of surprise'. The phrase could be applied as accurately to Armstrong's 1928 duets with Earl Hines as it could to Charlie Parker's pyrotechnic excursions in 1945 with kindred spirit Dizzy Gillespie; or to Eric Dolphy's 1960 opus *Out There*, the Art Ensemble of Chicago's 1973 classic *Fanfare For The Warriors*, alto-saxophonist Steve Coleman's radical M-Base experiments of the mid-1980s, or trumpeter Dave Douglas's compelling, Middle Eastern-flavored offering from 2001, *Witness*.

> ### Popular Melody
> Louis Armstrong – 'West End Blues' (1928)

Jazz has been called the quintessential American music, the ultimate in rugged individualism and the creative process incarnate. In its infancy, it was dismissed by one pointed newspaper editorial as 'a manifestation of a low streak in man's taste that has not yet come out in civilization's wash'.

Louis Armstrong, one of the twentieth century's most famous jazz artists, was one of the genre's earliest innovators.

INTRODUCTION

In more modern times, it has been hailed as one of the noblest forms of human expression, with a deep and direct connection to the soul. It is about individuals filling space with invention while negotiating their agendas within a group; an improvisational art that thrives on freedom of expression yet demands selfless collaboration.

New Orleans was the nexus for its genesis. A cultural melting pot where people of all nationalities lived side by side, New Orleans was one of the richest, most cosmopolitan cities in America during the early 1800s. It was in this integrated society that strains of melodies from the West Indies began to mingle with traces of African polyrhythms, carried over by slaves and European classical music played by Creoles (the free and prosperous light-skinned descendants of French and Spanish colonists and their African wives and mistresses). Many of these Creole musicians, who identified with their European and not their African ancestors, were classically trained. Added to the mix were minstrel tunes and plantation songs, work songs and spirituals, along with the constant sound of brass bands parading around the Crescent City at weddings, funerals and picnics, as well as during the six- to eight-week Carnival season leading up to Mardi Gras. This incredible hodgepodge of sound would eventually lead to ragtime at the outset of the 1890s.

In 1896, a landmark decision by the US Supreme Court would change the face of New Orleans music forever. This 'separate but equal' ruling institutionalized segregation between the races, effectively forcing classically trained Creole musicians into the black community, where they merged their technical fluency on various instruments with the blues-inflected music of black bands. Together, they would create a new music that began to emerge at the dawn of the new twentieth century. Something beyond ragtime or blues, it was initially called 'hot music', to convey its fiery nature, and later dubbed 'jass' (a name that came from the jasmine perfume favoured by prostitutes in Storyville). By 1907, around the time that the pianist-composer Jelly Roll Morton began to blend ragtime with minstrel songs, the blues and habanera dance rhythms from the Caribbean (which he described as the all-important 'Spanish tinge'), the term had eventually morphed into 'Jazz' and it has remained there to this day.

> **Popular Melody**
> Count Basie – 'One O'Clock Jump' (1937)

It was in New Orleans that Creole and African musical influences combined to create the musical style we know as jazz. This scene shows Canal Street in 1924, when New Orleans jazz was well under way.

While the facts of where jazz came from and how it evolved over time are indisputable, the question of where jazz is going – or, indeed, should be headed – is a topic of heated debate. On the one hand, staunch traditionalists believe jazz to be a precious, homemade American art music that ought to be preserved and disseminated intact. This 'curator' notion has led to the formation of various repertoire bands in the United States, chief among them the Lincoln Center Jazz Orchestra in New York (for which the trumpeter Wynton Marsalis serves as artistic director). Since its formation in 1988, the LCJO has taken on the task of presenting the works of jazz masters such as Duke Ellington, Sidney Bechet, Jelly Roll Morton, Thelonious Monk and others to largely subscription audiences at the prestigious Alice Tully Hall in the Lincoln Center complex.

Others maintain that the jazz tradition is one of innovation itself, and that the music must adapt to new times in order to survive. Indeed, many movements that came along throughout the course of jazz history were direct reactions to some previous, prevailing movement: as bebop was to swing, as hard bop was to the cool school, as the avant-garde movement was to mainstream jazz, and so on. Rather than supplanting a previous style, each new movement is an extension, that builds on the past while retaining some inherent qualities of previous styles. So, in Dizzy Gillespie's pyrotechnic trumpet work at the height of the bebop era in the late 1940s we can still hear something of Louis Armstrong; in Cecil Taylor's turbulent piano work we can still hear traces of his heroes Duke Ellington, Bud Powell and Fats Waller; in revolutionary, alto saxophonists such as Ornette Coleman and Eric Dolphy we can hear a direct connection to Charlie Parker.

Popular Melody

Roy Eldridge – 'Heckler's Hop' (1937)

Through the miracle of technology, we are now hearing something of the past masters (quite literally) in new hybrid forms such as hip hop jazz and smooth jazz. Countless beats from early 1960s Blue Note and Prestige soul-jazz recordings have been digitally sampled and looped to create the foundation for rhythm tracks on modern-day, cutting-edge recordings. The smooth jazz saxophone star Kenny G went one step further by brazenly 'dueting' with Louis Armstrong (via sampling) on 'What A Wonderful World', from his 1999 CD, *Classics In The Key Of G*.

Whether jazz remains an exclusive or inclusive art form, there is no denying the impact of other cultures on this quintessentially American music as it reaches ever outward. From its earliest manifestations at the turn of the twentieth century in the cultural gumbo of New Orleans, to the

---

After experimenting with the 'jungle sound', involving the heavily muted trumpet of Bubber Miley, the Duke Ellington Orchestra found nationwide fame and became an inspiration for generations of future jazz musicians.

Afro-Cuban jazz collaborations of Dizzy Gillespie and Machito in the 1940s, to the groundbreaking cross-pollination efforts of Stan Getz in the early 1960s with *Jazz Samba* and *Getz/Gilberto*, to the incorporation of Eastern rhythms and scales during the 1970s by fusion groups such as the Mahavishnu Orchestra and Weather Report, jazz has a history of embracing other cultural expressions.

Today, numerous jazz artists (such as trumpeter Roy Hargrove, alto saxophonist Steve Coleman and soprano saxophonist Jane Bunnett, among others) have travelled to Havana to soak up and document the authentic Afro-Cuban vibe in their music. Others, such as Panamanian pianist Danilo Pérez, Argentine pianist-composer-arranger Guillermo Klein, Czech bassist George Mraz, Cameroonian bassist Richard Bona, Norwegian alto saxophonist Jan Garbarek, Lithuanian pianist Vyacheslav Ganelin, Cuban piano sensation Gonzalo Rubalcaba, Chinese pianist/composer Jon Jang, Indian alto saxophonist Rudresh Mahanthappa, Pakistani guitarist Fareed Haque, Chinese baritone saxophonist Fred Ho, Vietnamese guitarist Nguyên Lê, Swedish keyboard player Esbjörn Svensson, Swiss-Dutch vocalist Susanne Abbuehl, Japanese pianist/composer/arranger and big band leader Toshiko Akiyoshi, Indian percussionist Zakir Hussain, Norwegian keyboard player Bugge Wesseltoft, Puerto Rican saxophonist David Sanchez, Brazilian percussionist Airto Moreira, Australian bassist Nicki Parrott, Irish guitarist David O'Rourke and Indian percussionist Trilok Gurtu (the list goes on and on) have mined the richness of their own cultural heritages to come up with other new and exciting hybrid forms of jazz. In the process, all have advanced the cause of jazz, taking the essence of the music to a new place through their bold experimentation and honest expression.

Popular Melody

Charlie Parker – 'Koko' (1945)

This living drama continues to unfold. Every trumpeter today, 100 years after the birth of jazz, still carries a little piece of Buddy Bolden, or King Oliver, or Louis Armstrong with him; every alto sax player a bit of Bird, every pianist something of Jelly Roll, every drummer a touch of Baby Dodds and so it goes on. Like Olympians carrying the eternal flame across the ages, they represent the past while charging full steam ahead into the future. In his own time and in his own way, each has made a unique contribution. This is the nature of jazz – continually flowing and changing, like the never-ending river.

Two of the greatest innovators in jazz, Charlie Parker (centre) and Miles Davis (right), together with bass player Tommy Potter. Parker and Davis were instrumental in bringing jazz forward to a new era in the 1940s.

The Roots

The first two decades of the twentieth century saw the beginning of America's modernization and rise as a global superpower. The gradual developments in communications and travel opened up the continent and broadened people's horizons.

Technological advances also led to the possibilities of mass-production, and items that had once been considered top-of-the-range luxuries, such as phonographs and motor cars, became popular middle-class possessions. As recording techniques began to improve, the first jazz records were issued and this burgeoning new music began to spread.

Although slavery had been abolished, Jim Crow segregation laws meant that African-Americans were often forced to live in poorer conditions than their white countrymen, and there was still a long way to go before racial equality would be achieved. A major influx of European immigrants around this time (from, in particular, Italy, Germany, Scandinavia and Eastern European countries) introduced new elements of language, music and cuisine, which influenced mainstream American culture and added variety.

Key Artists

Kid Ory
Clarence Williams

In Europe, the horrors of the First World War formed the focus of the 1910s. President Woodrow Wilson sent US troops to Europe during the last eighteen months of the war, and the fresh energy of the American soldiers helped to lead the Allied Powers to victory in 1918.

The Mississippi riverboat SS Capitol, *where jazz musicians of the 1910s and 1920s were able to ply their trade.*

Ragtime and the Blues Join Forces

'Jazz started in New Orleans,' Jelly Roll Morton (c. 1890–1941) opined solemnly in his monumental 1938 oral autobiography for the Library of Congress. Jazz also started in many other places across America – a new wave of musical sound, melded from turn-of-the-century African-American rivulets of song in the ragtime and the blues styles, reached middle America by the teens of the twentieth century. But in New Orleans, the music was nurtured by a vibrant culture of many nationalities and ethnic groups.

Ragtime was a jubilant, rhythmically propulsive music in syncopated march time, while the blues was a slow, emotionally forceful expression of personal sorrow. Forged together, these gifts from the African-American soul created a new music that rapidly circled the globe and became a primary expression of the modern American spirit. The world entered a new age, dancing and singing to the sounds of jazz.

[New Orleans] was just 'bout the most musical town in the country.'

Zutty Singleton

Ragtime gathered impetus in the American Midwest and the deepest blues emerged from the hot South. By 1918, the emerging new music had been named 'jass' (a slang term for sex). It fused the energy of ragtime with the depth of the blues. The new music emerged from differing sources. Ragtime spread as a piano music; affordable, mass-produced pianos had become the latest badge of middle-class prosperity and gentility, and the newly developed player pianos could reproduce ragtime's three-minute syncopated sonatas with eerie perfection. The blues were pronounced on the street by itinerant guitarists and harmonica players.

A Missouri pioneer and entrepreneur named John Stark heard black pianists playing their own works and decided to use his small music-publishing firm to proselytize America with their enticing, melodic music. In 1899, he published a piece by Scott Joplin (1868–1917), an up-and-coming young ragtime pianist who arrived in Missouri by way of Texas and Arkansas. It was named after a rough and ready Sedalia bar, the Maple Leaf Club. Joplin's 'Maple Leaf Rag' was a nationwide sensation, selling upwards of a million copies of Stark's sheet-music score. It was played everywhere by bands like those of John Philip Sousa and Arthur Pryor. Vaudevillians such as clarinettist-bandleader Wilbur Sweatman turned classic ragtime into popular music, as in his 'Down Home Rag' (1916). Ragtime was the reveille call for America's golden new twentieth century; we still dance to its bright syncopations.

The sheet music for 'Maple Leaf Rag' by Scott Joplin.

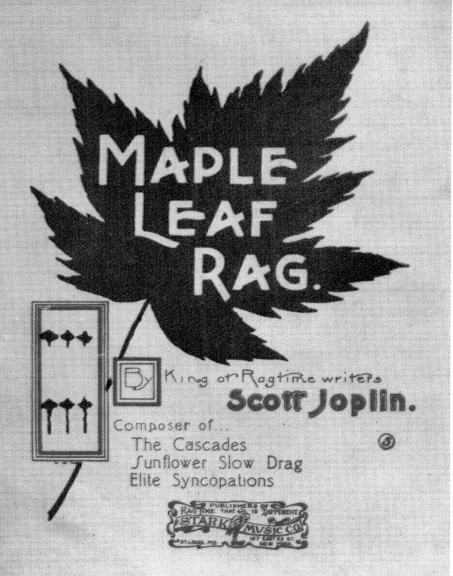

The Sounds of New Orleans

Other streams of music flowed as tributaries into the new jazz river. New Orleans had long, fertile traditions preserving all forms of black music. In Congo Square in the nineteenth century, generations of African-Americans gathered to sing, dance and drum, maintaining a lifeline to their homeland traditions.

One notable musician to absorb these influences was piano virtuoso and composer Louis Moreau Gottschalk, who grew up mesmerized by the sounds from Congo Square. Strains of Creole music from the gumbo of New Orleans' mixed culture – French, Spanish, American-Indian and African-American – emerged as a spicy remoulade: red hot peppers mixed with the more formal ballroom music from south of the city (Cuban, Caribbean and Latin-American rhythms such as the habañera, the tango, the meringue). Like the city's open-air markets, the music was redolent of tasty, tangy sounds, and in the teens a 'tango craze' hit the city; many tango halls opened and the dance fad reached everyone. Its presence can be heard in the insinuating Spanish tinge of Jelly Roll Morton's music, in his tangos such as 'Mama Nita', 'The Crave' and 'Creepy Feeling'.

Popular Melody

Robert Cole, James W. and J. Rosamond Johnson
– 'Under The Bamboo Tree' (1902)

At the beginning of the twentieth century, New Orleans was America's most exotic and cosmopolitan city, with a huge variety of cultures, languages, dialects and patois intertwining, especially in song. In the French Quarter, the long-established French Opera was a temple for popular entertainment, its airs mixing on the streets and squares with street vendors' cries and the bluesy honk of brass bands on parade. People might hum or whistle a blues melody, a minstrel tune, a lilting aria from Bizet or Gounod or an excerpt from the wildly popular melodramatic operas of Giacomo Meyerbeer.

Following the Civil War (1861–65), America had become a nation of town, village and municipal band music, with thousands of small bands echoing the monumental work of John Philip Sousa, whose many compositions and arrangements redefined and codified the literature for bands. His marches became national airs, and their steady tempos the vital pulse of the country. After 1870, brass instrumentation was modernized and standardized, and musical instruments became cheaper and easier to come by. The hearty sound of brass could be heard in the air everywhere.

John Philip Sousa, whose marches were performed by brass bands all over the US.

Brass Bands Take Over

New Orleans, a hot-weather city of constant, organized festivities teeming with social clubs, fraternal orders and non-stop partying, fairly demanded the brash urgency of brass-band music. Bands were in demand for lawn parties, parades (for Masonic cornerstone-layings and other ceremonial events), holiday celebrations and funerals.

The city marched and danced to brass-band music and many citizens eventually went to rest in their crypts heralded by a band. Ensembles such as the Eureka Brass Band, the Excelsior Brass Band, the Onward Brass Band and others had developed over decades and by the teens were known all over New Orleans. Across the river in Algiers, trumpeter Henry Allen Sr (1877–1952) led a famous brass band that taught many young players, including his son Henry 'Red' Allen (1908–67), the rudiments of the new hot music.

Known generally as 'social aid and pleasure clubs', hundreds of organizations existed to provide burial insurance that paid for a service, a wake, a funeral and a celebratory send-off – 'the end of a perfect death', as Jelly Roll Morton said. A band of 10 or 12 pieces assembled at the church to play hymns, then provided mournful dirges on the march to the burying ground. After the graveside service, the band left consecrated ground, struck up a lively ragtime march and led the mourners back to a funeral supper. Morton illustrated the 'jazz funeral' idea on his 1938 Library of Congress recordings and on a 1939 band recording of 'Oh, Didn't He Ramble', a rollicking and rude song descended from an even older English ditty, 'The Derby Ram'. His version runs the gamut from mourning to jubilation in three short minutes.

Popular Melody

Jelly Roll Morton – 'Original Jelly Roll Blues' (1915)

Various kinds of band music joined together to create a multicultural tradition. Circuses, travelling minstrel/tent shows, revival meetings, medicine shows and carnivals all featured bands in which New Orleans musicians apprenticed themselves. Trumpeters like William Geary 'Bunk' Johnson (1889–1949) and Ernest 'Kid Punch' Miller (1894–1971) hit the circus-band circuit and brought back more new music to New Orleans. Both men later fuelled the revival of New Orleans-style jazz that took off in the 1940s.

The New Orleans funeral march remains an important part of the city's musical heritage to this day.

A Swelling Flood of Music

Various founts of new music fed the surging tide of jazz in the teens. In Storyville, the few square blocks set aside for licensed prostitution (usually just called 'the District' in New Orleans), itinerant piano 'professors' (or 'ticklers') played dance tunes, blues, bawdy songs, bits of Creole badinage and all the latest pop music for customers in the gilded parlours of the big houses.

Jelly Roll Morton began his long career near the turn of the century as a kid piano player nicknamed 'Windin' Boy' – already a dedicated keyboard-and-song man whose idol was Tony Jackson, the 'man of a thousand tunes' that Morton called 'the world's greatest single-handed entertainer'. In his own piano jazz, which emerged from the solid roots of ragtime, Morton tried to capture the ebullience and sophistication of Jackson. Jelly Roll said he always tried to make the piano sound like a band, echoing the novel hot music beyond the District, in the dance halls of the city.

While brass bands, dance bands, ragtime pianists and blues singers retailed new and exciting musical forms, they inevitably traded and reconfigured them, absorbing the harmonies and rhythms heard in the dance halls, on riverboats, in the streets and picnic grounds, and in Lake Pontchartrain resorts. While attending the French Opera, the Lyric Theater or a fine restaurant, one might hear a theatre-pit orchestra or a 'sit-down' dance orchestra, such as the one John Robichaux fronted for many years, playing from printed scores.

Popular Melody

Jelly Roll Morton –
'Black Bottom Stomp' (1926)

These formal sit-down orchestras brought music to New Orleans from across the US, introducing musical comedy numbers such as Bessie McCoy's smash-hit song 'Yama Yama Man'. This number from the musical *Three Twins*, recalled an earlier transplant – the perennial theme song of Mardi Gras 'If Ever I Cease To Love' from *Bluebeard*, a burlesque comedy of 1872. Other music brought in by orchestras from afar included the New Orleans classic 'High Society', written by Porter Steele. This lively little march created a sensation when Robichaux's orchestra played it with a piccolo *obbligato* interpolated by New York arranger Robert Recker in 1901. Now, 'High Society' seems a product of spontaneous improvisation, but it was really part of a long tradition of arranged music feeding the developing jazz genre.

Basin Street, Storyville, New Orleans; Tom Anderson's café was a major musical centre.

The Influence of the Jazz Pioneers

Highly skilled teachers such as 'Professor' James Humphrey (1861–1937) of Magnolia Plantation, Creole violinist and trumpeter Peter Bocage (1887–1967) of Armand J. Piron's popular dance band and multi-instrumentalist Manuel Manetta (1889–1969) tutored generations of New Orleans' African-American players, including Humphrey's highly talented sons Percy (trumpet) and Willie (clarinet).

Other musicians mentored young followers, just as cornet virtuoso Joe 'King' Oliver (1885–1938) took Louis Armstrong (1901–71) under his wing and called him to the big time in Chicago in the 1920s. Throughout his long, amazing career as a world-renowned musician, Armstrong constantly acknowledged his debt to Oliver and the other jazz pioneers.

As much early jazz derived from musical scores as from invented or overheard music; in the city, musicians distinguished between readers ('musicianers') and illiterate improvisers ('routiners'). They said of untrained players: 'He couldn't read a note as big as a house!' and expressed as much regard for musical literacy and craftsmanship as they did for imagination and inventiveness. There was also a respect for the sort of drive and hustle embodied by Morton, who turned his hand to pool-sharking, pimping, and anything else going that would help to make ends meet. One white entrepreneur-agent, hustler and midwife to jazz was 'Papa' Jack Laine (1873–1966), a sometime drummer who ran a stable of brass bands and dance groups in New Orleans' white jazz community. These white musicians rubbed elbows with African-American players and quickly adopted their musical styles, bringing with them lyrical strains of Italian and French operas, folk ditties, the sounds of Mediterranean bands and dance music from old Europe, all transposed into jazz time.

Popular Melody
Bessie Smith – 'St Louis Blues' (1925)

Many of the later stars of white 'Dixieland' jazz – cornettist Nick LaRocca, the Brunis brothers, New Orleans Rhythm Kings trombonist George and his compatriot cornettist Paul Mares, among many others – rose to success through Laine's bands. Here they traded musical ideas and solidified the style that became the first jazz on record – the music of the Original Dixieland Jass Band, whose sensational New York recordings of 1917–18 changed the nation's musical soundscape overnight.

'Papa' Jack Laine – entrepreneur, drummer and bandleader.

Jazz Music Comes of Age

As the teens turned towards the twenties, jazz was maturing in New Orleans. Young players like cornettist Joseph 'Buddie' Petit (c. 1890–1931) developed flexible and infectious styles. Although unrecorded, Petit was influential on the next generation of jazzmen. Another unrecorded trumpet king was Chris Kelly, known for his soulful blues playing. These younger men recalled the earliest years of jazz in the city, when Charles 'Buddy' Bolden (1877–1931) led what was then called a 'ragtime' band and entranced the city. Bolden's band dominated the scene until his untimely mental collapse in 1907.

But the organization that older musicians recalled as the golden standard of music during the years of the First World War was the Oliver-Ory band. It was led by Edward 'Kid' Ory (1886–1973), the first great trombonist in jazz, and by Joe 'King' Oliver, at this stage largely unchallenged for the cornet crown. The band employed many upcoming 1920s jazz stars – Louis Armstrong, cornet; Johnny Dodds (1892–1940), clarinet; Warren 'Baby' Dodds (1898–1959), drums, and many others destined soon to leave the Crescent City for the big time. By 1918, Oliver had left New Orleans to follow a crowded northern migration to Chicago, and Kid Ory took the other standard way out, to California and fame in Los Angeles.

'When you come right down to it, the man who started the big noise in jazz was Buddy Bolden.... I guess he deserves credit for starting it all.'

Mutt Carey

Jazz musicians were also able to find work on the Mississippi riverboats; Fate Marable, the bandleader and pianist for the Streckfus Lines on paddlewheelers SS *J.S.*, SS *Capitol* and SS *Sidney*, had a plethora of sidemen that included such rising young luminaries as Louis Armstrong, Baby Dodds and banjoist Johnny St Cyr (1890–1966). These musicians spread new hot sounds to points north including St Louis, Missouri and St Paul, Minnesota. By 1920, New Orleans jazz was moving up the Mississippi River towards Chicago, before heading across the western territories and northeast to the new mecca of Harlem. Jazz was moving full speed ahead into its golden age, bringing an unparalleled army of talent and genius with it. In New Orleans the party was over – the old District was shut down as a public health menace during the First World War, while a new national culture of youth, speed and modernism was fuelled by the energetic sounds of jazz. In the next decade, the roots of jazz would produce the blossoms and fruit by which we now know the music best.

The only known photograph of Buddy Bolden (standing second from left), c. 1895.

The Teens

In America, in the teens of the twentieth century, change was the national keynote. Everywhere, science, industry, technology and commerce were reshaping American culture. Women were within grasp of the vote, temperance forces were starting the country on a vast experiment with Prohibition, and rapidly expanding cities and suburbs absorbed rural communities. Dress was changing from Victorian heavy to central-heating lite, women's hair got shorter – and their skirts did too.

Popular music was also beginning to shift. America had been singing and dancing to ragtime for a decade, and the new ragtime was faster, staccato and more urgent. White listeners learned blues harmonies for the first time; phonographs and piano rolls delivered more music to more homes.

'Bands in those days fighting all the time. One band get a job in the Love and Charity Hall, another band move right over there and play better through the windows.'

Bunk Johnson

In the mid-teens, new, one-step dances were popularized by Irene and Vernon Castle, an attractive dance team who fascinated the nation with wild new dances sporting animal names – the turkey trot, the grizzly bear, the buzzard lope. Gone were sedate cotillion numbers and even the old reliable two-step ushered in a generation earlier by John Philip Sousa and his 'Washington Post March' in 1889. Young dancers now not only touched each other but took a firm grip for the athletic shenanigans that followed the downbeat.

The Castles travelled widely, taught and tirelessly proselytized the new music. Their house orchestra was led by Harlem maestro James Reese Europe (1881–1919), a highly educated composer, bandleader and entrepreneur who formed the Clef Club in Harlem. Europe mentored a generation of geniuses, including Eubie Blake (1883–1983) and Noble Sissle (1889–1975) and other composers and players who shaped both jazz and musical show styles for the following decades. His orchestra was the clarion for the Harlem Renaissance of the 1920s, and a series of records spread the fast one-step music, with tunes like 'Castle House Rag' of 1914. Europe distinguished himself in the First World War as the leader of the 369th US infantry regiment band, nicknamed the 'Hell-Fighters'. They spread Europe's brand of syncopated marches and sizzling numbers including 'Memphis Blues', 'St Louis Blues' and 'Russian Rag'. They recorded in 1919, just days before Europe was killed by a crazed drummer in the band.

The people of America were soon dancing to the new jazz sounds.

The Original Dixieland Jass Band

The largest landmark of the decade, however, was the 1917 advent of the Original Dixieland Jass Band, a vaudeville-touring quintet of white New Orleanians.

The band opened in Reisenweber's Café in New York and cut landmark (and bestselling) records such as 'Livery Stable Blues', 'Tiger Rag', 'Ostrich Walk' and 'Bluin' the Blues', before branching out to tour in England and take London by storm. New Yorkers, trained by Europe and the Castles, knew how to dance to this frenetic, jerky music, and the records immediately swept the rest of the US and the world. Thus, the Jazz Age was launched by a crew of young white men from the rough Irish Channel district of New Orleans.

Racial Integration in Music

From its founding, New Orleans was notably an 'open city', with segregation only slowly making headway. People of all social and caste groups lived in mixed neighbourhoods and intermingled freely until Jim Crow and the rule of strict segregation tightened after the turn of the twentieth century. Ultimately, the poison of racism infected everything in US culture, but the power and glory of African-American music kept breaching social divides to free hearts and minds. Black and white musical co-operation and collaboration developed throughout the twentieth century until, in the words of a swing song, 'rhythm saved the world'.

> **Popular Melody**
>
> James Reese Europe – 'Castle House Rag' (1914)

Maestro James Reese Europe, who mentored future stars in his band, including Eubie Blake and Noble Sissle.

Key Artist: Kid Ory

Edward 'Kid' Ory was born in LaPlace, Louisiana in 1886. He learned trombone and led a group of young musicians, the Woodland Band, which he took to New Orleans around 1908. He played with veteran jazzmen in the following years and gained a reputation as a powerful ensemble player and inspired soloist, especially where the blues were concerned.

In the teens, Ory worked at Pete Lala's Café and developed a partnership with Joe 'King' Oliver, the top trumpet man and leader in the city. The Ory-Oliver bands showcased rising talents, including the Dodds brothers, Jimmie Noone and Bill Johnson. When Oliver left for Chicago, Ory migrated to Los Angeles, where he assembled a group of musicians who followed him throughout his long career – bassist Ed 'Montudie' Garland, guitarist Arthur 'Bud' Scott, trumpeter Thomas 'Mutt' Carey and clarinettist Wade Whaley. Later stalwarts included pianist Albert Wesley 'Buster' Wilson and drummer Minor 'Ram' Hall. In 1922, Ory's band made history as the first African-American New Orleans jazz band to record, cutting sides for the tiny Sunshine label in LA; they accompanied blues singers and made instrumentals including 'Ory's Creole Trombone'.

Key Tracks

'Muskrat Ramble' Louis Armstrong's Hot Five
'1919 Rag' Kid Ory's Creole Jazz Band

Chicago Beckons

Ory left for Chicago in the mid-1920s, becoming a star with King Oliver's Dixie Syncopaters and with Louis Armstrong's Hot Five and Hot Seven. With Oliver and Armstrong, Ory became the model for the traditional 'tailgate' players of the era. Tailgate playing describes a jazz trombone style in which the instrument fulfils a largely rhythmic and riff-tagging role beneath the more melodic cornets and trumpets. This remained the norm until virtuoso players such as Jack Teagarden came along and reinvented the trombone as a lead instrument. Ory also recorded with the New Orleans Wanderers and the New Orleans Bootblacks, as well as participating in Jelly Roll Morton's brilliant first Red Hot Peppers recordings. In the 1930s Ory found work too scarce to continue as a musician. He returned to California, where he was traced by Orson Welles in the early 1940s and brought back to prominence. A central figure in the revival of New Orleans-style jazz in the 1940s–60s, Ory led bands in California, touring and recording prolifically with many old cohorts to the end of his days in 1973.

New Orleans trombonist Kid Ory, with his Original Creole Jazz Band.

Key Artist: Clarence Williams

Clarence Williams was born in 1898 in Plaquemine, Louisiana, migrating to New Orleans in the teens to play piano and begin a long career as a composer, bandleader and musical promoter. He was manager of two early jazz venues – the Big 25 Club and Pete Lala's Café – hiring the best musicians in the city.

He opened a publishing business with Armand J. Piron, the leader of a popular dance band operating at the Lake Pontchartrain resorts. In 1919 he partnered with the savvy publisher-writer Spencer Williams. They gathered, annotated and copyrighted musical numbers that were floating in the air around the dance halls, bars and brothels of the city, publishing such enduring mega-hits as 'None Of My Jelly Roll' and 'Royal Garden Blues'.

'He was very important in coaching and teaching and working on our artists. He could somehow manage to get the best out of them….'

Frank Walker

Williams left for Chicago around 1917, pursuing publishing and becoming an agent for recording companies. In the 1920s he shifted to New York City as it became a hub for hot music. He assembled bands of friends from New Orleans for OKeh and Columbia Records, including the seminal Blue Five group, which united a young Louis Armstrong and Sidney Bechet. Among important songs he recorded were 'Cakewalking Babies From Home', 'Papa De Da Da' and 'Texas Moaner Blues'.

In his long career, Williams' gift for spotting fresh talent and potential musical hits was renowned. Among the first-rate musicians he assembled were trumpeters such as King Oliver, Jabbo Smith, Henry Allen, Ed Allen, Bubber Miley and Louis Metcalf. He recorded clarinettists such as Buster Bailey, Arville Harris and Albert Nicholas and trombonists Charlie Irvis and Ed Cuffee. He was the session piano player on many recordings but he was most comfortable as a musical director for OKeh Records, and an arranger and composer of jazz and pop tunes. With a fine ear for both novelty jazz material and songs that bridged the gap between pure jazz and pure pop, Williams was an important transmitter of New Orleans traditions to the East Coast musicians he met. In the 1930s, during the squeeze of the Depression, Williams closed his publishing office, turned to radio promotion and went on to run an antique store in Harlem. He died in 1965, having sold his vast catalogue to Decca Records in 1943.

Pianist, composer, arranger and musical director Clarence Williams (back left) with one of his bands.

A-Z of Artists

Papa Celestin (Trumpet, vocals, 1884–1954)

Oscar 'Papa' Celestin was a much-loved New Orleans fixture, who started out with the Algiers Brass Band at the turn of the century. In 1910 he founded the Original Tuxedo Jazz Orchestra with trombonist William 'Baba' Ridgley. Celestin recorded with OKeh and Columbia in the mid-1920s, and his recordings of 'Original Tuxedo Rag' and 'Black Rag' stand up well as sizzling hot jazz or dance music in comparison with the recordings that King Oliver made at the time with his Creole Jazz Band.

Unlike many of his peers, Celestin stayed in New Orleans. After the glory days of the Original Tuxedo Jazz Orchestra, he led bands on Bourbon Street, made records and played regularly for radio broadcasts. He was a sweet-toned trumpeter and a frog-voiced singer, vigorously selling sure-fire tunes like 'Li'l Liza Jane' and 'Bill Bailey'. His band featured elders including Alphonse Picou (clarinet), Bill Mathews (trombone), Ricard Alexis (bass) and Christopher 'Black Happy' Goldston (drums).

Will Marion Cook (Composer, arranger, violin, 1869–1944)

Will Marion Cook was a highly educated musician, studying at Oberlin Conservatory and the Berlin Hochschule für Musik with virtuoso Joseph Joachim. He worked as a composer with Bob Cole's All-Star Stock Company, a seminal force in early African-American musical comedy production.

Cook dreamed of working with the stellar African-American vaudeville team of (Bert) Williams and (George W.) Walker. In 1898, together with poet Paul Lawrence Dunbar, he wrote *Clorindy, or The Origin Of The Cakewalk*. Very successful, *Clorindy* set a new course for black musicals. This success assured Cook of his dream – he worked for Williams and Walker for more than a decade, while continuing to collaborate with Dunbar on *In Dahomey* (1903), *In Abyssina* (1906) and *In Bandanna Land* (1908). In 1918, Cook formed the New York (or American) Syncopated Orchestra, with settings for the new jazz music. In the 1920s he led Clef Club ensembles and worked with many important musicians, including pioneer big-band leader Fletcher Henderson and singer-actor Paul Robeson.

> ### Key Tracks
> 'Bill Bailey' Original Tuxedo Jazz Orchestra
> 'Clorindy' Will Marion Cook
> 'I'm Coming, Virginia' Will Marion Cook

The music for a song from Will Marion Cook's Clorindy, or The Origin Of The Cakewalk.

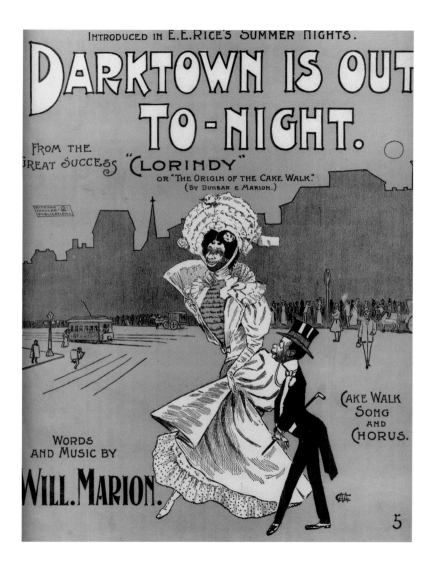

A-Z of Artists

Eagle Band (Instrumental group, 1900–17)

The Eagle Band, originally led by Buddy Bolden, was a popular and influential New Orleans ensemble. Frankie Duson (or Dusen) (1880–1940), a powerful tailgate trombonist, joined the band in 1906 and went on to take over the band when Bolden suffered a mental collapse the following year. Subsequently, Duson employed various Bolden alumni – Lorenzo Staulz, Brock Mumford, Frank Lewis and Edward Clem. He also chose younger sidemen who became major jazz stalwarts – Bunk Johnson, Joe Oliver, Sidney Bechet, Johnny Dodds and 'Big Eye' Louis Nelson. Drummers Baby Dodds, Henry Zeno and Abbey 'Chinee' Foster also played with the band. Duson was associated with the raggy and bluesy music of Bolden. Unfortunately for jazz history, Duson's bands never recorded.

Bunk Johnson (Trumpet, 1889–1949)

William Geary 'Bunk' Johnson, a New Orleans trumpeter was associated with Frankie Duson and other Bolden cohorts, and was famous as a showy, lyrical soloist. He played with Adam Olivier's orchestra in the city and then worked mainly in western Louisiana, and on the road with tent shows and other itinerant outfits. Johnson left music in 1933 but was rediscovered in New Iberia, Louisiana by William Russell and his co-authors of the influential *Jazzmen* in the late 1930s. After correspondence, Russell and friends rehabilitated Johnson and set him on the path to a new career with other New Orleans jazz veterans. In the early 1940s, Johnson led bands, recorded steadily for Russell's American Music label and toured, with a long stand in New York City from 1945–46. The band he led continued for decades under the leadership of clarinettist George Lewis, exerting a worldwide impact on the jazz revival.

Key Tracks

'Buddy Bolden's Blues' Eagle Band
'Careless Love' Eagle Band
'High Society' Bunk Johnson
'Tiger Rag' Bunk Johnson

Johnson generated controversy, epitomizing the acrimony between early jazz advocates ('Mouldy Figs') and zealots for the emerging modern jazz ('Modernists'). His example inspired the jazz revival of ensuing decades, and he joined the pantheon of New Orleans trumpet stars that included Bolden, King Oliver, Louis Armstrong and others. Struggling with alcoholism, Johnson declined in the late 1940s, leaving one final recording session which shows his personal concept of hot jazz.

Trumpeter Bunk Johnson, shown here playing with Leadbelly.

A-Z of Artists

Sara Martin (Vocals, 1884–1955)

Martin, an early classic blues singer, was signed by Clarence Williams for OKeh Records in 1922, at the beginning of the blues craze. While she was a pop-style singer, she was also able to pitch the blues in a rough-and-ready way. She recorded with Williams-led jazz groups, with such illustrious accompanists as King Oliver and Sidney Bechet (on some sessions she sang as 'Margaret Johnson' or 'Sally Roberts').

Martin was often accompanied by Thomas Morris (cornet) and Charlie Irvis (trombone), both blues specialists. On 'Death Sting Me Blues' (1928), Martin matches Joe Oliver's intensity, and on 'Atlanta Blues' (1923) she delivers the old folk melody with great dignity. Her diction was clear, and she had a good ear for plangent blues that were not over-worn. In 1929, she appeared on film with the immortal Bill 'Bojangles' Robinson in *Hello Bill*. She left show business in the Depression and returned to Louisville.

New Orleans Rhythm Kings (Instrumental group, 1922–25)

The New Orleans Rhythm Kings (NORK) were one of the major white groups in early New Orleans jazz; after a run at Chicago's Friar's Club in 1922, they recorded with Paul Mares (trumpet), George Brunis (trombone), Leon Roppolo (clarinet), Jack Pettis (alto sax), Elmer Schoebel (piano), Lew Black (banjo), Steve Brown (bass) and Frank Snyder (drums). Mares was a skilful, Oliver-esque lead, Roppolo a highly gifted clarinettist, Schoebel a fine arranger and composer, and Brown a topflight bassist. Sometime associates were drummer Ben Pollack, pianist Mel Stitzel and others.

> ### Key Tracks
> 'Atlanta Blues' Sara Martin
> 'Death Sting Me Blues' Sara Martin
> 'Graveyard Dream Blues' Sara Martin
> 'Panama' New Orleans Rhythm Kings
> 'Tin Roof Blues' New Orleans Rhythm Kings

The NORK's sound was different from the Original Dixieland Jass Band (ODJB), with slow blues and relaxed, mid-tempo tunes that swung. They emulated Joe Oliver's style, and recorded some of his music ('Sweet Lovin' Man'), some from the ODJB book ('Tiger Rag') and some basic New Orleans material ('Maple Leaf Rag'). They also recorded standards still played: 'She's Cryin' For Me' and 'Angry'. In 1923 the NORK made history, playing with Jelly Roll Morton on piano to create the first interracial band recording session on sides that included 'Sobbin' Blues'.

The Original Dixieland Jass Band (c. 1916) with the line-up that preceded their recording career: l–r Tony Spargo, Eddie Edwards, Nick LaRocca, Alcide 'Yellow' Nunez, Henry Ragas.

A-Z of Artists

Original Creole Orchestra (Instrumental group, 1912–18)

Freddie Keppard's Original Creole Orchestra toured extensively during the teens as an early harbinger of authentic New Orleans jazz, reaching big-time vaudeville's prestigious Orpheum circuit. Powerful pioneer trumpeter Keppard (1889–1933) had with him Creole clarinettists George Baquet, 'Big Eye' Louis Nelson and Jimmie Noone, pioneer bassist Bill Johnson and multi-instrumentalist Dink Johnson as a drummer.

The band created a sensation among vaudeville audiences. While the band did not record, Sidney Bechet appropriated a piece of mock-orientalia from Keppard, 'Egyptian Fantasy', and recorded the track. The band broke up in 1918 and Johnson set about finding a replacement for Keppard; he settled on King Oliver. Keppard went to Chicago in the 1920s, playing with important orchestras run by Charles 'Doc' Cook. He recorded with the Cook big band and with a small washboard band, demonstrating hot styles from wah-wah to plunger blues to a stirring open horn of startling volume.

Original Dixieland Jass Band (Instrumental group, 1917–25)

The Original Dixieland Jass (or Jazz) Band were five young white musicians from working-class uptown New Orleans – Nick LaRocca (cornet), Larry Shields (clarinet), Eddie Edwards (trombone), Tony Spargo (real name Sbarbaro, drums) and Henry Ragas (piano). All alumni of 'Papa' Jack Laine's stable of bands, they went to Chicago and then to New York, where their music created a sensation. The word 'jazz' or 'jass' was not spoken in polite circles, but their frenetic and wild music made it suddenly acceptable.

Key Tracks

'Saltydog Blues' Original Creole Orchestra
'Jazz Me Blues' Original Dixieland Jazz Band
'Fidgety Feet' Original Dixieland Jazz Band

After making important recordings – including 'Livery Stable Blues'/'Dixie Jass One Step' (1917), the first jazz recording released – and conquering New York society, in 1919 the band went on to a stand in Britain (with Billy Jones on piano), before returning to the US. They disbanded in the mid-1920s but were reunited briefly (with ragtimer J. Russel Robinson on piano) in 1936, making a *March Of Time* short film and cutting new recordings of the ODJB standards, including 'Clarinet Marmalade' and 'Original Dixieland One-Step'. They also recorded with a large swing band backing them.

Trumpeter Freddie Keppard, leader of the Original Creole Orchestra.

The Twenties

The Roaring Twenties, or Jazz Age, was a time of great economic prosperity and extravagance in America. Consumerism reigned and an increasing number of people had access to cars and other luxury goods. Advances in recording technology and the rise of the radio brought the music of the day into people's homes.

Jazz enjoyed widespread popularity and its artists became major stars. The rise of Hollywood and Tin Pan Alley added to the sense of glamour and excitement, and to the general feeling that America was several paces ahead of the rest of the world.

The Great Migration of labourers from the South to the northern cities, in search of better wages and new beginnings, reached its peak. This further enabled the absorption of African-American music genres into the mainstream, as migrants brought with them the sounds of their homelands.

Key Artists

Louis Armstrong
Bix Beiderbecke
Duke Ellington
Jelly Roll Morton
King Oliver

Other aspects of 1920s American culture were less rosy. Prohibition, in force from 1919–33, led to bootlegging, corruption and the sale of rot-gut alcohol, creating a wealthy and powerful underworld. Racism was rife, particularly in the South where white supremacists such as the Ku Klux Klan terrorized African-Americans and their supporters. In Europe, the growth of Communism and its right-wing alternative Fascism was creating increasingly uncomfortable political tensions.

Then, on 24 October 1929, the New York Stock Exchange crashed. The Jazz Age had come to an abrupt end.

1920s Chicago, which became the thriving centre of jazz music after the Great Migration of labourers from the South.

From Crescent City to Windy City

In the 1920s, with many seminal jazz figures migrating north, the music's epicentre shifted from its birthplace in New Orleans to Chicago. One of the events that caused this mass exodus of pioneering musicians from the Crescent City was the official closing of Storyville, the city's red-light district, in 1917.

In 1898, in an attempt to control prostitution, alderman Sidney Story had proposed a city ordinance to confine illegal trafficking to an area of New Orleans bordered on the north by Robertson and on the south by Basin Street. He was determined that such vice would be contained within this area, which became known as Storyville. It flourished as a red-light district for 20 years, providing many musicians with gainful employment in the various sporting houses that flourished there. In 1898, there were about 2,200 registered prostitutes working and advertising their services in Storyville; by 1917, that number had dwindled to 388. Storyville was eventually closed by the Navy on the grounds that it was illegal to operate houses of prostitution within five miles of a military institution.

'Chicago was really jumping around that time [1923]. The Dreamland was in full bloom. The Lincoln Gardens, of course, was still in there. The Plantation was another hot spot at that time. But the Sunset, my boss' place, was the sharpest of them all, believe that.'

Louis Armstrong

Clarinet great Sidney Bechet (1897–1959) was among the first to leave the Crescent City and head north. In 1917, just as New Orleans' stringent vice laws came into effect, he hooked up with the Bruce & Bruce Stock Company for a whirlwind tour of the Midwest, ending up in Chicago in November of that year. Meanwhile, trombonist and prominent bandleader Edward 'Kid' Ory (1886–1973) went west in 1919 and ended up in Los Angeles, where in 1922 he led the first African-American New Orleans group to make a record (under the name Spike's Seven Pods of Pepper Orchestra). Cornettist Joseph 'King' Oliver (1885–1938), a sideman in Ory's New Orleans group, also left for Chicago in February 1919, followed in 1923 by itinerant musician Jelly Roll Morton (1890–1941); both became key figures on the Windy City's hot jazz scene.

New Orleans clarinet virtuoso Sidney Bechet, one of the first jazz artists to leave the Cresecnt City.

The Jazz Age Begins

Chicago held the promise of a new life for the southern black population, which left behind the cotton fields for the blast furnaces, factories and slaughterhouses of the big northern cities. It was also an attractive destination for working jazz musicians, many of whom worked in the gangster-owned speakeasies created in reaction to the Volstead Act of 1919 outlawing the manufacture and sale of alcohol.

What followed was the 'Roaring Twenties', a decade marked by a new vitality in the wake of the First World War and underscored by a prevailing air of good times, in spite of the repressive era of Prohibition. The Jazz Age was a time when young people sought illegal booze, revelry and hot music.

In Chicago, jazz matured at the hands of its finest composers and practitioners, including Bechet, Ory, Oliver, Morton, Louis Armstrong (1901–71) and others who held forth on the city's predominantly black South Side, on a nine-block stretch of State Street known as 'The Stroll'. There, jazz lovers could choose between the Lincoln Gardens, Pekin Inn, Dreamland Ballroom, Plantation Café, Sunset Café and other spots where hot jazz flowed nightly. It was in this black neighbourhood that the young, white jazz-seeking teenagers who attended Austin High School on Chicago's white, middle-class West Side congregated to hear King Oliver's Creole Jazz Band, featuring Louis Armstrong and Johnny Dodds (1892–1940). By 1923, Chicago had become the centre of the jazz universe.

Popular Melody

Louis Armstrong's Hot Five – 'Muskrat Ramble' (1926)

The Harlem Renaissance

The mass migration of blacks from the South also fed the growth of population in Harlem. This influx of people helped to create the Harlem Renaissance, a period of unprecedented creative activity among African-Americans in all fields of art. From 1920–30, great works were done by writers and poets, painters, composer-bandleaders such as Noble Sissle (1889–1975), Eubie Blake (1883–1983) and Duke Ellington (1899–1974); and icons such as Bill 'Bojangles' Robinson, and Ethel Waters (1896–1977). Two other geniuses who came up in Harlem during this incredibly rich period in African-American history were Thomas 'Fats' Waller (1904–43) and Louis Armstrong. They were good friends whose paths crossed frequently in Chicago and New York, socially and professionally, throughout the 1920s.

A 1926 Charleston competition; the jazz dance craze took 1920s society by storm.

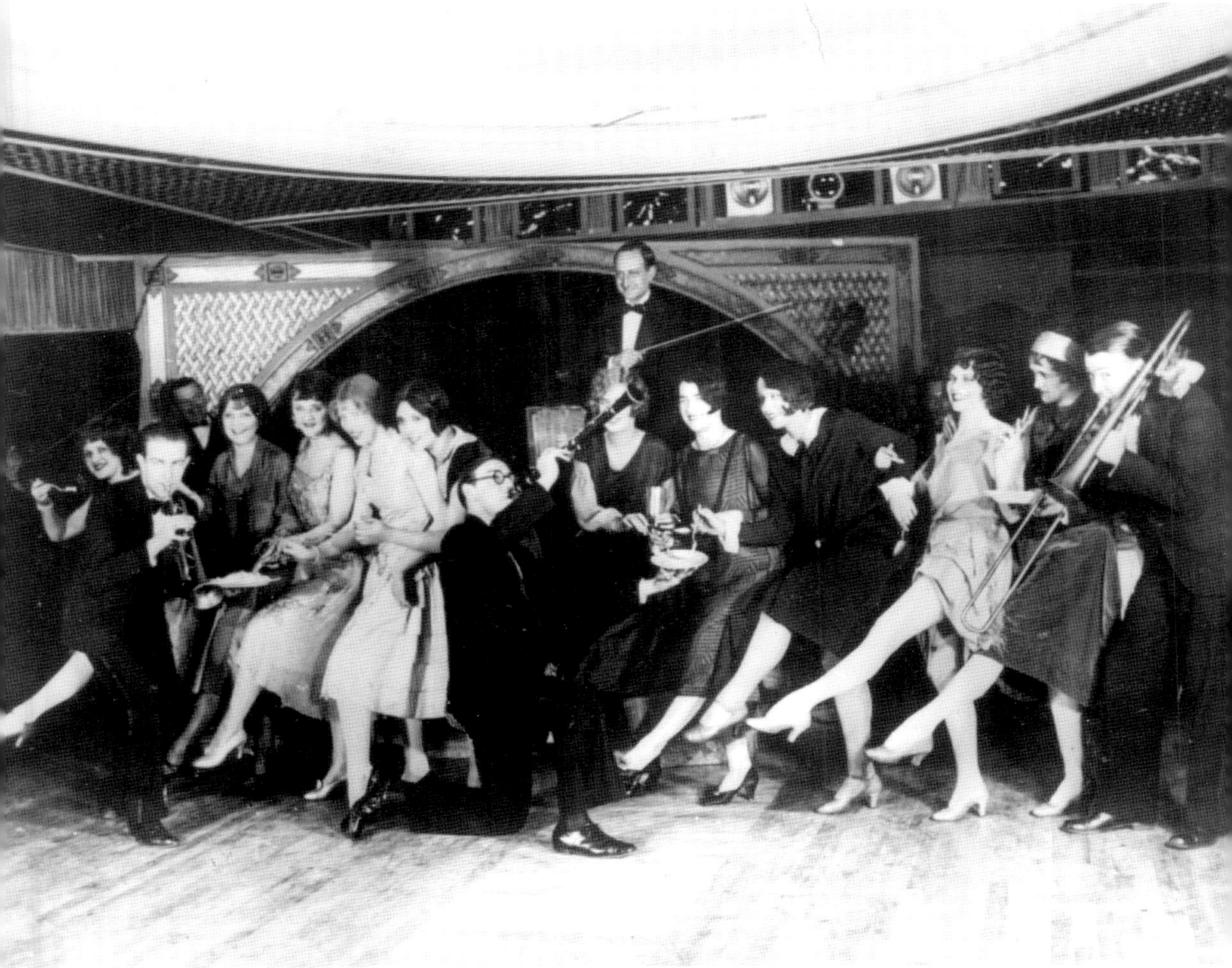

Waller and Armstrong

Fats and Louis first met in 1924 while moonlighting with Clarence Williams' Blue Five band at the Hoofer's Club in Harlem. They appeared together on live radio broadcasts and at late-night jams at Connie's Inn (also in Harlem).

In 1925, before Armstrong went back to Chicago to record his revolutionary Hot Five sessions, they appeared together on a recording date for Vocalion by Perry Bradford's Jazz Phools. In 1927, the two kindred spirits met up again in Chicago for a series of gigs at the Vendome Theater with Erskine Tate's band. During his brief stay in the Windy City, Waller also sat in on several late-night jam sessions at the Sunset Café with Armstrong's band, which by 1927 included pianist Earl Hines (1903–83).

The Jazz Scene Relocates Again

By the end of the 1920s, the centre of jazz had shifted again, from Chicago to New York. Here, Duke Ellington was leading the way with his sophisticated Cotton Club Orchestra, while Armstrong and Bix Beiderbecke (1903–31) were setting the pace for up-and-coming young trumpeters Jabbo Smith (1908–91), Henry 'Red' Allen (1908–67), Jimmy McPartland (1907–91) and Red Nichols (1905–65).

> **Popular Melody**
>
> James P. Johnson – 'Charleston' (1923)

Meanwhile, the stock market crash of 29 October 1929 signalled a symbolic end to the raucous, freewheeling, thrill-seeking Jazz Age. As the Great Depression loomed, Americans would soon turn to the ebullient dance music of the Swing Era to heal their woes. While Ellington and Armstrong would spearhead a transition from 'jungle music' and classic jazz into the new Swing Era, others such as Jelly Roll Morton, King Oliver and Kid Ory would fall out of favour in the 1930s, their New Orleans jazz now perceived as archaic and corny by the swing set.

Louis Armstrong (second from right) with Erskine Tate's Band at Chicago's Vendome Theater.

Key Artist: Louis Armstrong

An incomparable figure in the history of jazz, Armstrong played with an unprecedented virtuosity and bravura. In the early 1920s, he shifted the emphasis of jazz from ensemble playing to a soloist's art form, while setting new standards for trumpeters worldwide.

The sheer brilliance of his playing is best exemplified by his epochal masterworks from the 1920s, such as 'Potato Head Blues', 'West End Blues', 'Hotter Than That', 'Tight Like This', 'Cornet Chop Suey' and 'Weather Bird' – all marked by a passionate, robust attack, dramatic, slashing breaks and a remarkable flexibility and range. As Miles Davis put it, 'You can't play anything on your horn that Louis hasn't already played'.

Satchmo Joins King Oliver

Born in New Orleans on 4 August 1901, Armstrong began playing cornet after being sent to the Colored Waif's Home in 1913. Nicknamed 'Dippermouth' or 'Satchelmouth' (shortened to Satchmo) because of his wide, toothy grin, Armstrong came up playing in parade bands, in bars around Storyville and on steamboat excursions with Fate Marable. In late 1918, he replaced his mentor King Oliver in Kid Ory's band and honed his skills in that oufit for the next few years. On 8 August 1922, Armstrong joined King Oliver's Creole Jazz Band in Chicago, where he caused an immediate stir at Lincoln Gardens. Louis made his recording debut on 6 April 1923 (soloing on 'Chimes Blues'); he remained with Oliver's band throughout that year before moving to New York in early 1924 to join Fletcher Henderson's band during its residency at the Roseland Ballroom.

The Rosetta Stone of Jazz

After returning to Chicago in 1925, Armstrong recorded the first of his historic Hot Five sessions for OKeh Records with pianist (and Armstrong's second wife) Lil Hardin Armstrong, trombonist Kid Ory, clarinettist Johnny Dodds and banjo player Johnny St Cyr. There followed some Hot Seven sessions in 1927, featuring Armstrong's hometown friend Warren 'Baby' Dodds on drums, and a second Hot Five

Above: Perhaps jazz music's most emblematic star, Louis Armstrong. Right: The house in Perdido Street, New Orleans in which Armstrong grew up.

session in 1928 with Earl Hines replacing Hardin on piano. Often referred to as 'the Rosetta Stone of Jazz', the Hot Five and Hot Seven recordings are the most exciting and influential in jazz music, if not in the entire twentieth century. Armstrong's all-star ensembles set the ground rules for the direction jazz was to take, establishing it as a basis for improvisation and virtuosic solo playing within a group. He also introduced wordless 'scat' singing and steered jazz towards the more fluid rhythms of swing.

'What he does is real, and true, and honest, and simple, and even noble. Every time this man puts his trumpet to his lips, even if only to practice three notes, he does it with his whole soul.'

Leonard Bernstein

Following these revolutionary recordings, Armstrong began gradually to focus on entertainment at the expense of art. He had already hinted at a more good-humoured direction with his ribald, vaudevillian playfulness on the intro to 'Tight Like This' and in his frisky repartee with pianist Earl Hines to start off 'A Monday Date', both from his Hot Seven recordings of 1928. It was a direction that stern jazzophiles would come to view with increasing indignation over the years.

In 1929, Armstrong gave a crowd-pleasing performance in *Hot Chocolates*, which had its initial run at Connie's Inn in Harlem before moving to the Hudson Theatre on Broadway. It was in that show that Satchmo introduced 'Ain't Misbehavin'', the Fats Waller-Andy Razaf tune that became his first big hit. Armstrong was featured with Leroy Smith's group, at first performing from the pit but eventually taking his spot on stage, to the delight of audiences. His gravel-throated charisma helped to make *Hot Chocolates* the hottest ticket in town.

Armstrong Follows a New Route

In that same pivotal year of 1929 Armstrong cut the pop song 'I Can't Give You Anything But Love', charting a new course away from the cutting-edge Hot Fives and Hot Sevens, and steering more toward the mainstream entertainment by emphasizing his signature vocals. Armstrong would pursue this direction throughout the 1950s and 1960s with various aggregations of his All-Stars band. By then he had become a beloved yet sometimes controversial icon, a featured player in movies – including *Paris Blues* (in which he appeared with Duke Ellington) and *Hello, Dolly* – and a worldwide ambassador of jazz. After his death in 1971, his home in Queens, New York was preserved as an archive and museum.

Next Page: The Colored Waif's Home band, featuring Louis Armstrong (back row, indicated by a white arrow).

Key Artist: Bix Beiderbecke

The most strikingly original and authoritative voice on cornet since Louis Armstrong, Leon 'Bix' Beiderbecke set the example for a generation of aspiring white jazz players during the 1920s. His meteoric rise to fame was followed by a dramatic fall from grace that led to his ultimate death from alcoholism at the age of just 28 in 1931.

A Self-Taught Genius

Born in Davenport, Iowa on 10 March 1903, Beiderbecke rebelled against his strait-laced parents and his own upper-middle-class upbringing by becoming a jazz musician, a path that his parents found abhorrent. Inspired by recordings of the Original Dixieland Jass Band from New Orleans (and particularly the playing of the group's trumpeter and bandleader Nick LaRocca), Beiderbecke began playing cornet aged 15. Completely self-taught, he developed a distinctive tone and biting attack along with flawless intonation, a natural sense of swing and an uncanny command of blue notes. Contemporaries such as Hoagy Carmichael later said that the notes coming out of Beiderbecke's horn sounded like they were hit rather than blown, like a mallet striking a chime.

In 1923 Bix joined the Indiana-based Wolverines (named after Jelly Roll Morton's 'Wolverine Blues'), and in 1924 they cut a series of classic sides for the Gennett label, including 'Tiger Rag', 'Royal Garden Blues', 'Jazz Me Blues', 'Copenhagen' and Hoagy Carmichael's first tune, 'Free Wheeling'. Those recordings were absorbed and analyzed note for note by a group of jazz-hungry young Chicagoans collectively known as the Austin High School Gang, whose ranks included cornettist Jimmy McPartland, saxophonist Bud Freeman, clarinettist Frank Teschemacher, drummer Dave Tough and trombonist Jim Lannigan. It also included other young Windy City players such as trumpeter Muggsy Spanier, drummer Gene Krupa, clarinettist Benny Goodman and banjoist Eddie Condon.

Above: Jazz cornet genius Bix Beiderbecke, who took Chicago by storm.

Bix and Tram

In 1925 Beiderbecke moved to Chicago and began sitting in with all the great New Orleans players there, including King Oliver, Jimmy Noone and Louis Armstrong, whom Beiderbecke had first heard playing on a riverboat in 1920 with Fate Marable's band, in his hometown of Davenport. In the early part of 1926, Bix joined a band led by C-melody saxophonist Frankie 'Tram' Trumbauer at the Arcadia Ballroom in St Louis, and by summer of that year the two were playing in Jean Goldkette's Orchestra at the Graystone Ballroom in Detroit. In late 1927, Bix and Tram were recruited by Paul Whiteman, who led the most successful dance band of the day. Though unworthy of his moniker 'King of Jazz', Whiteman did respect the superb artistry that Beiderbecke demonstrated with his horn and featured him frequently on recordings from 1927–29. Bix's brief eight-bar statements within the context of popular Whiteman fare such as 'Marie', 'Louisiana', 'Sweet Sue' and 'Mississippi Mud' were brilliant gems of well-constructed, lyrical improvisation.

'Bix's breaks were not as wild as Armstrong's, but they were hot and he selected each note with musical care. He showed me that jazz could be musical and beautiful as well as hot.'

Hoagy Carmichael

At his peak, around 1927–28, Bix was fêted by his fellow jazz musicians, white and black alike. Perhaps his most famous and most widely imitated solo came on a 1927 Trumbauer-led small group recording of Bix's 'Singin' The Blues', which trumpeters of the day studied assiduously. Louis Armstrong refused to record the track himself, believing that Bix's solo could not be improved upon. Beiderbecke's other famous compositions included 'Davenport Blues' and a Debussy-inspired solo piano piece, 'In A Mist' – one of two such works that he recorded.

The Alcohol Takes its Toll

In the autumn of 1929, Beiderbecke had a nervous collapse; he was sent back to Davenport and entered a sanatorium to help him with his alcohol problems. Off the Whiteman payroll by the spring of 1930, he tried making a comeback with some recordings as a leader but died of pneumonia, exacerbated by alcoholism, on 6 August 1931. Seven years after his death, Beiderbecke was the inspiration for *Young Man With A Horn*, a novel by Dorothy Baker that was adapted for a 1950 Warner Bros. film starring Kirk Douglas.

Next Page: Bix (seated far right) in his first group – the Wolverines.

Key Artist: Duke Ellington

Universally acknowledged as one of the twentieth century's emblematic composers, Edward Kennedy 'Duke' Ellington used his longstanding touring orchestra as a tool to create wholly unique tonal colours and a distinctive harmonic language in jazz.

From the late 1920s to the early 1970s he composed many tunes that have become standards, as well as exquisite three-minute jazz concertos, dance band repertoire, popular suites, sacred concerts, revues, tone poems and film soundtracks. His most famous titles – including 'Mood Indigo', 'Satin Doll', 'Sophisticated Lady' and 'It Don't Mean A Thing (If It Ain't Got That Swing)' – have become embedded in the English language.

The Duke Makes his Name

Born in Washington, DC on 29 April 1899, Ellington was influenced by ragtime piano players and other popular performers of the day, including James P. Johnson, the father of Harlem stride piano. Nicknamed 'Duke' for his dapper appearance, he composed his first pieces – 'Soda Fountain Rag' and the risqué blues 'What You Gonna Do When The Bed Breaks Down?' – as a teenager and in 1919 formed his first group, the Duke's Serenaders. By 1923, Ellington had settled in Harlem in the midst of the area's thriving cultural renaissance. His first gig came as a sideman in the Washingtonians, a sextet led by banjo player and fellow Washington, DC native Elmer Snowden. After a brief stint in 1924 at the Hollywood Club, Ellington took over the band (which featured hot trumpeter James 'Bubber' Miley and drummer Sonny Greer) and played at the Kentucky Club in midtown Manhattan. His first recordings with the group in 1924 were 'Choo Choo (Gotta Hurry Home)' and 'Rainy Nights (Rainy Days)'.

A Golden Opportunity in Harlem

A pivotal year in Ellington's career was 1927, when he took over residency at the Cotton Club in Harlem. That same year he also recorded his first masterpieces 'Black and Tan Fantasy' and 'East St Louis Toodle-Oo' (both composed with Bubber Miley) along with 'Creole Love Call'. In 1928, he

Above: Duke Ellington – pianist, composer, bandleader and one of jazz music's most important figures. Right: Harlem's Cotton Club, where Duke Ellington's Orchestra held a three-year residency.

'I like any and all of my associations with music – writing, playing, and listening. We write and play from our perspective, and the audience listens from its perspective. If and when we agree, I am lucky.' **Duke Ellington**

recorded 'The Mooche', one of his signature pieces of 'jungle music', marked by Miley's growling trumpet and the plunger-mute trombone work of Joseph 'Tricky Sam' Nanton.

Ellington remained at the Cotton Club until 1930, then took his orchestra to Hollywood to appear in the Amos 'N Andy film *Check And Double Check*. The subsequent decade saw Ellington's flowering, as he produced hundreds of recordings, played countless concerts and broadcasts and became a sophisticated international figure – in his terms, 'beyond category'. Key to Ellington's art was his use of specific musicians – including baritone saxophonist Harry Carney, alto saxophonist Johnny Hodges, trumpeters Cootie Williams and Rex Stewart, trombonist Juan Tizol, bassist Jimmy Blanton, drummer Sonny Greer, and clarinettists Barney Bigard, Jimmy Hamilton and Russell Procope – as individual tones on his compositional palette. He often transformed improvised riffs or half-baked themes into enduring, full-blown works, and in 1938 initiated a remarkable close collaboration with co-composer Billy Strayhorn. In the 1940s Ellington premiered ambitious works, such as 'Black, Brown And Beige' – a musical history of African-Americans – at New York's Carnegie Hall.

A Long and Varied Career

Although not immune from industry-wide downturns and changes in audience tastes, Ellington toured and recorded prolifically throughout the 1950s and 1960s, filling his orchestra with new soloists – such as trumpeter Clark Terry, drummer Louie Bellson, trombonist Quentin Jackson and tenor saxophonist Paul Gonsalves – when his longtime sidemen died, retired or moved on. His appearance at the 1956 Newport Jazz Festival led to a *Time* magazine cover, a new contract with Columbia Records and the bestselling

Ellington At Newport, which featured Gonsalves' fabled 27-chorus solo on 'Diminuendo And Crescendo In Blue'. Ever the open-minded modernist, Ellington recorded with John Coltrane, Max Roach and Charles Mingus in the 1960s. His later masterpieces included 'The Far East Suite' (1966), marked by modal and Asian-inflected motifs, and the 'New Orleans Suite' (1970). Ellington was revered worldwide as a genius and giant of contemporary music long before his death in 1974.

Next Page: The hugely popular Duke Ellington Orchestra, shown here in Chicago in 1934.

Key Artist: Jelly Roll Morton

Ridiculed as a braggart, pimp, card shark and pool hustler, the audacious, self-proclaimed inventor of jazz Jelly Roll Morton was also hailed as a pioneering composer, gifted arranger, dazzling pianist and the greatest entertainer that New Orleans ever produced. He was one of the first jazz musicians to strike a perfect balance between composition and collective improvisation, bridging the gap between ragtime and jazz.

Ferdinand Lamothe Becomes Mr Jelly Roll

Born on 20 October 1890, Ferdinand Joseph Lamothe was a Creole of mixed French and African ancestry. He was among the earliest piano players in the bordellos of the Storyville district, where he mixed elements of ragtime, minstrel and marching-band music, foxtrots and French quadrilles, opera and salon music along with Latin American-influenced rhythms, which he called 'the Spanish tinge'.

By 1907, after re-christening himself 'Jelly Roll Morton', he began to travel the black vaudeville circuit around the Gulf Coast. By 1911 his travels had brought him up to New York, and the following year he made trips through Texas and the Midwest. Morton settled in Chicago in 1914 and remained in this new centre of hot jazz until 1917, during which time he composed and published his earliest numbers, including 'Jelly Roll Blues', 'New Orleans Blues' and 'Winin' Boy Blues'.

Morton's Red Hot Peppers

Morton travelled to California during the summer of 1917 and remained there throughout 1922, working his way up and down the West Coast from Tijuana to Vancouver with pickup bands. By May of 1923 he was back in Chicago and in June made his first recordings – 'Big Fat Ham' and 'Muddy Water Blues' – for the Paramount label. In July, he cut sides with the New Orleans Rhythm Kings ('Sobbin' Blues', 'Mr Jelly Lord', 'Milenburg Joys' and 'London Blues'), along with some solo piano pieces ('Wolverine Blues', 'New Orleans Joys', 'Grandpa's Spells', 'The Pearls' and 'King Porter

Above: The multi-talented Jelly Roll Morton.

Stomp'), for Gennett Records. In 1924, Morton recorded two piano-cornet duets, 'Tom Cat Blues' and 'King Porter Stomp', with his New Orleans colleague King Oliver. Morton recorded prolifically throughout 1926–27 with two different editions of his Red Hot Peppers, cutting classic New Orleans-flavoured sides such as 'The Chant', 'Black Bottom Stomp', 'Sidewalk Blues', 'Dead Man Blues', 'Jelly Roll Blues' and 'Grandpa's Spells' in 1926 with a group featuring Kid Ory, Omer Simeon and Johnny St Cyr, and 'The Pearls', 'Jungle Blues' and 'Wild Man Blues' in 1927 with a band that included both Johnny and Baby Dodds.

'He was fussy on introductions and endings and he always wanted the ensemble his way but he never interfered with the solo work..... His own playing was remarkable and kept us in good spirits.'

Omer Simeon

When the centre of jazz shifted to New York, Morton relocated there and from 1928–30 recorded several sides for the Victor label, including lesser-known tunes such as 'Low Gravy', 'Deep Creek', 'Tank Town Bump' and 'Smilin' The Blues Away'. For these New York sessions, Morton recorded with a new edition of the Red Hot Peppers, featuring trumpeters Henry 'Red' Allen and Bubber Miley, trombonists Geechie Fields and J.C. Higginbotham, clarinettists Omer Simeon and Albert Nicholas, bassist Pops Foster and drummers Paul Barbarin and Zutty Singleton.

A Jazz Musician's Testament

By 1930, Morton's style was considered old-fashioned and his work opportunities declined. He moved to Washington, DC in 1935 – the same year in which Benny Goodman's rendition of Morton's 'King Porter Stomp', arranged by Fletcher Henderson, ushered in the Swing Era – but throughout the decade Morton laboured with little success to regain his earlier status. Although his compositions were performed regularly, he did not receive royalties. In 1938, folklorist Alan Lomax recorded a series of interviews for the Library of Congress in which Morton reminisced about his New Orleans upbringing and his colourful career, while also providing examples of various piano styles. Lomax later used these interviews for an oral biography of Morton, which was released posthumously as *Mister Jelly Lord*. In 1939, Morton recorded eight sides for Bluebird in an all-star session that included New Orleans musicians Sidney Bechet, Sidney de Paris, Zutty Singleton, Henry 'Red' Allen and Albert Nicholas. He made his last recordings in January 1940 and died in poverty and obscurity at the age of 50 in Los Angeles on 10 July 1941.

Next Page: The mid-1920s recordings of Morton's Red Hot Peppers are classics, combining the spirit of New Orleans with the modernism of Chicago Jazz.

Key Artist: King Oliver

One of the cornet kings of early New Orleans – along with Buddy Bolden, Freddie Keppard and Bunk Johnson – Joseph 'King' Oliver helped to define the bravura spirit of hot jazz through his work in Chicago during the 1920s with his Creole Jazz Band. He is said to have earned the sobriquet 'King' by besting Keppard in a cutting contest one night in Storyville.

A King And His Mute

Born in Abend, Louisiana on 11 May 1885, Joseph Oliver began working around New Orleans as a cornettist in 1907 with the Onward Brass Band and later with the Eagle Band. By 1917, he became the star cornettist in a popular band led by Kid Ory. One of the early masters of the mute, Oliver created a whole lexicon of vocal effects on his horn during his two-year stint with Ory's band, which influenced a generation of musicians including trumpeter Bubber Miley and trombonist Tricky Sam Nanton – both of whom would play decisive roles in the Duke Ellington Orchestra in the 1930s. When Oliver went north to Chicago in February 1919, Ory hired his 18-year-old protégé Louis Armstrong as his replacement on cornet (Armstrong idolized Oliver and always referred to him as 'Papa Joe').

Above: King Oliver, who taught Louis Armstrong the basics of ensemble cornet playing and improvisation.

Oliver Rocks Lincoln Gardens

In Chicago, Oliver established himself in Bill Johnson's band at the Dreamland Ballroom. Following a year-long stay in California, he returned to Chicago in June 1922 and started playing regularly with his Creole Jazz Band at the Lincoln Gardens on Chicago's South Side. The original line-up of the Creole Jazz Band included trombonist Honoré Dutrey, bassist Bill Johnson, clarinettist Johnny Dodds, drummer Baby Dodds and pianist Lil Hardin. In July he sent for Louis Armstrong, who joined the group in Chicago on 8 August. Oliver's Creole Jazz Band made its first recordings in April 1923 at the Richmond, Indiana studios of Gennett Records. Included in the batch of Oliver originals that they cut that day were 'Snake Rag', 'Zulu's Ball', 'Just Gone', 'Chimes Blues', 'Canal Street Blues' and 'Dippermouth Blues', which showcases Oliver's wah-wah technique.

Oliver Loses His Protégé

Lil Hardin and Louis Armstrong were married in February 1924 and Hardin had plans for her new husband, advising him on various matters and ultimately convincing him to leave his mentor's side and join Fletcher Henderson's Orchestra in New York. Shortly after Armstrong's exit, the Creole Jazz Band fell apart; in December 1924 Oliver recorded a pair of piano-cornet duets ('King Porter Stomp' and 'Tom Cat Blues') with Jelly Roll Morton for the Autograph label. In 1925, he took over Dave Peyton's band, which had a residency at the Plantation Café, and renamed it the Dixie Syncopators. From 1927–28, the Dixie Syncopators recorded prolifically for the Vocalion and Brunswick labels, and when the Plantation Café was destroyed by fire in 1929, the band went to New York and worked at the Savoy Ballroom. Oliver unwisely turned down an offer to become the house band at the Cotton Club in Harlem (the gig went to Duke Ellington's Orchestra, which became famous via the club's radio broadcasts) and Luis Russell later took over Oliver's band, renaming it the Luis Russell Orchestra.

'Joe would stand there fingering his horn with his right hand and working his mute with his left, and how he would rock the place....'

George Wettling

Oliver's last recordings as a leader were in 1931 for the Victor, Brunswick and Vocalion labels, although he was suffering from a gum disease and rarely played himself, hiring other cornet players for the sessions. The New Orleans jazz legend spent his last years touring the South and finally settled in Georgia, where he worked as a janitor in a pool hall up until his death in 1938.

Next Page: King Oliver (centre) with his band and assorted musical instruments.

A-Z of Artists

Henry 'Red' Allen (Trumpet, 1908–67)

The son of bandleader Henry Allen Sr, Henry 'Red' Allen was one of the greatest trumpeters to come out of New Orleans. He moved to New York in 1927 to join King Oliver's Dixie Syncopators and in 1929 he was signed to the Victor label. He played with Luis Russell's Orchestra from 1929–32, then in 1933 joined Fletcher Henderson's Orchestra. Following a stint with the Mills Blue Rhythm Band (1934–37), Allen returned to the Russell Orchestra. He then led his own bands through the 1940s and 1950s, participated in the 1957 CBS TV special *The Sound of Jazz* and toured Europe in 1959 with Kid Ory. Allen experienced a renaissance in the 1960s before succumbing to cancer.

Josephine Baker (Vocals, dancer, 1906–75)

Born Freda Josephine McDonald, the St Louis-born entertainer danced in the 1921 Sissle/Blake musical *Shuffle Along* before gaining a bigger role in their *Chocolate Dandies* in 1924, leading to appearances at the Cotton Club. The following year, she introduced 'le jazz hot' to Paris in *La Revue Négre* with her exotic dancing and onstage sexuality. After working with the Red Cross and French Resistance during the Second World War she staged a major comeback in 1973, culminating in a 1975 performance at New York's Carnegie Hall.

Sidney Bechet (Soprano saxophone, clarinet, 1897–1959)

A child prodigy who worked with various bands around New Orleans, the Creole clarinettist thrilled audiences with his soaring tone, forceful attack, penetrating solos, dazzling facility and unusually fast vibrato. In 1917, Bechet and King Oliver played together briefly in Kid Ory's band until Bechet relocated to Chicago. The following year, while on a European tour with Will Marion Cook's Southern Syncopated Orchestra, Bechet discovered the unsual straight soprano saxophone. Bechet made his first recordings in 1923 with the Clarence Williams Blue Five and continued to record prolifically throughout the 1920s and 1930s, scoring a hit in 1938 with his bluesy rendition of George Gershwin's 'Summertime'. The New Orleans revival of the 1940s made him an international star and he lived out his final years in France, where he was feted as a national hero.

Key Tracks

'It Should Be You' Henry 'Red' Allen
'Avec' Josephine Baker
'Summertime' Sidney Bechet

Flamboyant stage star Josephine Baker poses on an exotic set in 1933.

A-Z of Artists

Irving Berlin (Piano, songwriter, 1888–1989)

Born Israel Beilin in Siberia, Berlin's family relocated in 1893 to New York, where he broke into vaudeville. He published his first song in 1907 and in 1911 had his first major hit with 'Alexander's Ragtime Band'. One of America's most prolific melodicists, Berlin wrote hundreds of tunes that became standards, including 'Always', 'Cheek To Cheek', 'White Christmas' and 'There's No Business Like Show Business' from his successful musical *Annie Get Your Gun*. His songs have been interpreted by musicians from Bessie Smith to Charlie Parker to Cassandra Wilson.

Eubie Blake (Piano, composer, 1883–1983)

James Hubert Blake wrote his first piece, 'The Charleston Rag', in 1899. The Baltimore native started out playing piano in sporting houses and with travelling medicine shows in the early 1900s. He also worked with bandleader-composer James Reese Europe before teaming up on the vaudeville circuit with lyricist Noble Sissle in 1915 – they were billed as 'The Dixie Duo'. In 1921 they collaborated on the first all-black musical, *Shuffle Along*, which produced the hit song 'I'm Just Wild About Harry' and paved the way for several other all-black productions during the 1920s and 1930s. After three decades of inactivity, Blake emerged with a triumphant two-record set on Columbia, *The Eighty-Six Years of Eubie Blake* (1969), which sparked a Blake revival and led to the highly successful 1978 Broadway musical revue, *Eubie* (which subsequently travelled to London). Blake continued performing until he was 98.

Key Tracks

'Puttin' On The Ritz' Irving Berlin
'Memories Of You' Eubie Blake
'Willow Tree' Louisiana Sugar Babies

Garvin Bushell (Clarinet, bassoon, 1902–91)

Jazz's first double-reed specialist on bassoon, Bushell played with Mamie Smith's Jazz Hounds before a two-year stint with Sam Wooding's Orchestra (1925–27). In 1928 he formed the Louisiana Sugar Babies with Fats Waller and Jabbo Smith, and he later worked with Otto Hardwick (1931), Fess Williams (1933), Fletcher Henderson (1935–36), Cab Calloway (1936–37) and Chick Webb (1938). In 1959 he replaced Omer Simeon in Wilbur de Paris's New Orleans Jazz Band, and in 1961 recorded live in a large ensemble with John Coltrane at the Village Vanguard.

Prolific composer Irving Berlin (left) discusses one of his songs with actor, dancer and singer Fred Astaire.

Ragtime Violin

EASTER PARADE

by
Irving Berlin

FOR SALE BY ALL DEALERS

A-Z of Artists

Eddie Condon (Banjo, guitar, 1905–73)

Originally from Indiana, Condon became associated with Chicago's Austin High School Gang, a group of white West-Side teenagers who emulated King Oliver's Creole Jazz Band and created their own take on hot jazz. In 1927, Condon co-led a band with William 'Red' McKenzie (which also included Bud Freeman, Frank Teschemacher, Gene Krupa and Jimmy McPartland) that helped to define the driving, freewheeling Chicago jazz sound of the Roaring Twenties. Condon also worked with Red Nichols & his Five Pennies and with McKenzie's Mound City Blue Blowers during the late 1920s.

Condon's considerable wit and charm made him an ideal spokesperson for the 1940s revival of traditional jazz. His all-star concerts in New York's Town Hall were broadcast weekly on the radio from 1944–45. He opened his own club, Condon's, in New York in 1945 and in 1949–50 hosted the first jazz television show, *Eddie Condon's Floor Show*. Condon continued to record, tour, write about and promote jazz until his death.

Johnny Dodds (Clarinet, 1892–1940)

The premier New Orleans clarinettist of the 1920s, Dodds played in Kid Ory's band from 1912–19 and then alongside Louis Armstrong and his own brother, Warren 'Baby' Dodds, in Fate Marable's riverboat band. Dodds left New Orleans in January 1921 to join King Oliver's Creole Jazz Band in Chicago, taking part in that influential band's classic 1923 recordings for Gennett.

Popular Melody

King Oliver – 'Dippermouth Blues' (1923)

Dodds played a key role in Armstrong's legendary Hot Five and Hot Seven sessions from 1925–27, and his virtuoso solos and distinctive, liquid tone also grace recordings by Jelly Roll Morton's Red Hot Peppers, the New Orleans Wanderers, the Chicago Footwarmers and his own Black Bottom Stompers, featuring Armstrong. He worked regularly in Chicago throughout the 1930s while also running a cab company with Baby Dodds. He led his final session on 5 June 1940, before passing away two months later.

Johnny Dodds – possibly the finest clarinettist in New Orleans jazz.

A-Z of Artists

Warren 'Baby' Dodds (Drums, 1898–1959)

The grandfather of jazz drumming, Baby Dodds played in Fate Marable's riverboat band from 1918–21 before joining King Oliver's Creole Jazz Band and relocating to Chicago. He remained there for the rest of his career, collaborating with Jelly Roll Morton's Red Hot Peppers and Armstrong's Hot Seven, as well as trombonists Kid Ory and Miff Mole, trumpeter Bunk Johnson and clarinettists Jimmie Noone, Sidney Bechet and Dodds' brother Johnny. His soloist style influenced countless drummers, including Gene Krupa, Max Roach and Roy Haynes.

George 'Pops' Foster (Bass, 1892–1969)

Known for his powerful, slap bass sound and signature solos, Foster worked with the Magnolia Band and A.J. Piron before playing in Fate Marable's riverboat band (1918–21) and collaborating with Kid Ory and others during the 1920s. In 1928 he played with King Oliver's Dixie Syncopators in New York and then joined the Luis Russell Orchestra. Foster was in demand during the 1940s New Orleans revival and from 1956–61 he played with Earl Hines in San Francisco. Foster remained active into the mid-1960s.

'[Baby Dodds] had a rhythm entirely his own, and I feel that as a drummer he had more personality than any other specialist on any other instrument....'

Tommy Brookins

Bud Freeman (Tenor saxophone, clarinet, 1906–91)

Freeman was one of the Austin High School Gang, a group of white, jazz-seeking teenagers who were obsessed with the hot jazz scene on Chicago's South Side. He recorded in 1927 with the McKenzie-Condon Chicagoans, then moved to New York to work with Red Nichols' Five Pennies.

He eventually developed his own style on the tenor saxophone that offered a fresh alternative to Coleman Hawkins and Lester Young. Freeman became a swing star with the Tommy Dorsey band in 1936 and the Benny Goodman Orchestra in 1938. He was also the house saxophonist at Commodore Records in the 1930s. Freeman reunited with Eddie Condon in 1945 and continued to play freewheeling Chicago-style jazz with the World's Greatest Jazz Band (1968–71) and as a leader into the early 1980s.

Bandleader Fate Marable (seated at the piano) with his Capitol Revue featuring Warren 'Baby' Dodds on drums.

A-Z of Artists

George Gershwin (Piano, composer, 1898–1937)

One of the most enduringly popular composers of the twentieth century, Gershwin composed such enduring melodies as 'Summertime', 'Embraceable You' and 'Let's Call The Whole Thing Off'. His tuneful songs with their rich harmonic progressions are ideal for improvisation and were popular with jazz musicians including Louis Armstrong, Art Tatum, Oscar Peterson, Coleman Hawkins and Miles Davis.

A self-taught pianist, 15-year-old Gershwin was the youngest songwriter on Tin Pan Alley. He and his lyricist brother Ira scored their first big hit in 1919 with 'Swanee' for Al Jolson. From 1919–33 they produced a succession of musicals, including the first Pulitzer Prize-winning musical comedy, *Of Thee I Sing* (1931). In 1924, George wrote *Rhapsody In Blue* as a concerto for piano and the Paul Whiteman Orchestra. His success with this work led to his 1935 'folk opera' *Porgy & Bess*. The Gershwins went to Hollywood in 1936 but George died of a brain tumour the following year. Ira continued to work as a lyricist until retiring in 1960.

Key Tracks

'Summertime' George Gershwin
'It's Been So Long' Edmond Hall
'Harlem on Saturday Night'
  Lil Hardin Armstrong

Edmond Hall (Clarinet, 1901–67)

Raised in a musical family (his father Edward also played clarinet), Hall played around New Orleans during the early 1920s before departing to New York in 1928 to work with Alonzo Ross. He worked with Claude Hopkins, Lucky Millinder, Joe Sullivan and Zutty Singleton in the 1930s; with Teddy Wilson and Eddie Condon through the 1940s; and toured with Louis Armstrong's All-Stars from 1955–58. He reunited with Condon in the 1960s and made his final recording in 1967 at John Hammond's New York Spirituals To Swing concert.

Lil Hardin Armstrong (Piano, vocals, arranger, 1898–1971)

Memphis-born pianist Lillian Hardin joined King Oliver's Creole Jazz Band in Chicago in 1921 and married fellow band member Louis Armstrong in 1924. She played on Armstrong's Hot Five and Hot Seven recordings and also received some composer credits. After the couple divorced in 1938, Lil subsequently worked as the house pianist at Decca Records and recorded up until 1961. She died during a performance of 'St Louis Blues' at a Louis Armstrong memorial concert in Chicago.

A publicity poster for Gershwin's 1935 'folk opera' Porgy & Bess.

THE THEATRE GUILD PRESENTS
PORGY and BESS
MUSIC BY
GEORGE GERSHWIN
LIBRETTO BY
DUBOSE HEYWARD
LYRICS BY
DUBOSE HEYWARD and IRA GERSHWIN
PRODUCTION DIRECTED BY
ROUBEN MAMOULIAN
GERSHWIN PUBLISHING CORPORATION
& NEW DAWN MUSIC CORPORATION
609 Fifth Avenue, New York, N. Y. 10017
CHAPPELL & CO INC

A-Z of Artists

Coleman Hawkins (Tenor saxophone, 1904–69)

'Hawk' played with Mamie Smith's Jazz Hounds in 1922 before joining Fletcher Henderson's band in New York. Louis Armstrong's presence in the band had a major effect on Hawkins' playing; by marrying a swing feel to his heavy tone, informed by his advanced understanding of harmony and chords, Hawkins became a star soloist and the pre-eminent saxophonist of his time.

Returning to the US in 1939 following a sojourn in Europe (during which he worked with Django Reinhardt and Stephane Grappelli), Hawkins recorded 'Body And Soul' – a masterpiece of melodic improvisation and one of the first pure jazz recordings to become a commercial hit. Hawkins was the first prominent Swing era artist to make the transition to bebop, playing with Thelonious Monk, Dizzy Gillespie and Don Byas. In 1948 Hawk made another milestone recording, 'Picasso', a stunning, unaccompanied solo. He recorded prolifically in the 1950s and 1960s with John Coltrane, Roy Eldridge, Duke Ellington, Max Roach, Sonny Rollins and Pee Wee Russell, among others.

Fletcher Henderson (Piano, arranger, bandleader, 1897–1952)

The Georgia native came to New York in 1920 and worked at a music publishing company owned by Harry Pace and W.C. Handy. When Pace left in 1921 to form the Black Swan record label, Henderson followed as house pianist and arranger. In 1923 Henderson's session band, which included young talents such as Coleman Hawkins, landed a steady gig at the Club Alabam, and in 1924 began an engagement at the Roseland Ballroom; Louis Armstrong joined the same year.

From 1925–28, Henderson's swinging ensemble was among the finest in jazz, but the Depression took its toll and by 1935 Henderson was writing crack arrangements for the Benny Goodman Orchestra that essentially helped to launch the Swing Era. Henderson led his own small groups during the 1940s and in 1950 co-led a sextet with Lucky Thompson before being sidelined by a stroke.

Key Tracks

'Stampede' Coleman Hawkins
'One Hour' Coleman Hawkins
'Rocky Mountain Blues' Fletcher Henderson
'Sugar Foot Stomp' Fletcher Henderson

Saxophonist Coleman Hawkins, shown here with Miles Davis in the 1940s.

A–Z of Artists

Jack Hylton (Piano, bandleader, 1892–1965)

Prominent British bandleader and booking agent Hylton began recreating the 'symphonic jazz' of Paul Whiteman's Orchestra in 1920. In 1933 Hylton booked the Duke Ellington orchestra to tour Europe for the first time. He toured the US with American musicians in 1935, reformed his British band in 1936 and toured through the 1930s before disbanding in 1940.

James P. Johnson (Piano, composer, 1894–1955)

The seminal figure among the Harlem stride pianists, Johnson was a mentor to Fats Waller and composer of 'The Charleston', which launched a Jazz Age dance craze. Count Basie, Duke Ellington and Art Tatum were also directly influenced by his skilful stride and compositions, including 'You've Got To Be Modernistic'. His 'Carolina Shout' became proving ground for other stride pianists of the day.

'Evidence of [Eddie Lang's] genius can be heard on all of our early OKeh recordings....'

Frank Trumbauer

Tommy Ladnier (Cornet, trumpet, 1900–39)

A stylistic descendant of King Oliver, Ladnier learned under Bunk Johnson and played in various bands around New Orleans. Around 1917 he moved to Chicago, where he worked with Jimmie Noone and King Oliver. In 1925 he toured Europe with Sam Wooding's band and the following year joined Fletcher Henderson in New York. In 1932, Ladnier formed the New Orleans Feetwarmers with Sidney Bechet before dropping off the scene, re-emerging in 1938 with Mezz Mezzrow until his premature death from a heart attack.

Eddie Lang (Guitar, 1902–33)

Philadelphia native Salvatore Massaro joined the Mound City Blue Blowers in 1924 and by the mid-1920s had become jazz's first in-demand session guitarist and jazz's first guitar hero. In 1926, he teamed up with Joe Venuti for some classic guitar-violin duet sessions. After recording prolifically during 1927, he teamed up with Lonnie Johnson for some historic duet recordings in 1928 and in 1929 joined Paul Whiteman's Orchestra, which featured a young Bing Crosby. When Crosby left to launch his solo career in 1932, Lang became his full-time accompanist until his untimely death the following year.

Guitar virtuoso Eddie Lang, who formed a fruitful musical partnership with violinist Joe Venuti.

A-Z of Artists

George Lewis (Clarinet, alto saxophone, 1900–68)

Lewis (born George Louis Francis Zeno) led bands in New Orleans in the 1920s, but he remained in the Crescent City while many of his colleagues headed north to Chicago, where the Jazz Age was being forged on the city's South Side. Lewis did not record until the 1940s (in sessions that teamed him with New Orleans trumpeter Bunk Johnson) and he later became a prominent figure in the New Orleans revivalist movement of the 1950s.

McKinney's Cotton Pickers (Instrumental group, 1926–34)

Formed in 1926 by drummer Bill McKinney (1895–1969), this Ohio-based big band improved significantly after hiring arranger Don Redman from Fletcher Henderson's band in the summer of 1927. For the next four years, until Redman left in 1931, McKinney's Cotton Pickers rivalled both Henderson's and Duke Ellington's orchestras for ensemble precision. The band's trumpeter and principal soloist John Nesbitt (a close friend of Bix Beiderbecke) also contributed potent arrangements throughout the 1920s.

Key Tracks

'Burgundy Street Blues' George Lewis
'Milenberg Joys' McKinney's Cotton Pickers
'Cherry' McKinney's Cotton Pickers
'Sentimental Journey' Jimmy McPartland
'Mystery March' Jimmy McPartland

Jimmy McPartland (Trumpet, 1907–91)

Part of the Chicago-based Austin High School Gang, along with Bud Freeman, Frank Teschemacher, Jim Lannigan and Dave Tough, McPartland was inspired by recordings of the New Orleans Rhythm Kings and Bix Beiderbecke, who he replaced in the Wolverines in 1925. He joined Ben Pollack's band in 1927 and recorded with the McKenzie-Condon Chicagoans that same year. McPartland worked steadily through the 1930s in Chicago and continued leading Dixieland sessions for the next four decades.

Cornettist Jimmy McPartland was a soldier during the Second World War, and took part in the 1944 D-Day invasion of Normandy.

A-Z of Artists

James 'Bubber' Miley (Trumpet, 1903–32)

A key figure in the Duke Ellington Orchestra of 1926–28, Miley played a lead role on such classic pieces of early Ellingtonia as 'East St Louis Toodle-Oo', 'Black And Tan Fantasy' and 'Creole Love Call'. His uniquely expressive, growling trumpet style was influenced by the plunger mute approach of King Oliver, and served as one of the signatures of Ellington's 'jungle sound'. Miley formed his own band in 1930 but shortly afterwards died of tuberculosis, aged 29.

Punch Miller (Trumpet, cornet, 1894–1971)

One of the leading New Orleans cornettists during the 1920s, Ernest 'Punch' Miller moved to Chicago in 1926 and found work with fellow New Orleanians Freddie Keppard and Jelly Roll Morton, as well as with Tiny Parham and Albert Wynn's Gutbucket Five. He spent the 1930s in New York before returning to Chicago. In 1956, Miller returned to New Orleans; he recorded his last sessions in the mid-1960s with trombonist George Lewis.

Miff Mole (Trombone, 1898–1961)

A vital figure of the 1920s, Irving Milfred Mole was among the earliest trombonists with the virtuosity to express fully developed musical lines on an instrument largely still relegated to glissandos and rhythm accents. Mole elevated the instrument to first-chair status on hundreds of records and solos, many recorded with Red Nichols. He left jazz to work in radio after 1929, played in various traditional groups after the Second World War, and was reunited with Nichols in 1956 on the television show *This Is Your Life*.

Sam Morgan (Trumpet, 1895–1936)

An early practitioner of New Orleans jazz, Morgan travelled the Bay St Louis-Pensacola-Mobile circuit and played Crescent City venues, including the Savoy on Rampart Street, before suffering a stroke in 1925. He recovered and in 1927 made recordings at the Werlein's Music Store on Canal Street for the Columbia label, including 'Mobile Stomp', 'Bogalousa Strut' and his vocal feature, 'Short Dress Gal'. Morgan continued to play until he had a second stroke in 1932.

Popular Melody

Duke Ellington – 'East St Louis Toodle-Oo' (1926)

The name Red Nichols gave his groups, 'Five Pennies', was a play on his surname (five pennies make a nickel) and often had more than five members.

A-Z of Artists

Red Nichols (Cornet, 1905–65)

As a child, Nichols played in his father's brass band. After moving to New York in 1923 he teamed up with trombone player Miff Mole, and this marked the start of a long musical partnership. With Mole, Nichols recorded various line-ups under different names, the most common of which was Red Nichols & his Five Pennies. He worked prolifically on Broadway and radio as well as on tour and in the studio.

Jimmie Noone (Clarinet, 1895–1944)

The most fluid and graceful of the classic New Orleans clarinettists, Noone worked with trumpeter Freddie Keppard (1914) and also with the Young Olympia Band (1916) before following Keppard to Chicago in 1917. A member of King Oliver's first Creole Jazz Band (1918–20), he also played in Doc Cooke's Dreamland Orchestra (1920–26) before forming his popular Apex Club Orchestra in 1928. Noone led bands throughout the 1930s and joined Kid Ory in 1944.

Key Tracks

'Avalon' Red Nichols & his Five Pennies
'Sweet Lorraine' Jimmie Noone
'He's The Last Word' Ben Pollack
'My Papa Doesn't Two Time' Don Redman

Ben Pollack (Drums, 1903–71)

A member of the Chicago-based New Orleans Rhythm Kings, Pollack formed his own band in 1926 and by 1928 was employing such promising young players as Benny Goodman, Jimmy McPartland, Jack Teagarden and Glenn Miller. When Pollack's orchestra disbanded in 1934, its membership became the core group for Bob Crosby's orchestra. Pollack became the musical director for Chico Marx in the early 1940s and continued to play Dixieland music with his Pick-A-Rib Boys into the 1960s.

Don Redman (Alto saxophone, clarinet, vocals, composer, arranger, 1900–64)

Renowned for crafting the polished sound of the mid-1920s Fletcher Henderson Orchestra, Redman's innovative arrangements pre-dated the Swing Era by a decade. His sophisticated compositions were significantly affected by the trumpet work of Louis Armstrong, who played in Henderson's Orchestra throughout 1924. The conservatory-trained arranger left Henderson's band in 1927 to become musical director of McKinney's Cotton Pickers for four years, then led his own big band from 1931–41.

A photo card for Ben Pollack's Park Central Hotel Orchestra, which included Jack Teagarden and Benny Goodman.

Ben Pollack
AND HIS PARK CENTRAL HOTEL ORCH

A-Z of Artists

Zutty Singleton (Drums, 1898–1975)

Arthur 'Zutty' Singleton was one of the first New Orleans drummers, along with Baby Dodds, to develop a melodic approach to the kit and the concept of the extended drum solo. He played in the second configuration of Louis Armstrong's Hot Five, appearing on OKeh recordings cut in 1928 (including the landmark 'West End Blues'), and then moved to New York the following year. In the 1930s he played with Fats Waller, Eddie Condon and Bubber Miley, while also leading his own band.

After moving to Los Angeles in 1943, he demonstrated his versatility by working with a variety of artists including bluesman T-Bone Walker, Dixielander Wingy Manone and jivester Slim Gaillard (appearing on 'Slim's Jam' with bebop icons Charlie Parker and Dizzy Gillespie). He spent the early 1950s in Europe working with Hot Lips Page, and through the 1960s could be found playing drums at Jimmy Ryan's club in New York.

Noble Sissle (Vocals, composer, bandleader, 1889–1975)

Sissle worked with bandleader James Reese Europe from 1916–19, before teaming up with Eubie Blake; together Sissle and Blake wrote hits for Sophie Tucker and the successful all-black musicals *Shuffle Along* (1921) and *Chocolate Dandies* (1924). Sissle led his own bands in Europe during the late 1920s before returning to America in 1931 and forming a new group that featured singer Lena Horne. Between 1938 and 1950, Sissle's orchestra held forth at Billy Rose's Diamond Horseshoe Club in New York.

Key Tracks

'Barney's Bounce' Zutty Singleton
'Shuffle Along' Noble Sissle
'Black And Tan Fantasy' Jabbo Smith
'Jazz Battle' Jabbo Smith & his
   Rhythm Aces

Jabbo Smith (Trumpet, 1908–91)

This Georgia-born trumpeter (real name Cladys Smith) was on the New York scene by the age of 17 in 1925, working with Charlie Johnson's house band at Small's Paradise. In 1927 he played on Duke Ellington's 'Black And Tan Fantasy' and later that year joined James P. Johnson and Fats Waller in Chicago for a production of *Keep Shufflin'*. By 1929, Smith was being touted as competition for Louis Armstrong on the strength of recordings with his Rhythm Aces for Brunswick.

New Orleans drummer Zutty Singleton, whose versatility enabled him to play both traditional and developing styles of jazz, as well as blues music.

A–Z of Artists

Pine Top Smith (Piano, vocals, 1904–29)

A seminal figure in the development of boogie-woogie piano, Clarence 'Pine Top' Smith worked the southern club and vaudeville circuit during the early 1920s. In 1928 he moved to Chicago, where he roomed with Meade 'Lux' Lewis and Albert Ammons. Smith recorded his signature 'Pine Top's Boogie-Woogie' for Vocalion in 1928. The following year he was shot in a Chicago dancehall and died aged just 25.

Johnny St Cyr (Guitar, banjo, 1890–1966)

Johnny St Cyr played around New Orleans as a teenager with A.J. Piron and the Superior, Olympia and Tuxedo bands. He joined Kid Ory's band in 1918 and later played in Fate Marable's riverboat band. In 1923 he moved to Chicago, where he joined King Oliver's Creole Jazz Band. He played on Armstrong's historic Hot Five and Hot Seven sessions (1925–27) and also recorded with Jelly Roll Morton's Red Hot Peppers (1926). St Cyr led a small Dixieland band at Disneyland from 1961 until his death.

Frankie Trumbauer (C-melody and alto saxophone, 1901–56)

Known as 'Tram', Trumbauer was a player of impeccable technique. He first recorded in 1923 with the Benson Orchestra of Chicago and by 1926 was playing alongside cornettist Bix Beiderbecke in Jean Goldkette's Orchestra. Bix and Tram were reunited as star soloists in Paul Whiteman's orchestra in 1927. Trumbauer remained until 1932, during which time he was also on the bandstand with Eddie Lang, Joe Venuti, Andy Secrest, Mildred Bailey and Bing Crosby.

> **Popular Melody**
> Bix Beiderbecke – 'Riverboat Shuffle' (1927)

His second hitch with Whiteman lasted from 1933–36, and was followed by a stint with the Three Ts, featuring Charlie and Jack Teagarden. Trumbauer continued to record in the early 1950s.

Joe Venuti (Violin, 1903–78)

Venuti teamed up with guitarist Eddie Lang in 1926 for some classic duet sessions on OKeh. They reprised their intimate chemistry on 1928 sessions and worked together through the 1920s and 1930s on recordings for Jean Goldkette, Paul Whiteman, Red McKenzie and Roger Wolfe Kahn. In 1933 Venuti led small group sessions and in 1935 fronted a big band. He experienced a major comeback in the 1970s.

Bix Beiderbecke with his good friend and musical collaborator, saxophonist Frankie 'Tram' Trumbauer (right), in 1928.

A-Z of Artists

Fats Waller (Piano, vocals, composer, 1904–43)

Thomas Wright 'Fats' Waller developed his playing style during the early 1920s under the tutelage of Harlem stride pianists James P. Johnson and Willie 'The Lion' Smith. The son of a Baptist preacher, he began playing in the church and by the age of 15 was the house organist at the Lincoln Theatre. He first recorded for OKeh aged 18 and shortly thereafter met lyricist Andy Razaf, who became a key collaborator on popular tunes such as 'Honeysuckle Rose', 'Ain't Misbehavin'' and '(What Did I Do To Be So) Black And Blue' as well as successful musicals *Keep Shufflin'* and *Hot Chocolates*.

By 1924 Fats was well known for his piano rolls, radio broadcasts and extroverted, off-the-cuff, jivey performance style. He also flaunted dazzling piano work on many instrumentals, including 'A Handful Of Keys', 'Smashing Thirds' and 'Jitterbug Waltz'. Waller recorded with a sextet in the mid-1930s and by 1940 was a household name.

'Some little people has music in them, but Fats, he was all music, and you know how big he was.'

James P. Johnson

Paul Whiteman (Violin, bandleader, 1890–1967)

Erroneously dubbed 'The King Of Jazz' by press agents, Whiteman led his first dance band in San Francisco in 1918. Arriving in New York in 1920, he assembled some of the city's top musicians and gained popularity with hits such as 'Japanese Sandman' and 'Whispering'. In 1924 his orchestra premiered George Gershwin's *Rhapsody In Blue*. Whiteman's best band (1927–30) included such superb soloists as Frankie Trumbauer, Bix Beiderbecke, Eddie Lang and Joe Venuti, and launched crooner Bing Crosby's career.

Sam Wooding (Piano, arranger, bandleader, 1895–1985)

Wooding led his Society Syncopators in the early 1920s before travelling to Berlin in 1925 with the *Chocolate Kiddies* revue. One of the first wave of expatriate American jazz musicians to live abroad, he spent the remainder of the 1920s in Europe playing with bands that featured star soloists such as Doc Cheatham and Tommy Ladnier. He returned to the United States in 1935 but had little success swimming against the tide of the Swing Era.

Bandleader Paul Whiteman, whose orchestral line-up at various times included Bix Beiderbecke, Eddie Lang and Bing Crosby.

The Thirties

Following the stock exchange crash of 1929, America and, in turn, the rest of the world, entered a period of economic downturn. A decline in production and trade led to high levels of debt and unemployment, and many people faced financial ruin.

Furthermore, the Dustbowl storms in the agricultural areas of Oklahoma, Texas and Arkansas left hundreds of thousands of people homeless, and the migration northwards continued as the southerners sought better prospects in the northern cities.

Radio was still a growing medium, with increasingly inventive programming, and by the end of the decade 80 per cent of US citizens owned a set. While the recording industry and record sales went into a temporary decline, live music prospered and the joyful sounds of jazz resonated in dancehalls everywhere. In an effort to lift America's spirits, a committee organized the New York World's Fair in 1939 – an ambitious undertaking that presented exhibits from all over the world, and in which artefacts from history mingled with inventions for the future.

Key Artists

Count Basie
Charlie Christian
Roy Eldridge
Benny Goodman
Lester Young

In Europe, dictators such as Hitler, Mussolini and Stalin were fuelling the political turmoil that led to the Second World War. The preparations for rearmament in Europe and the US, and the subsequent outbreak of war in 1939, enabled the gradual rebuild of the economy and created opportunities for work.

During the Great Depression, the American unemployed were forced to queue for their bread.

The Vituosos Take Over

Jazz entered the 1930s as a clunky, two-cylinder Model A and soared out a stainless-steel zephyr gliding on the wind. Three factors shaped this spectacular transformation: an aggressive quest for virtuosity, the power of mass public acclaim and a conscious spirit of modernity.

Much of the evolution of jazz in the 1930s can be explained in terms of a steeply rising arc of instrumental virtuosity. Jazz players had become conscious during the previous decade of the possibilities that instrumental technique could bring to the music. Louis Armstrong (1901–71) had shown that beautifully wrought high notes, growing out of a carefully plotted emotional logic, could bring stately dramatic power to a simple blues. In the 1930s instinct was inspired by skill, which searched for new hills to climb. Armstrong turned away from the blues and applied himself to the more challenging medium of popular song. The best younger players, previously in awe of Armstrong's technique, promptly mastered it and then extended it. With the high notes achieved, faster and more fluid notes chasing more daring ideas became the norm. In the 1930s the *legato* eighth-note replaced the hammered quarter-note as the centre of jazz phrasing. Roy Eldridge (1911–89) and Harry James (1916–83) showed that one could create a totally original and modern voice within the Armstrong model and take it to new places. Eldridge and Charlie Shavers brought a fresh and ferocious precision to their playing that became the benchmark of virtuosity in the 1940s and formed a technical foundation without which bebop's complexities could not have been mastered.

'The big bands needed individualists ... we grew up with jazz, felt strongly about our music and each of us developed in his own way, becoming both distinct individuals and soloists. We weren't just another sideman!'

Bud Freeman

On piano, Art Tatum (1909–56) brought to bear a level of technique so colossal that it would be a generation before others caught up; Teddy Wilson (1912–86) provided a more practical route into the future for most. Tatum and Wilson made their first records in 1933, and each made his right hand the primary focus of his style, playing single-note lines that complemented the rhythmic fluency of swing. But Wilson's gentler, more symmetrical virtuosity made him more accessible and, accordingly, more directly influential.

Teddy Wilson's accessible yet highly original piano style made him a very influential musician.

The Reign of the Big Bands

When Benny Goodman (1909–86) combined his clarinet virtuosity with the arranging skills of Fletcher Henderson (1897–1952), big-band jazz became the dominant popular music of the late 1930s. Big bands had occupied a major place in popular music since the end of the First World War but, except those led by Duke Ellington (1899–1974), Henderson, Earl Hines (1903–83) and a few others, most were white bands conducted by entertainers who played instruments only incidentally, if at all.

Goodman changed much of that in 1935–36. By 1939, Goodman had opened the door for a procession of bandleader virtuosos. They included Artie Shaw (1910–2004), Count Basie (1904–84), Tommy Dorsey (1905–56), Chick Webb (1909–39), Woody Herman (1913–87), Teddy Wilson, Glenn Miller (1904–44) and others – all brilliant players whose names became the great musical brands of the decade.

While the big swing units reached mass audiences, a self-proclaimed jazz elite held itself apart. Rejecting big bands as commercial distortions of the real thing, they insisted that the only true jazz was improvised small-group music with roots in the style of the late 1920s. Commodore Records became home to this alternative, as well as the first label founded exclusively to record jazz. Formed in 1938 by Milt Gabler, it concentrated on spirited Dixieland sessions and drew from a stock company that included Eddie Condon (1905–73), Pee Wee Russell (1906–69), Wild Bill Davison, and Bud Freeman (1906–91). A year later Blue Note Records became the country's second jazz-only label, emphasizing traditional black artists such as Sidney Bechet (1897–1959) and Meade 'Lux' Lewis (1905–64).

Popular Melody

Bing Crosby with Joe Sullivan/Mildred Bailey & her Swing Band – 'Someday Sweetheart' (1934)/(1935)

These labels were part of a larger trend – a rising recognition that jazz had a history before 1935. Two music magazines in America (*Down Beat* and *Metronome*) and one in England (*Melody Maker*) became the most influential publications guiding contemporary taste and exploring jazz roots. As fans read about jazz history, they grew curious about listening to it as well. At Columbia Records in 1940 George Avakian produced the first series of jazz reissue albums (four 78-rpm records), starting with long out-of-print performances by Armstrong, Henderson, Bessie Smith (1894–1937) and Bix Beiderbecke (1903–31).

Bandleaders such as Benny Goodman and Harry James (on trumpet) were set to change the character of American music.

Jazz Music Gains Wider Recognition

By 1939 jazz was becoming increasingly conscious of itself as a 'serious' art form. Thus, it deserved a place at the table among the higher arts – a claim based partly on the notion that the best jazz musicians now commanded a level of virtuosity equal to the finest classical players.

Mainstream music critics were called upon to recognize jazz on a par with the European masters. At least one classical critic, Winthrop Sargeant of the *New Yorker*, took up the task. His *Jazz, Hot And Hybrid*, published in 1938, was the first serious musicological study of jazz. Among the most basic changes that made many of these advances possible was an early shift in the rhythm section. By 1932 the banjo and tuba were disappearing, replaced with the more supple sounds of guitar and string bass. Drummers began to untie the rigidity of 1920s two-beat rhythm, giving the pulse a lightness and swiftness that was essential to a swing feel. By the mid-1930s, jazz's rhythm engine was revving out its lumpy two-beat tradition to a driving 4/4 swing, revising the most basic laws of motion in jazz.

The Jazz Age Meets the Machine Age

The spirit of the 1930s was dominated by new possibilities of technology. In one brief 18-month period, from 1934–36, America saw its first diesel streamliners, the Chrysler Airflow car, the DC-3 aircraft and the Golden Gate Bridge amongst other technological innovations. In the midst of this fixation with stylized modernity and motion, the smooth, rhythmic momentum of swing became an extension of the same spirit of efficiency that found beauty in sleek designs. In jazz terms, swing reached a perfection of form by 1939 with the Count Basie band. Jazz soon spilled out into daily life through radio, movies and advertising. The top white swing bands played on their own radio shows and in Hollywood, swing quickly found its way on to the screen. Louis Armstrong appeared in *Pennies From Heaven* (1936). Benny Goodman's music mingled with Paramount's *Big Broadcast of 1937* and Warner Bros.' *Hollywood Hotel* of the same year, and at MGM the link between jazz and the jitterbug dance fad became the basis for Artie Shaw's first film, *Dancing Co-Ed* (1939). In this convergence of modernistic expressions lies perhaps the best explanation of why jazz managed to swiftly become the popular music of America.

> **Popular Melody**
> Artie Shaw & his Orchestra – 'Carioca' (1939)

Manhattan's magnificent Chrysler Building typified the streamlined forms that dominated modern design in the US during the 1930s.

Key Artist: Count Basie

If swing in its most characteristic form was a hot and hard-driving music, William 'Count' Basie showed that there was a cooler and softer side to the music, an alter ego that even at swift tempos could move with a relaxed, almost serene restraint that subliminally mirrored the streamlined design forms of the Machine Age, in which science and art seemed to mingle.

For Basie this was surely an outcome of chance, not intent. He was born in Red Bank, New Jersey on 21 August 1904 and never finished high school, preferring a life in show business and music. He arrived in New York in 1924 and came to know the reigning Harlem pianists of the day – James P. Johnson, Willie 'The Lion' Smith and Fats Waller – mastering their dense, two-handed stride style. But for his own style to emerge he needed to escape those powerful influences. Stranded in Kansas City, Basie joined the Blue Devils, led by bassist Walter Page, in 1927.

The Kansas City Scene

The American Southwest was a jazz environment unto itself, alive with regional bands that worked from Chicago to Texas. In the Blue Devils Basie met the core of players who would be with him in Chicago and New York. In 1929 Basie joined the Bennie Moten orchestra. He had recorded nine sessions with Moten by the end of 1932, none of which provide a clue to the pianist that would emerge when he next recorded in 1936.

A lot happened during that four-year blackout. After Moten's sudden death in 1935, Basie took a job at the Reno Club in Kansas City, hiring players from the old Moten unit as well as former Blue Devils. By early 1936 many of the key men were in place, including Walter Page, Jo Jones and Lester Young. Broadcasting nightly from Kansas City, the signals found their way north through the cold night air to Chicago, where they caught the ear of critic John Hammond. Writing in *Down Beat*, he called the band 'far and away the finest in the country' with a rhythm section 'more exciting than any in American orchestral history'.

Above: Accomplished pianist and revolutionary bandleader Count Basie. Right: Kansas City in the 1930s, where Count Basie's band caught the attention of music critic John Hammond.

> *'Count is ... just about the best piano player I know for pushing a band and comping for soloists. I mean the way he makes different preparations for each soloist and the way, at the end of one of his solos, he prepares an entrance for the next man.'*

Freddie Green

That summer Hammond drove to Kansas City and was not disappointed. The band was soon on its way to Chicago, where Hammond recorded a small Basie unit featuring Lester Young in the landmark 'Lady Be Good'. Suddenly here was the spacious, minimalist Basie piano style, always implying more notes than were played and allowing the rhythm section to shine through with a transparent clarity.

Basie Rhythm

Rhythm guitarist Freddie Green joined Jones and Page to complete the unique Basie rhythm team. Page and Green became the quiet pulse keepers. With a rhythm section so subtle and implicit, the arrangements often held back, offering it space. Many of the band's most characteristic charts would begin softly with a chorus or two of rhythm and Basie's see-through piano, then unfold in steadily expanding layers of riffs (e.g. 'One O'Clock Jump'). The band reached New York in January 1937 and hit its stride in the summer of 1938 during an engagement at the Famous Door. Basie's group recorded more than 60 sides for Decca, then moved to Columbia in 1939 where it remained until after the war. This forms the collective body of work on which the Basie reputation continues to rest.

The Basie Sound Develops

In the early 1950s many of the players who had given the band its voice had left and Basie reformed in 1952 with a new band whose book institutionalized the essence of the Basie sound, but without relying on the cult of the irreplaceable soloist. It became an arrangers' band, in which brilliant writers such as Neal Hefti, Ernie Wilkins, Frank Foster, Thad Jones and Sammy Nestico set the pace. Yet the 'new testament' Basie band would host many fine players and enjoy a steadily growing success from the 1950s through the 1980s. During that time the band recorded extensively for Verve, Roulette and Pablo as Basie watched his

fame ascend into legend. The band has continued to tour successfully, under leaders including Thad Jones, Frank Foster, Grover Mitchell and since 2004 Bill Hughes – all alumni of the 1950s Basie bands.

Next Page: The Count Basie Band moved to Chicago and then to New York, where they accumulated an extensive following.

Key Artist: Charlie Christian

Charlie Christian was the last great figure to emerge from the jazz scene of the 1930s. He not only brought a perfectly formed approach to his music, but also an entirely new musical platform – the electric guitar. His career in the big time was brief, but Christian was a lighthouse whose beam still illuminates anyone with serious intentions on the instrument.

Charles Henry Christian was born on 29 July 1916 in Dallas, Texas to Clarence and Willie Mae Christian, both professional musicians. When Clarence lost his sight in 1918, he turned to playing the guitar, which he also taught to his three sons. By the time Charlie was 10 his father had died and the family had moved to Oklahoma City, where he began working part-time as a pianist. During his teens his future looked grim: at 15 Christian was a lanky high-school dropout and at 16 he was an unexpected father, trying to get by in the dust bowl of the Great Depression. But beneath the bashful, diffident exterior stirred an emerging savant of whom it was said that he could hear around corners with flawless logic. In Oklahoma City he was able to make his way, landing regular jobs in clubs.

'If Charlie had lived, he would have been real modern.'

Kenny Clarke

Christian Joins Benny Goodman

Sometime in the mid-1930s Christian bought a Gibson ES150 electric guitar. No recordings exist by which to chart his development, but there is no question that travelling musicians took notice as Christian worked for $2.50 a night in Oklahoma City. One of the players who heard him while passing through in 1939 was Mary Lou Williams, pianist with the Andy Kirk orchestra.

Meanwhile, Benny Goodman was eager to reinvigorate his band. He was clearly intrigued by the possibilities of the electric guitar and tried out several players on his radio programme, but none was up to the clarinettist's virtuosity. That summer Williams told critic John Hammond about Christian. Hammond flew out to see him, was astonished and shortly afterwards brought him to Los Angeles, where Goodman was playing. In August Christian first sat in with Goodman's quintet. Nothing could have prepared Goodman for what he heard. Christian was immediately hired and for the rest of his short career, the Benny Goodman Sextet and Septet were his professional homes.

Electric guitar virtuoso Charlie Christian, who found fame with the Benny Goodman quintet.

He could not have found a more perfect environment. Goodman and vibraphonist Lionel Hampton were brilliant players who recognized one of their own and the Sextet, with its openness to developing original material, offered an ideal creative mandate. Furthermore, Goodman reached a vast national audience and gave his protégé a generous spotlight. Within weeks, both Christian and the electric guitar were famous. His solos were so inventive in concept and flawless in performance that they seemed to foreclose all future alternatives in one sweeping, inclusive stroke. As 1940 began he stood like a lone colossus on the commanding heights of a dawning, electrified instrumental empire.

Christian's Style

Except for the use of accent chords or recurring triads in his largely set solo on 'Stardust', Christian was a horn-like soloist who played through chords, creating single-note contours that would climb and ebb with a gliding, unbroken flow. He might punctuate with a slicing glissando or unexpectedly riff on a tone pair, i.e. a single note alternating two strings for a variation in timbre. He was also frighteningly prolific at tossing off concise musical figures, many of which became the basis for the classic pieces originating in the Goodman groups: 'Air Mail Special', 'Seven Come Eleven', 'Shivers', 'A Smooth One' and others.

Away from the Goodman Sextet, Christian's appetite for the jam session was voracious. Several warm-ups were caught during his Columbia sessions, and he took part in a dazzling jam at Carnegie Hall with Count Basie, Lester Young and others in December 1939. He was also recorded playing long solos at Minton's Playhouse in Harlem in 1941, performances that catch him at his most relaxed and unguarded. He died in March 1942 from tuberculosis. Almost immediately, a group of direct disciples emerged: Barney Kessel, Herb Ellis, Remo Palmieri, Irving Ashby and Les Paul. Today, distinguished contemporary players such as Russell Malone and Howard Alden carry on the Christian line.

Jazz pianist Mary Lou Williams heard Christian play in Oklahoma City and spread the news of his talents.

Key Artist: Roy Eldridge

While Louis Armstrong remained a pre-eminent jazz symbol in the public mind through the 1930s, and inspired many imitators, younger musicians were coming up who could navigate the trumpet with great agility and dexterity. They would break through the perimeters that Armstrong had established in the 1920s and take the music to new places. In the 1930s no player consolidated those advances or more spectacularly than Roy Eldridge, known throughout his career as 'Little Jazz' because of his short stature and high power.

Eldridge's Heroes

Born in Pittsburgh, Pennsylvania on 30 January 1911, David Roy Eldridge came to music with great youthful exuberance, first on drums and then trumpet. In his eagerness to progress, he played by ear at first. It was his older brother Joseph who disciplined his progress and instructed him in matters of theory and the logic of chord sequences, which the young trumpeter acquired by learning the basics of the piano. During his formative years in the late 1920s he avoided the influence of Armstrong, preferring instead to master the speed and precision of saxophonist Coleman Hawkins. Although he began playing professionally around 1927, Eldridge's development as a player is not documented until 1935, when he recorded with Teddy Hill and on three Teddy Wilson-Billie Holiday sessions. Here he emerges as a seasoned player with a big, clean sound and sharp attack.

'When I was growing up, all I wanted to play was swing. Eldridge was my boy. All I ever did was try to play like him but I never quite made it.'

Dizzy Gillespie

An Exuberant Playing Style

In 1935 he joined Fletcher Henderson in Chicago and not only showed what he could do, but let loose unimagined possibilities for the trumpet. Starting with Armstrong's sense of dramatic pacing, Eldridge added a wildly exuberant recklessness that threw fast, complex phrasing and penetrating high notes together with meticulous precision. Eldridge was a competitive player and thrived on the stimulation of the encounter. The Henderson band gave him his first important foil: tenor saxophonist Chu Berry. On a simple riff piece, 'Jangled Nerves', Berry solos with swift, glancing eighth notes, setting a rapid pace.

Exuberant trumpeter Roy Eldridge, who battled it out with Louis Armstrong in Fletcher Henderson's band.

Then Eldridge bores in with a ferociously suppressed intensity that soon explodes into stabbing high notes, seasoned with a striking dissonance. In the late 1930s it made musicians' heads spin, including that of a young Dizzy Gillespie, who soon showed Eldridge's impact in his first recorded solos.

Faster, Higher!

After leaving Henderson, Eldridge remained in Chicago and formed his own band, which unleashed the full force of his virtuosity. A number of live radio performances from the Three Deuces in Chicago (1937) and the Arcadia in New York (1939) have survived, which offer some of the most breathtaking trumpet solos ever recorded. Interestingly, he performed several Armstrong showpieces, including 'Shine' and 'Mahogany Hall Stomp'. They were homages to the past but also parodies, serving notice that a new generation of elite virtuosos, eager for risk, was now in charge.

Eldridge broke up his band in late 1939, freelanced on record dates, then joined Gene Krupa in 1941, where he gained national prominence (finally topping *Down Beat*'s Readers' Poll in 1942). But he also found his talents restricted to a few showcase numbers. One of them, the beautiful 'Rocking Chair', became one of his most requested pieces. He worked with Artie Shaw in 1944–45 before bebop marginalized him for a period late in the decade. In the 1950s he became part of Norman Granz's Jazz at the Philharmonic tours, recording frequently for Granz's Verve label, and was featured on *The Sound Of Jazz* with Billie Holiday et al. He later recorded with Pablo Records in the 1970s and 1980s, before health problems forced him to give up playing. Roy Eldridge died in February 1989.

Dizzy Gillespie (left) was greatly influenced by the innovative playing of Roy Eldridge.

Key Artist: Benny Goodman

Benny Goodman was the first of the great bandleader virtuosos of the 1930s to achieve global success. Through a combination of personal connections, nerve, enormous talent and sheer luck, he parlayed a sequence of opportunities in 1934–35 into a payoff that changed American music.

After forming his first band in New York in 1934, he won a coveted place on NBC's weekly *Let's Dance* radio show late that year, and then a record contract with RCA Victor. In 1935 a national tour took him to the Palomar Ballroom in California, where his music finally caught the ear of America and the world.

Benjamin David Goodman was born on 30 May 1909 in Chicago, Illinois and took up the clarinet when he was 10. His progress was so swift that by the age of 13 he had a union card and was soon earning $58 a week playing in the Jules Herbeveaux Orchestra. Goodman's first recordings, made with Ben Pollack's orchestra in December 1926, find him self-assured with a smooth, powerful attack and sparkling sound. Although he was part of the Chicago jazz scene and influenced by its heat, his prodigious technique gave him professional choices that many of his jazz contemporaries lacked.

'It wasn't just that his own improvisation was marvelous, the spirit, the verve, the vitality, even humor he played with, but the sheer technical mastery. He played that thing like it was a yo-yo.'

Mel Powell

He could rip into raw, hard-driving solos influenced by Johnny Dodds and Frank Teschemacher but also, when the job required, play polite solo interludes with restraint.

New York Beckons

Moving to New York in 1928, Goodman prospered in radio, theatre and recording work. He was making such a good living by the early 1930s that he had little incentive to fight a growing public indifference to jazz. If Goodman was not committed to 'the cause', however, a young critic and producer named John Hammond was. He approached Goodman in 1933 and provided him with moral support, frequent jazz recording dates and a sense of renewed confidence to pursue the jazz route.

Above: Important bandleader and clarinet virtuoso Benny Goodman (right) jams with Stan Getz and others.

Swing's the Thing

Throughout 1934–35 Benny Goodman became the first white bandleader to bring the swinging spirit of the great black orchestras – Chick Webb, Benny Carter, Duke Ellington and Fletcher Henderson – to a mass audience. He used the Henderson model, bought many of Henderson's arrangements and sharpened the intonation and attack without suffocating any of the rhythmic energy. To this he added his own brilliant clarinet solos. Suddenly jazz music sounded fresh and new to millions of young dancers, who started to listen. By the time Goodman reached Chicago in December, the whole country was talking about 'swing'.

The arrival of swing awakened a sustained consciousness about jazz and, indirectly, about race. The Goodman tide lifted all boats, black and white, and also became a wedge of direct social progress. More than a decade before Jackie Robinson broke the colour line in baseball, Goodman integrated music by bringing Teddy Wilson (1935), Lionel Hampton (1936) and Charlie Christian (1939) into his small groups. Before the end of the decade Fletcher Henderson joined the full Goodman band on piano, becoming the first black musician ever to play as a regular member of a white orchestra. Although politically liberal, Goodman's instincts were musical, not ideological.

Jazz Goes Legit

In January 1938 Goodman's famous concert in Carnegie Hall seemed to sanctify jazz with a new status and 'legitimacy'. Although Carnegie Hall was the crowning event of Goodman's prime years, other accomplishments would follow: the brilliant sextets and big band of 1939–41 with Charlie Christian and Cootie Williams, innovative new charts by Eddie Sauter and Mel Powell, and the late wartime sextet with Red Norvo. After the Second World War Goodman attempted to embrace bebop and performed a clarinet concerto written for him by Aaron Copeland, before wisely returning to the style in which he was most comfortable. From the 1950s into the 1980s he worked when he liked, in a state of semi-retirement.

As a soloist he never fell into set routines, which led to some inconsistency. But an indifferent performance at one concert was often repaid at the next with inspired solos that seemed to surprise Goodman as much as they did the audience.

Musically active until the end, Benny Goodman died in New York in June 1986. His private papers and recordings are archived at Yale University.

Next Page: (l–r) Artie Shaw, Benny Goodman, Duke Ellington, Chick Webb (back), George Hall and Raymond Scott.

Key Artist: Lester Young

Of all the great solo architects of the 1930s, none personified the smooth, penetrating sweep through space and time more ideally or organically than tenor saxophonist Lester Young. His fluid, unforced phrasing and undulating attack were matched to a cool, satin skin of sound that seemed to dispel all friction by decompressing the emotional density of the prevailing tenors into a piping, almost hollow echo.

Young's streamlined contours would have risen to the top in any context, but when joining with the elegant modernity of the Count Basie rhythm section in 1936, Young found his perfect soul-mate; he defined the essence of swing at its most pure and became one of the most influential jazz voices of the decade.

A Musical Background

Born in Woodville, Mississippi on 27 August 1909, Lester Willis Young grew up in a musical family that toured and performed together. He experimented with the trumpet, violin and drums as a boy before finally focusing on the tenor saxophone by 1922. Four years later the Young family relocated to Minneapolis, Minnesota, but Lester grew restless working under his father's hand. When he turned 18 he went out on his own, touring with a variety of regional bands in the upper Midwest. He worked briefly with the Blue Devils in 1930 and with Basie for the first time in the Bennie Moten band in 1934. But Young didn't stay long; he moved through several other groups, then returned to Basie in 1936, just as the bandleader was on the verge of being discovered by John Hammond.

Early Records

Young's career rose swiftly with Basie's, and vice versa. His record debut, made with a small Basie group in October 1936, produced two of the great swing classics of the decade – 'Lady Be Good' and 'Shoe Shine Boy' – and there would be more where that came from. A steady stream of Basie band records poured out, plus many small group sessions, produced by Hammond, that brought Young together with Billie Holiday, Teddy Wilson, Benny Goodman, Charlie Christian and others. The 54 sides made with

Above: Tenor saxophone great Lester Young, one of the most influential jazz soloists of the 1930s. Right: Young with his patron and organizer of 'Jazz At The Philharmonic', Norman Granz.

Holiday between January 1937 and November 1938 carried a particular and persistent fascination – and not merely because the records caught both artists at the peak of their powers. They also seemed to capture a quality of looming melancholy in the relationship of two gentle but flawed temperaments, for whom doom due to fragility seemed written on the wind. The music survives in a nimbus of legend.

Young's dry, feathery lyricism and fluid laws of motion immediately set him apart from the flock, as the other musicians recognized a new and original tenor voice. His ideas were oblique and unexpected. He would spread a phrase out over several bars, then suddenly pause over a lingering, out-of-tempo note, or interrupt himself with an impulsive arching swoop. In a broadcast performance of 'I Got Rhythm' from the Southland Café, Young bounces along on a sleek, unbroken F over four continuous bars of rhythmic variations. By the end of the 1930s Young had not only become the first serious alternative to the big-toned, romantic tenor; he also seemed to have opened a door into post-war modernism, where the hot would soon make room for the cool.

Leaving Basie

Young left Basie in 1940, returned briefly in 1944, and was then drafted into the army. During basic training he was caught in possession of marijuana and confined to military prison until December 1945. Although he seemed to recover much of his pre-war form in a series of Jazz At The Philharmonic (JATP) concerts in the spring of 1946, it was soon apparent that Young's sound had taken on a thicker, denser texture. Also, his easy fluency seemed to settle into a series of set signature phrases and figures.

Fans and critics disagree on the merits of Young's later work, but there is little dispute that a younger generation of light-toned players based their style and sound largely on his innovations in the 1930s. Although they continued to revere him, they passed him by to become the stars of the post-war cult of the cool: Al Cohn, Zoot Sims, Alan Eager, Dexter Gordon and above all Stan Getz. Norman Granz became Young's most consistent patron, despite the fact that Young's declining health had an increasingly severe impact on his playing. After the mid-1950s his performances were unquestionably a shadow of their former selves. A final reunion with Billie Holiday in December 1957 on *The Sound Of Jazz*, a CBS Television special, would acquire in the years ahead a special poignancy. Today many feel that they see in the performance the star-crossed character of their brief lives, caught with a touching transparency. Young died on 15 March 1959 in New York.

Next Page: Bennie Moten's (seated right), shown here in 1929, was where Young met bandleader Count Basie (seated left).

A-Z of Artists

Billy Banks (Vocals, 1908–67)

A crooner and scat singer, Billy Banks was a protégé of agency impresario Irving Mills. He headlined a handful of legendary records in 1932 by the Rhythmakers – less interesting for his vocals than for the punchy, eccentric work of the all-star band, which included Henry 'Red' Allen, Pee Wee Russell, Fats Waller, Eddie Condon, Pops Foster, Tommy Dorsey and Zutty Singleton. Banks also recorded with the Mills Blues Rhythm band in the 1930s before leaving for Europe in 1952. He later settled in Tokyo, where he ran a club.

Danny Barker (Banjo, guitar, educator, 1909–94)

Daniel Moses Barker carried forth the musical traditions of New Orleans, playing with a number of traditional bands in the 1920s and 1930s before marrying Louise Dupont (a.k.a. Blue Lu Barker) in 1930. They recorded several sides together in 1938, including Baker's own song 'Don't You Make Me High', revived in the 1970s by Maria Muldauer. After working with several big bands in the 1930s (including those of Lucky Millinder and Cab Calloway), he was a New Orleans revival activist, leading a youth band that included Wynton Marsalis.

Key Tracks

'Mean Old Bed Bug Blues' Billy Banks
'Don't You Make Me High' Danny Barker
'Marie' Bunny Berigan
'I Can't Get Started' Bunny Berigan

Bunny Berigan (Trumpet, vocals, 1908–42)

Rowland Bernard Berigan's warm sound and fluent style made him a major figure of the Swing Era. To some extent, his alcohol-related death at 33 has unduly enhanced his legacy, lifting a solid talent to the level of tortured artist-genius. Berigan arrived in New York in 1929 and became a sought-after session player. He played in Benny Goodman's 1935 band, leaving memorable solos on 'King Porter Stomp' and 'Sometimes I'm Happy'.

With Tommy Dorsey in 1937 he scored two more classics – 'Marie' and 'Song Of India'. Berigan assembled his own band and recorded his most famous showpiece, 'I Can't Get Started'. His solo began with a series of reflective breaks and then broke into a majestic high note statement, before falling to a low-register denouement and epilogue. Laid out with strong dramatic pacing, it shows Berigan's debt to Louis Armstrong. In 1939 Berigan dissolved his band, rejoined Dorsey briefly in 1940, and then resumed with his own orchestra.

Bandleader Cab Calloway, who worked with Danny Barker in the 1930s.

A-Z of Artists

Chu Berry (Tenor saxophone, 1908–41)

Inspired by Coleman Hawkins' big sound, Leon 'Chu' Berry honed a more rapid, streamlined tenor attack. He recorded with Benny Carter in 1933 and joined Fletcher Henderson three years later. In 1937 he topped *Down Beat*'s first national poll of leading musicians and joined Cab Calloway's orchestra, where he remained until his death. Berry also participated in numerous small groups. A versatile musician, he was equally at home skating over the beat at fast tempos, surging effortlessly through mid-tempos or playing romantic ballads in the Hawkins tradition.

Cab Calloway (Bandleader, vocals, entertainer, 1907–94)

Cabell Calloway's orchestra was one of the most successful black bands of the 1930s. He arrived in Chicago in the late 1920s and found his niche as a singer, then went to New York, where the band that he fronted replaced Duke Ellington's at the Cotton Club. He cultivated a jive-talking persona that appeared to a mixed racial audience. After 1935 he brought in a succession of important soloists (Ben Webster, Chu Berry and Dizzy Gillespie), but his vocals remained the focus of the band's sound. After the war he gave up the band to concentrate on club, theatre and movie work until the end of his life.

'The problem of expressing the contributions that Benny Carter has made to popular music is so tremendous it completely fazes me, so extraordinary a musician is he.'

Duke Ellington

Benny Carter (Alto saxophone, arranger, trumpet, vocals, 1907–2003)

One of the great arrangers and soloists in jazz history, Bennett Lester Carter wrote some of the first big-band music to fully realize the flowing, *legato* ensemble of the coming swing movement. His saxophone ensembles were smooth projections of his solo style. 'Lonesome Nights' and 'Symphony In Riffs' were so advanced when Carter recorded them in 1933 that they still sounded at home in the late 1930s and early 1940s when Artie Shaw, Tommy Dorsey, Gene Krupa and Cab Calloway recorded their versions. Carter worked in Europe during 1935–38 and returned to lead a series of excellent bands. After settling in California in 1942, Carter prospered in film and worked to integrate musicians in Hollywood. He continued to record and perform into his 90s.

Benny Carter, a hugely influential player but a relatively unsung hero of jazz music.

A-Z of Artists

Doc Cheatham (Trumpet, vocals, 1905–97)

Adolphus Cheatham played in countless bands and groups in the 1920s, before settling in the Cab Calloway orchestra in 1931. He remained with Calloway until 1939, after which he resumed work with a variety of bands. He didn't emerge as a soloist until the 1960s, working with George Wein, Benny Goodman and others. His singing style was suited to both cabaret and jazz clubs; he performed regularly in New York throughout the rest of his long life.

Jimmy Dorsey (Bandleader, alto saxophone, clarinet, 1904–57)

Jimmy Dorsey freelanced in New York in the early 1930s, recording frequently with brother Tommy as the Dorsey Brothers Orchestra. They formed a working band in 1934 but split up in 1935. Jimmy carried on, backing Bing Crosby on radio and recording prolifically for Decca. He came into his own in the 1940s and in 1957 he scored an unexpected hit with 'So Rare'.

Tommy Dorsey (Bandleader, trombone, trumpet, 1905–56)

With the breakup of the Dorsey Brothers Orchestra, Tommy Dorsey hired the Joe Haymes orchestra *en masse* and built a new band. The Dorsey band of 1935–39 drew its identity from the swing of drummer Dave Tough, soloists Bud Freeman, Bunny Berigan, Yank Lawson and Johnny Mince, and singers Jack Leonard and Edythe Wright. Late in 1939, Sy Oliver joined as arranger and reinvented the band, which became a showboat of talent. In 1953 the Dorsey brothers reunited and in 1956 their *Stage Show* introduced Elvis Presley to a national television audience.

Key Tracks

'What Can I Say After I'm Sorry' Doc Cheatham
'What A Diff'rence A Day Made' The Dorsey
  Brothers Orchestra
'A-Tisket, A-Tasket' Ella Fitzgerald

Ella Fitzgerald (Vocals, 1917–96)

Sixteen-year-old Ella Fitzgerald joined Chick Webb's band in 1934 and became its biggest attraction. After Webb's death in 1939 she became titular leader of the orchestra, which continued until 1942; she then worked as a solo artist. After the war Fitzgerald revealed an uncanny talent for bebop scat singing; it drew the attention of Norman Granz, who began adding her to his Jazz At The Philharmonic shows. She rose to become the reigning interpreter of twentieth-century American songs.

Tommy (left) and Jimmy Dorsey (right) with drummer Buddy Rich.

A-Z of Artists

Stephane Grappelli (Violin, piano, 1908–97)

Largely self-taught, Stephane Grappelli's virtuosity came to the attention of the world in 1934 through records with Django Reinhardt and the Quintet of the Hot Club of France. His refined sound was decorative on ballads but could push with an alert and driving attack of formidable power on jazz standards such as 'Tiger Rag', 'Shine' and 'I've Found A New Baby'.

In Paris and London Grappelli recorded with many visiting American players, including violinist Eddie South in 1937. Their repertoire, which ranged from Gershwin to Bach, produced some of the most dazzling and intriguing violin duets ever recorded. The Quintet never appeared in America, although it was heard on several radio broadcasts. Grappelli lived in London during and after the war, but his reputation faded. In 1969 George Wein brought him to the Newport Jazz Festival for his American debut. Still at the top of his form, he continued to tour and record for another 28 years.

Bobby Hackett (Trumpet, cornet, guitar, 1915–76)

After Bobby Hackett was praised in *Down Beat* by Boston critic George Frazier in 1937, he headed to New York and settled into a group of neo-traditional players loosely associated with Eddie Condon. Although a lifelong fan of Louis Armstrong, Hackett's gentle, fluid lyricism made him a more logical descendent of Bix Biederbecke, whom he represented in a historical section of Benny Goodman's 1938 Carnegie Hall concert. Hackett recorded with his own big band in 1939. His association with Condon brought him into an informal stock company of players who recorded for Dixieland-oriented Commodore Records.

Key Tracks

'Tiger Rag' Stephane Grapplli
'I've Found A New Baby' Stephane Grappelli
'Embraceable You' Bobby Hackett
'Strings Of Pearls' Bobby Hackett

He joined Glenn Miller in 1941 and played the famous cornet bridge on 'String Of Pearls'. During the 1940s he divided his time between radio staff work and jazz. Hackett's placid improvisations found a large audience in the 1950s as the featured solo voice on many mood music albums conducted by Jackie Gleason. He also worked prominently with Goodman, singer Tony Bennett and Vic Dickenson in his later years.

The Quintet of the Hot Club of France, with Django Reinhardt (second from left) and Stephane Grappelli (second from right).

A-Z of Artists

John Hammond (Critic, producer, 1910–86)

John Hammond was the most influential jazz critic, producer and social activist of the politically charged 1930s. A Vanderbilt descendant raised in social prominence and luxury on New York's East Side, Hammond rebelled against his class, producing jazz records and pressing for racial integration. He played a key role in the careers of Fletcher Henderson, Benny Goodman, Billie Holiday, Lionel Hampton, Count Basie and Charlie Christian – bringing them together on occasions – and later Aretha Franklin, Bob Dylan and Bruce Springsteen.

Lionel Hampton (Vibraphone, drums, piano, 1908–2002)

During his early years Lionel Hampton worked as a drummer. He began experimenting with the vibraphone around 1930, but few bandleaders wanted its unorthodox sound. In 1936 Benny Goodman heard Hampton and immediately invited him to join Gene Krupa and Teddy Wilson, making the Goodman Trio a quartet. In 1937 he began a parallel series of remarkable sessions under his own name on Victor that would involve most of the greatest soloists of the period. After leaving Goodman in 1940, Hampton formed his own band, which recorded his definitive version of 'Flying Home' in 1942, featuring tenor saxophonist Illinois Jacquet. He continued leading bands and touring the world well into the 1990s.

Key Tracks

'Flying Home' Lionel Hampton
'Piano Man' Earl Hines
'A Monday Date' Earl Hines

Earl Hines (Piano, bandleader, 1903–83)

Earl 'Fatha' Hines was the key transitional figure between the early ragtime and stride styles and the essentials of modern piano. He stripped away much of the density of 1920s piano, replacing it with more linear octaves and edgy single-note lines with the right hand while softening the rhythmic accompaniment with the left. Hines established his reputation in Chicago in the late 1920s, recording solos and classics such as 'Weather Bird' and 'West End Blues' with Louis Armstrong. He led the house band at Chicago's Grand Terrace Café from 1928–40. Hines turned it into a first-class orchestra and the band's peak years came on its Victor recordings (1939–42). Hines gave up the band in 1947, toured with Louis Armstrong until 1951 and then fell in to obscurity. In 1964 a New York solo concert returned him to prominence; for the next 19 years he toured and recorded prolifically.

Earl Hines emerged in Louis Armstrong's company, introducing 'trumpet-style' piano.

A-Z of Artists

Johnny Hodges (Alto and soprano saxophones, 1907–70)

Saxophonist Johnny Hodges was fortunate enough to forge an early relationship with Sidney Bechet; while playing at Club Bechet in New York he won the attention of Duke Ellington, who signed him in 1928. Hodges' sweeping tone and scooping glissandos remained a vital part of Ellington's orchestra for around 40 years, with only a few periods of absence as he experimented with small groups and other ventures. Hodges was admired by many other saxophonists, including Ben Webster and John Coltrane.

Spike Hughes (Bass, bandleader, critic, 1908–87)

As editor for *Melody Maker* and producer at British Decca, Spike Hughes recorded many dance and novelty sides during 1930–32 but had ambitions in jazz. During a New York visit in 1933 he augmented Benny Carter's band with Coleman Hawkins and recorded 14 of his own arrangements as Spike Hughes & his Negro Orchestra. Notwithstanding Hughes' many excellent solos, John Hammond wrote that he 'could not write music that swung'. At this, Hughes decided to return to journalism and producing, and never recorded again.

Key Tracks

'Good Queen Bess' Johnny Hodges
'Day Dream' Johnny Hodges
'Bugle Call Rag' Spike Hughes
'Dark Eyes' Jo Jones
'Goin' To Chicago Blues' Jo Jones

Jo Jones (Drums, 1911–85)

Few players have defined a big band from the drum chair as strongly as Jonathon 'Jo' Jones did with Count Basie. When the first Basie records came out in 1937, their rhythm section was both a revelation and a revolution – and brought jazz drumming into a new, more sleek modernity. A master of the steely hi-hat cymbal, Jones coaxed from it a supple, relaxed whoosh, sliding accents slightly to either side of the beat. It swung with an uncanny crackle and power and became the principle mainspring of his time.

Jones had first worked with Basie in the Blue Devils in 1929. He joined the Basie band in Kansas City and remained during its prime years from 1936–44, during which he also recorded many dates with Teddy Wilson and Billie Holiday. Jones returned to Basie in 1946, by which time new drummers were carrying his innovations into bebop. From the 1950s onwards he freelanced and taught an army of young students, becoming known as 'Papa' Jo Jones in his later years.

Three of the great innovators in jazz during the 1930s – (l–r) Teddy Wilson, Jo Jones and Lester Young – reuniting at a Norman Granz session in 1956.

A-Z of Artists

Jonah Jones (Trumpet, vocals, 1909–2000)

By the time Jonah Jones came to prominence on New York's 52nd Street, he had developed a fierce, intense attack that suggested Roy Eldridge without the high notes. He played and recorded with Stuff Smith from 1936–40 and on sessions with Teddy Wilson, Billie Holiday and Lionel Hampton. He worked with Cab Calloway from 1941–52. In 1957 he began recording for Capitol and had several hits, including 'Baubles, Bangles And Beads' and 'On The Street Where You Live', which combined a shuffle rhythm with his muted trumpet.

Gene Krupa (Drums, 1909–73)

Possibly the most famous jazz drummer, Gene Krupa played in the 'press roll' style of Chicago, where he first recorded in 1927. He was a traditionalist and kept time largely on the snare, with either sticks or brushes, playing two-beat on bass drum. He joined Benny Goodman in 1934 and became a key factor in the band's historic success.

Popular Melody

Benny Goodman –
'Sing Sing Sing' (1937)

As a soloist, he combined technique, imagination and flash that made him the centre of attention. Much of that technique infused Goodman's trio and quartet pieces. But his *tour de force* would forever be 'Sing Sing Sing', a nine-minute collage of riffs linked by Krupa's rock-solid tom-toms and recurring solo interludes. He left Goodman in 1938 to form his own band, which became a great success in the 1940s with Roy Eldridge and Anita O'Day. Krupa scaled back to a trio in 1951 and worked in that format for the next 20 years.

Jimmie Lunceford (Bandleader, arranger, 1902–47)

While working as a music teacher in Memphis, Mississippi-born Lunceford formed a band called the Chicksaw Syncopators. They first recorded in 1930 and after four years of touring gained a residency at the Cotton Club and became the Jimmie Lunceford Orchestra. Renowned for its polished stage presence, the band was nevertheless musically tight and trumpeter Sy Oliver's arrangements secured a signature 'Lunceford sound'. Pay disputes split the original line-up in the early 1940s, but Lunceford continued to lead the orchestra until his death.

Jimmie Lunceford's band was renowned for its elaborate stage shows.

A-Z of Artists

Wingy Manone (Trumpet, vocals, 1900–82)

Born in New Orleans, Joseph 'Wingy' Manone's rousing trumpet and gravelly vocals were (as with his fellow Italian-American, Louis Prima) confidently cast from the Armstrong matrix. After scoring a hit with 'Isle Of Capri' in 1935, he became a fixture on New York's 52nd Street before moving to California in 1940 to join Bing Crosby's circle of cronies. His 1930 disc 'Tar Paper Stomp' is the first recorded appearance of the blues riff that would become familiar in 1939 as Glenn Miller's 'In The Mood'.

Irving Mills (Music publisher, producer, manager, 1884–1985)

Publisher Irving Mills was early to recognize the potential in black music. He formed Mills Music, Inc. with his brother in 1919 and enjoyed a business relationship with Duke Ellington from 1926–39 that brought a procession of Ellington songs into the Mills catalogue. He also formed the Mills Blue Rhythm Band in 1931 and developed it into a fine orchestra before it evolved into the Lucky Millinder band in 1938. Mills Music, Inc. was sold in 1965.

Hot Lips Page (Trumpet, vocals, 1908–54)

Oran Thaddeus Page surfaced in the Bennie Moten band as a powerful blues player, often using a plunger mute. He was with the as-yet unknown Count Basie in 1936 and might soon have left Kansas City as one of that fabled band of brothers had he not been approached by Joe Glaser. Glaser was Louis Armstrong's personal manager, and he saw in Page's playing and singing another Armstrong; he signed him and took him to New York.

> ### Key Tracks
>
> 'Shine' Wingy Manone
> 'Isle Of Capri' Wingy Manone
> 'Uncle Sam Blues' Hot Lips Page
> 'St James Infirmary' Hot Lips Page
> 'Pagin' Mr Page' Hot Lips Page

In 1938 Page fronted a band and recorded two sessions for Victor that showcased him as an Armstrong clone. Page's solos were polished, regal and majestic, using many of the spectacular glissandos and dramatic breaks familiar on Armstrong's Decca records. But stardom never came and the band soon broke up. He joined Artie Shaw for five months in 1941–42, reaching his biggest audiences and posting some of his best performances ('There'll Be Some Changes Made'). He freelanced in traditional and small swing groups in the 1940s.

Hot Lips Page (left) plays with Freddie Moore (back left), Sidney Bechet (right) and Lloyd Phillips (back right) in New York.

A-Z of Artists

Walter Page (Tuba, bass, 1900–57)

By the end of the 1930s Walter Page had brought the usually subordinate roll of the bass to a position of critical importance without substantially expanding its time-keeping function. As a component of the unique Count Basie 'all-American' rhythm section from 1936–42, he produced a large, round but never percussive attack, whose ringing tone would remain a Basie hallmark. He also presaged an expanded melodic roll for the bass in 'Pagin' The Devil', made in 1938 with a Basie contingent a year before the arrival of virtuoso bassist Jimmy Blanton.

Django Reinhardt (Guitar, 1910–53)

One of the reasons that Django Reinhardt dominated conversations about the guitar so completely in the 1930s was his fortunate timing. He arrived on the world jazz scene through the Quintet of the Hot Club of France in 1934 – a year after the death of Eddie Lang and five years before the arrival of Charlie Christian. Belgian by birth, he became a jazz star without ever going to the United States. Reinhardt travelled in a gypsy caravan, yet absorbed American jazz pop and jazz standards, including 'Avalon', 'The Sheik Of Araby' and dozens more.

Key Tracks

'Blue Devil Blues' Walter Page
'Bellville' Django Reinhardt
'Panama' Luis Russell

The Hot Club Quintet had a salonish, continental quality with a chugging rhythm section of two guitars and bass (with no drums). It was an ideal anchor for the improvisations of Reinhardt, whose trajectories had a swift, spun-glass delicacy full of notes quivering with an intense vibrato that was equal parts emotion and ethnic flavouring. After the war he made his only trip to the US, recording with Duke Ellington in 1946.

Luis Russell (Bandleader, pianist, 1902–63)

Luis Russell first worked in New Orleans, then in Chicago with King Oliver, where he began moving the New Orleans sound towards a big-band format. Between 1929–31 he led one of the best early swing-oriented bands in the country. Its major soloists were J.C. Higginbotham and Henry 'Red' Allen, who also recorded with the band separately under his name in a number of Armstrong-inspired pieces. In 1935 Armstrong himself took over, effectively ending the Russell band as an independent entity.

Belgian gypsy guitarist Django Reinhardt, who created his own unique playing style.

A-Z of Artists

Pee Wee Russell (Clarinet, 1906–69)

Great musicians are often judged by the reach of their influence on others, but Charles Ellsworth Russell's clarinet was one of a kind, so personal and eccentric that it offered little to any would-be disciples. He arrived in New York in 1927 from the Midwest, where he had played with Bix Beiderbecke and other Chicago-area musicians. There he built a solid reputation playing a relatively standard hot clarinet with Red Nichols.

By the time he joined Louis Prima on 52nd Street in 1935, however, his tone had taken on a tart growl and his phrasing swung with a lumpy, off-centre quirkiness that seemed to thumb its nose at notions of virtuosity. It gave his playing an 'authentic' quality that appealed to renegade jazz fans in rebellion against the professionalism of swing. From the late 1930s on, he was part of Eddie Condon's stock company of traditionalists. He made his most characteristic records for Commodore from 1938–45.

Artie Shaw (Clarinet, bandleader, composer, 1910–2004)

If the 1930s comes down to about half a dozen great brand names, Artie Shaw's is surely one of them. After much freelancing in the early 1930s and several years of band-building, Shaw (née Arthur Arshawsky) hit his stride just as Benny Goodman peaked in 1938. But no one ever confused these two unique, clarinet-playing masters. Shaw had a big, broad-shouldered lyricism that could turn diamond-hard in high registers.

Key Tracks

'It All Depends On You' Pee Wee Russell
'The Last Time I Saw Chicago' Pee Wee Russell
'Begin The Beguine' Artie Shaw
'Stardust' Artie Shaw
'Frenesi' Artie Shaw

His lines were long, bobbing and eloquently fluent. Many clarinettists committed his 'Stardust' solo to memory. When drummer Buddy Rich joined in 1939, the band acquired a supercharged power. But if Shaw loved music and the perquisites of stardom, he disliked the spotlight. He abandoned music in a huff at the end of 1939, returning sporadically between bouts of writing and well-publicized marriages and leading the Gramercy Five in 1953–54. Ultimately, and still in his prime, he disowned the clarinet itself in 1955.

Clarinettist Pee Wee Russell (bottom right) was a member of jazz supergroup the Rhythmakers, who recorded a legendary session in 1932.

Jazz Archives   N° 101

THE RHYTHMAKERS

1932

featuring
HENRY "RED" ALLEN • TOMMY DORSEY • PEE WEE RUSSELL
FATS WALLER • EDDIE CONDON • GENE KRUPA • ZUTTY SINGLETON

A-Z of Artists

Stuff Smith (Violin, 1909–67)

Inspired by Joe Venuti in the 1920s, Joe Hezekiah Leroy Smith and his sextet (with Jonah Jones) became a sensation on 52nd Street early in 1936. In contrast to the polish of Venuti, Smith turned the violin in a more barrelhouse direction, making it swing with an unremitting swagger. He was also the first to play amplified violin and is remembered for his comic homage to marijuana, 'You'se a Viper'. Norman Granz re-introduced Smith successfully in 1957.

Willie 'The Lion' Smith (Piano, 1897–1973)

In the 1920s Willie 'The Lion' Smith was an obscure master of Harlem stride (a virtuoso style that evolved out of ragtime after 1919) whose brilliant technique influenced countless young pianists who heard him in person. His legend began to emerge in 1935 as stride was fading in to nostalgia and he started to record regularly. For the next four decades, he would be celebrated as a living piece of jazz history – derby and cigar intact. His compositions, such as 'Echoes of Spring' and 'Passionette', show an unexpected, impressionistic strain.

Muggsy Spanier (Cornet, 1906–67)

Francis Joseph Spanier was an early part of the group of young white Chicagoans who in the late 1920s opened up and amended the original New Orleans styles that had come north during the Roaring Twenties. He had a hot, jabbing, poking attack, often coloured by the use of a plunger mute. When Spanier recorded a number of Commodore sessions in 1939–40 with his own Dixieland group, he helped to restore traditional jazz to prominence.

Key Tracks

'Time And Again' Stuff Smith
'Blow, Blow, Blow' Stuff Smith
'Morning Air' Willie 'The Lion' Smith
'Finger Buster' Willie 'The Lion' Smith
'At The Jazz Band Ball' Muggsy Spanier

Willie 'the lion' Smith, so-called beacuse of his heroism during the First World War, was one of the big three of stride piano.

A-Z of Artists

Rex Stewart (Cornet, 1907–67)

After honing a vocabulary of unorthodox trumpet techniques with Fletcher Henderson between 1926–33, Rex William Stewart switched to cornet and joined Duke Ellington. In an orchestra of distinctive voices, his was among the most unique. He played with a sharp, biting attack in the middle register. His tone had a slightly sour, almost sarcastic attitude, capable of some bizarre extremes. A typical solo on Henderson's 'Underneath The Harlem Moon' (1933) ended with an odd, sub-tone exclamation.

Seven years later, on 'Menelk' with Ellington, he built that into a long, onomatopoeic interlude evoking the sense of a lurking lion. His most famous trademark was squeezing notes through half-depressed valves, which gave his phrasing on 'Boy Meets Horn' (1938) and other pieces an impacted, almost crushed sense of implosion. But he could also swing with a relentless drive, nowhere more so than on his famous exchanges with Cootie Williams on 'Tootin' Through The Roof' (1939). He left Ellington in 1946 for freelancing and a later career as memoirist and critic for *Down Beat*.

Key Tracks

'Boy Meets Horn' Rex Stewart
'Swamp Mist' Rex Stewart
'Tea For Two' Art Tatum
'Sweet Lorraine' Art Tatum
'Body And Soul' Art Tatum

Art Tatum (Piano, 1909–56)

In the arms race of virtuosity that drove jazz in the 1930s, no player was more dazzling than Art Tatum. The piano had a history of virtuosos, but none approached the levels of sheer athletic aptitude that Tatum tossed off with such nonchalance. It came so naturally that he often seemed bored by his own wizardry, hurtling through a procession of sharp contrasts in tempo and style that changed every few bars, under a hail of arpeggios that dropped like confetti.

Tatum, born in Toledo, Ohio with only partial vision, came out of the stride tradition but extended it in so many directions as to create a comprehensive keyboard vocabulary that continues to astonish. His solo showpieces, such as 'Tiger Rag', were intended to intimidate if not terrorize, and in the 1930s he was heard on record and radio mostly in a solo setting. But he was a consummate ensemble player, working with a trio in the 1940s. In the 1950s he recorded a huge body of solo and ensemble work for Norman Granz.

Forward-thinking pianist Art Tatum stretched the limits of piano-playing with his innovative style.

A-Z of Artists

Jack Teagarden (Trombone, vocals, 1905–64)

Arguably the greatest trombonist in jazz history, Jack Teagarden might have been the dominant player of the 1930s. He made his reputation in the late 1920s with Ben Pollack and Red Nichols, but a lack of ambition and desire for security led him to decline the invitation of an obscure clarinettist launching a new band and choose instead a five-year contract with Paul Whiteman. Within months, Benny Goodman had become destiny's child and Teagarden was watching from the sidelines. He was blessed with one of the best white blues voices of all time, effortlessly singing classics such as 'Basin Street Blues' in a melodic, laid-back drawl. In 1939 he formed his own big band, then in 1940–45 made some of his finest records with small swing groups. He toured with Louis Armstrong from 1947–51 and played with his own groups thereafter.

Chick Webb (Drums, bandleader, 1909–39)

Associated with the Savoy Ballroom from 1927, the Chick Webb band built a large audience in Harlem. In the 1930s arranger Edgar Sampson became the chief architect of its swinging style, which was propelled by Webb's dynamic drumming and flashy solos, crackling with rim shots. He inspired Gene Krupa, Buddy Rich and other white big-band drummers. When Ella Fitzgerald joined in 1934, she became the band's principal attraction, expanded its audience and took over after Webb's early death.

'Through [Jack Teagarden's] completely new style the entire concept of what jazz trombone could sound like was being changed....'

Artie Shaw

Teddy Wilson (Piano, 1912–86)

Teddy Wilson was the most influential pianist of the 1930s. Wilson's style was centred almost wholly in his right hand, which spun smooth, bobbing, single-note lines and tranquil arpeggios, bringing him into perfect alignment with the sleek aerodynamics of swing. This was evident in his first recordings with Benny Carter (1933). But Wilson found his ideal companionship in the clean rigour of the Benny Goodman Trio and Quartet, which brought him national fame in 1935 and a parallel recording career under his own name that produced a number of jazz classics. Wilson left Goodman in 1939, formed an excellent but short-lived big band and recorded prolifically during the 1940s, often with Goodman, Edmond Hall and Red Norvo; he continued to perform and record until the end of his life.

Trombonist Jack Teagarden, who revolutionized the instrument's status within jazz music.

The Forties

The 1940s was dominated by the events of the Second World War. Following the Japanese attack on Pearl Harbor in 1941, the US was no longer able to remain separate from the military action taking place elsewhere in the world and entered the conflict. The war ended following the dropping of two atomic bombs on Japan in 1945.

On the home front, many positions that had been left open by the young men who had left for war were filled by women and African-Americans, prompting a feeling of liberation and initiating a radical, if necessary, change in working culture. As the men returned home, often traumatized by their experiences but also enlightened by their travels, the ensuing baby boom further aided America's recovery from the Great Depression.

Radio continued to dominate people's lives and was used for propaganda purposes as well as entertainment. Big band and swing were the most popular music forms, and live performances and dancing were encouraged, helping to maintain a positive feeling during the hard times. Jazz was also becoming increasingly popular in Britain and the rest of Europe. Bebop music was beginning to take shape, leading jazz music off in unprecedented directions and to new heights of dexterity.

Key Artists

Dizzy Gillespie
Woody Herman
Billie Holiday
Charlie Parker

As a devastated Europe began to rebuild its cities, populations and economies, the United States and Soviet Union took centre-stage as the two world superpowers. The political tension and competitive atmosphere between them became known as the Cold War and would last until the 1980s.

Swing devotees dance in the Savoy Club, Harlem.

Wartime Stringencies Hit the Big Bands

The 1940s plunged the world into a cataclysmic war that left its scars on every aspect of life and precipitated huge changes across the globe. Jazz was also affected; the decade saw the decline of the swing bands that had ruled the roost in the previous decade and the emergence of a new style of music – bebop.

Swing had definitely been king in the 1930s, when the uplifting music of the big bands was seen as an antidote to the miseries of the Great Depression. As it happened, the economic upturn generated by the wartime economy did the big bands little good, but their popularity continued through the 1940s, when bandleaders such as Woody Herman (1913–87), Benny Goodman (1909–86), Glenn Miller (1904–44), Stan Kenton (1911–79) and Harry James (1916–83) remained the pop stars of their day.

'We often talked in the afternoon [at Minton's]. That's how we came to write different chord progressions and the like…. As for those sitters-in that we didn't want, when we started playing these different changes we'd made up, they'd become discouraged after the first chorus….'

Kenny Clarke

The 1940s took its toll on all of these bands, as well as those led by the great African-American leaders such as Duke Ellington (1899–1974) and Count Basie (1904–84). The drafting of musicians in significant numbers, the closure of dance halls around the country, recording bans called by the American Federation of Musicians in 1942–43, the difficulties of producing records under wartime stringencies, increased transport problems – all of these factors combined to make big bands less and less financially viable as the decade progressed.

At the height of the Swing Era, singers had been largely an adjunct to the big bands, but the 1940s saw the growth of the singer as a popular phenomenon in his or her own right, exemplified by the likes of Bing Crosby, Frank Sinatra (1915–98), Nat 'King' Cole (1917–65), Ella Fitzgerald (1917–96), Sarah Vaughan (1924–90), Dinah Washington (1924–63) and Billie Holiday (1915–59). These figures paved the way for the rise of the modern pop star.

Pianist Stan Kenton divided critical opinion with his ambitious big-band innovations.

A New Creative Force

The emergence of bebop as a major new creative force in jazz took place against the backdrop of the decline of the swing bands, but the music was essentially an evolution from swing rather than a revolutionary departure. Lester Young (1909–59), Coleman Hawkins (1904–69), Ben Webster (1909–73), Art Tatum (1909–56), Jimmy Blanton and many others had already laid some of the groundwork for the harmonic and rhythmic rethinking that would become central to bebop.

The new music evolved in after-hours jam sessions at clubs such as Minton's Playhouse and Monroe's Uptown House in New York, and later in the jazz clubs of 52nd Street. The recording ban, wartime shortages of shellac and lack of interest from record companies meant that much of it went unrecorded. Charlie Parker (1920–55) and Dizzy Gillespie (1917–93) led the way in launching the new sounds, and the arrival of bebop began a new jazz war. The late 1940s also saw a Dixieland revival centred around Eddie Condon's (1905–73) club on 52nd Street and a slanging match developed between both the practitioners and the fans, polarized along traditionalist vs modernist lines and conducted in a hail of disparaging remarks that generated a lot of publicity for jazz music. The traditional revival also had its counterparts in Europe, notably in England, where jazz groups such as the Crane River Band gained ground in the wake of the war.

Popular Melody

Duke Ellington/Blanton-Webster Band
– 'Cotton Tail' (1940)

Bebop brought new harmonic and rhythmic ideas in to jazz and cemented the role of the virtuoso soloist and improviser. The seedy club-land in which bebop thrived exacerbated the problems with drugs that were all but endemic in its circles, while pervasive racism and police harassment continued to plague the lives of the musicians. However, the clubs on 52nd Street did allow the development of mixed-race audiences in an America that was still heavily segregated, especially in the southern states. The high artistic demands of the music contrasted vividly with the low esteem in which both the artists' work and their lifestyles were held. Parker and Gillespie led the way in establishing the principal musical foundations of bebop. Gillespie claimed that the name came from his habit of singing as yet untitled tunes to the other players using nonsense syllables, although other theories exist.

Dizzy Gillespie on the corner of 52nd Street – the centre of the 1940s New York jazz scene.

Bebop and the Birth of the Cool

The bebop musicians took the 4/4 time signature of swing and added a plethora of new rhythmic accents to it, with drummers such as Kenny Clarke (1914–85) and Max Roach (b. 1924) preferring to 'ride' their cymbals and mark strict time with their hi-hats, rather than state a regular beat on the bass drum.

That crucial rhythmic development went hand in hand with a new focus on extended harmonies, using much more complex substitute chords and chromatic intervals as the basic building blocks of improvisations. It afforded great scope for melodic, harmonic and rhythmic invention that was exploited by musicians such as Parker, Gillespie, Bud Powell (1924–66), Thelonious Monk (1917–82) and others. That harmonic expansion was a fundamental strength of bebop, but also its built-in weakness. The musicians tended to use chord structures based on standard tunes or blues as the basis for their new melody lines, and bebop evolved as a music of great sophistication built on a repetitive and limited structure, which ultimately led to musicians exploring more experimental areas a decade later.

New York City, specifically Harlem and midtown from 42nd Street to 52nd, was very much the crucible for bebop. Bebop also travelled outwards, notably to the West Coast, where musicians including Dexter Gordon (1923–90), Art Pepper (1925–82) and others made their own contributions to the evolving form in LA's Central Avenue clubs. Bebop also touched the swing bands, its influence discernible in the ensembles of Duke Ellington, Woody Herman, Artie Shaw (1910–2004) and Benny Goodman. By the late 1940s, bebop was the new artistic force in jazz. The 1950s would see bop move to a more central position, through the emergence of the related forms of hard bop and soul jazz on the jukeboxes of the African-American community.

Popular Melody

Louis Jordan – 'Reet, Petite And Gone' (1946)

The end of the decade also saw the first stirrings of another development that would play a key role in the 1950s; the Nonet sessions of 1949–50 under the leadership of Miles Davis (1926–91), later dubbed the 'Birth Of The Cool', took an alternative approach to the well-established mores of bebop, using careful arrangements by the likes of Gerry Mulligan (1927–96) and Gil Evans (1912–88), and a less involved interplay of musical textures that would be taken up in the West Coast and cool jazz movements of the coming decade.

The British jazz scene grew following the Second World War. Here Harry Hayes (on clarinet) leads a recording at London's Columbia studios, 1947.

Key Artist: Dizzy Gillespie

John Birks 'Dizzy' Gillespie shares the credit for creating bebop with Charlie Parker, but his place in the history of twentieth-century music rests on a considerably wider achievement. He was born in Cheraw, South Carolina in 1917 and acquired his nickname in the 1930s. He moved to New York and worked in big bands with Teddy Hill, Lionel Hampton and Cab Calloway (the latter relationship ending acrimoniously after a notorious altercation over a spitball).

He was a prime mover in the jam sessions at Minton's Playhouse in Harlem, which became the forcing ground for the subsequent evolution of bebop. His speed and facility in the high register reflected the influence of Roy Eldridge, but he quickly displayed an increasingly original musical conception that came to fruition in the seminal group that he led with Charlie Parker in 1946.

Flying with Bird

The collaboration remains one of the crucial episodes in jazz history and laid the template for the new music that would both illuminate and divide the post-war jazz scene. Bebop demanded formidable technical abilities as well as imagination; Gillespie's pyrotechnic brilliance was the perfect foil for Parker's genius, and was underpinned by a more thorough understanding of harmonic theory than many of his contemporaries routinely possessed. Their partnership, which included further recordings and occasional reunions, such as the famous Massey Hall concert in Toronto in 1953, put bebop on the musical map and assured their joint status as jazz immortals. While Parker burnt himself out and died prematurely, Gillespie went on to become a respected elder statesman of the music.

Musically, he knows what he is doing backwards and forwards.... So the arranging, the chord progressions and things in progressive music, Dizzy is responsible for.'
Billy Eckstine

The Cuban Connection

As bebop was coalescing, Dizzy was assembling what would become a celebrated big band – one that made an equally important contribution to the development of modern jazz. Gillespie was a prime mover in the creation of Afro-Cuban jazz (or 'Cubop'), a style that brought Cuban folk and popular idioms into a jazz context. His interest was sparked

Right: Dizzy Gillespie's trumpet had a curious, upright bell made to his specification by the Martin company.

by Cab Calloway's lead trumpeter Mario Bauzá, who introduced him to percussionist Chano Pozo in 1947. Pozo was fatally shot in a bar in 1948 after contributing to Gillespie's classic Afro-Cuban recordings 'Manteca', 'Guarachi Guaro' and 'Cubana Be, Cubana Bop'. Latin tunes were well-established in jazz, but this was the first band to integrate real Afro-Cuban polyrhythms within the new bebop idiom, and others followed suit, including Machito, Tadd Dameron, Charlie Parker and Bud Powell.

The Cuban influence remained a strong element in Gillespie's music. He adopted his trademark upturned trumpet bell in 1953 and broke new ground in 1956 by taking jazz bands on State Department-sponsored tours to Africa, the Near East, Pakistan and South America, as well as Europe.

Politics and People

Gillespie became increasingly aware of his African roots and of the civil rights campaigns in America, even running for President in 1964 under a 'politics ought to be a groovier thing' banner. Astute enough to avoid the pitfalls of involvement with the drugs that plagued the bebop community, Gillespie was a natural showman as well as a brilliant musician, and is one of the select band of jazzmen who became household names.

An attempt to join the fashionable jazz-rock fusion movement in the 1970s was a rare lapse of judgement, and was quickly abandoned. He continued to lead both large and small groups throughout the rest of his career, including the United Nation Orchestra (the use of the singular reflected his adherence to the Baha'i faith and their belief in the unity of peoples), which he led from 1988 until his death from cancer in 1993.

Next Page: Gillespie (far left) directs his big band.

Key Artist: Woody Herman

Woodrow 'Woody' Herman (originally Herrmann) led several of the most exciting big bands in jazz history, hitting peaks of achievement in the 1940s that few have equalled. Born in Milwaukee, Wisconsin in 1913 to German immigrants, Herman began his stage career in vaudeville as a child, but his ambition was to lead his own band. He played alto, tenor and baritone saxophone and the clarinet, as well as singing. He worked for a number of bands before joining Isham Jones in 1934.

He fulfilled his ambition to become a bandleader almost by default in 1936, when Jones unexpectedly broke up his band in Knoxville. The players decided to continue as a co-operative band, and Herman was elected as leader of the group. Known as the Band That Plays The Blues, they began to win a big following. 'Woodchoppers Ball' was a huge hit in 1939, selling some five million copies ('It was great,' Herman said later, 'the first thousand times we played it').

New Directions for the Herd

In the early 1940s, more sophisticated arrangements gradually began to usurp the less formal 'head' structures that had been the band's staple format. Arrangers such as Dave Matthews, Neal Hefti and Ralph Burns had changed the sound of the band by the time it was officially known as Herman's Herd (later referred to as the First Herd) from 1943. By late 1945 the band was regularly winning popularity polls and setting new box-office records. Igor Stravinsky wrote his *Ebony Concerto* for them, and the concerto was premiered at Carnegie Hall in March 1946, alongside Ralph Burns's 'Summer Sequence', later completed by the famous Stan Getz feature 'Early Autumn'. The Woodchoppers, a small band drawn from the ranks of the orchestra, also achieved success. The band's notable players included trumpeter Conte Condoli, trombonist Bill Harris, saxophonist Flip Phillips, pianist Ralph Burns, and drummers Dave Tough and then Don Lamond. Herman eventually broke up the First Herd at the height of its popularity in December 1946, for domestic reasons.

'It was marvellous ... to work with Bill and Chubby and Flip, Ralph, Pete, and, of course, Sonny and Davey, too. That was an exciting group to be with. Ideas and whole new tunes sprang out of that group like sparks.'

Woody Herman

Woody Herman, a fine reedsman and celebrated bandleader.

Four Brothers

The break-up proved a temporary departure. Herman had formed his Second Herd by October 1947 with a new generation of stars in the making, including the famous 'Four Brothers' saxophone section of Stan Getz, Zoot Sims, Herbie Steward (soon to be replaced by Al Cohn) and Serge Chaloff. Their three-tenors-plus-baritone setup was the Second Herd's distinctive signature sound.

The band reflected a more overt bebop influence than the First Herd, but was also plagued by a less welcome borrowing from bebop – heroin addiction. Moreover, despite the Second Herd's significant musical success, the economies of the music business had turned against big bands and Herman incurred large financial losses. Several key players departed in 1949 and by the end of the year Herman had accepted the inevitable and broken up the band, forming a septet instead.

The Herd Swings On

But Herman could not stay away from big bands for long. The Third Herd ran for much of the 1950s and toured in Europe in 1954 and South America in 1958. The brief Anglo-American Herd made an impact on jazz in the UK in 1959, and the Swinging Herd line-up of the 1960s continued the band's traditions of strong soloists and meaty arrangements. Herman later added soprano saxophone to his roster, dabbled in jazz rock and became involved in the development of formal jazz education, although his bands had been providing a schooling for young musicians from the outset in any case.

His final years were plagued by a long-running dispute with the tax authorities, and eventually all his property and assets were seized by the government. He continued to lead his band until his death in 1987, after which saxophonist Frank Tiberi took over leadership of the Woody Herman Orchestra, which remains active.

The saxophone section from the Second Herd.

Key Artist: Billie Holiday

Billie Holiday was entirely untrained as a singer, but drew on the example of popular recording artists such as Bessie Smith and Louis Armstrong in developing her musical approach. She was able to make much of poor songs as well as great ones. Her phrasing, intonation, attention to the weight and nuance of lyrics, and her lightly inflected, subtly off-the-beat rhythmic placement were all highly individual and became widely influential.

Her early life is confusing. Recent biographical research has confirmed that she was born in Philadelphia in 1915 and was known by several names, the most frequently used being Eleanora Fagan. She was known as Billie from childhood, and took the surname Holiday from her largely absent father, guitarist Clarence Holiday. She was jailed for prostitution in New York in 1930, and began her singing career shortly afterwards in clubs in Brooklyn and then Harlem.

Lady Day and Lester

Producer John Hammond heard her perform and arranged for her to record with Benny Goodman in 1933. She made her professional debut at the Apollo Theater in Harlem in 1934, and in 1935–42, with pianist Teddy Wilson, began the series of recordings that made her name, working alongside major jazz musicians such as trumpeters Buck Clayton and Roy Eldridge and saxophonist Lester Young (who bestowed her with the nickname 'Lady Day'). Young was regarded as her closest musical associate, and there was undoubtedly a special chemistry at work in their collaborations.

'What comes out is what I feel. I hate straight singing. I have to change a tune to my own way of doing it.'

Billie Holiday

Her fame was largely confined to the African-American community at that stage, but spells with Count Basie in 1937 and Artie Shaw in 1938 brought her to wider notice and, in the latter case, helped to break the bar on black musicians working with white bands that was still very much in force. Her standing with intellectuals, leftists and radicals was boosted by her appearances at the interracial Café Society in 1939 and her recording of 'Strange Fruit', a song about southern lynchings that quickly attained cult status.

Jazz and blues singer Billie Holiday, whose distinctive voice was filled with emotion, passion and tragedy.

God Bless' The Child

A swing-spiritual based on the authentic proverb
"GOD BLESSED THE CHILD THAT'S GOT HIS OWN"

Words and Music by ARTHUR HERZOG, Jr. *and* BILLIE HOLIDAY

75¢
in U.S.A.

Edward B. Marks Music Corporation
136 West 52nd Street   New York, N. Y. 10019

Printed in U.S.A.

Success Turns Sour

Trademark ballad performances, including 'God Bless The Child', 'I Cover The Waterfront', 'Gloomy Sunday' (all 1941) and 'Lover Man' (1944), had made her a big name by the mid-1940s. She played her only minor acting role on film in 1946, as a maid opposite Louis Armstrong in *New Orleans*.

Her drug use led to imprisonment on drug charges in 1947 (recent research has suggested that she may have been set up, although her addiction was real enough). Her relationships with men were rarely to her advantage, emotionally or financially. Her career slipped in the wake of her jail sentence, in large part because she could no longer work in clubs in New York without the Cabaret Card, which was automatically denied to musicians convicted of drug charges.

Hard Times

Her health and her voice began to show the ravages of a hard life and drug abuse, but she was still capable of memorable performances in the 1950s, including a treasured clip made for the television special *The Sound Of Jazz* in 1957, in which she sang her 1939 hit 'Fine And Mellow' with a stellar cast of jazzmen, including Lester Young. Her late recordings and performances were often harrowing, but even her final recordings have the power to move the listener profoundly – in some respects, they may even be heard as more powerful emotional testimonies than her classic but sunnier recordings of the 1930s and 1940s.

She died in New York in 1959, having left an auto-biography, *Lady Sings The Blues* (1956), which has been seen as self-serving. Recently, biographer Stuart Nicholson has suggested that the book – but not the 1972 feature film loosely based on it – may be a more accurate depiction of her life than once seemed likely.

Sheet music for Holiday's 1941 hit 'God Bless The Child'.

Key Artist: Charlie Parker

Charlie Parker, also known as 'Yardbird' or 'Bird', was a largely self-taught musical genius with acute self-destructive tendencies. His career exemplified both the creative power and the destructive social ethos of bebop. His music burned as brightly as any in jazz, but his lifestyle sent out the wrong message to too many young musicians, despite his frequent warnings to stay away from drugs.

Louis Armstrong had begun the evolution of jazz from an ensemble's to a soloist's music two decades earlier, but bebop brought that process to fruition and Parker was its supreme exponent. His influence was all-pervasive and continues to be so on contemporary musicians, affecting not only saxophonists, but players on every instrument.

'The way he got from one note to the other and the way he played the rhythm fit what we were trying to do perfectly.... He was the other half of my heartbeat.'

Dizzy Gillespie

Forging the New Sound

Parker was born in Kansas City on 29 August 1920. He played in the city's famous jam sessions, wore out the recordings of Lester Young, picked up basic harmony lessons from local musicians and made remarkable progress after suffering some early slights from established players. He made his recording debut with Jay McShann's band in 1941, before working with Earl Hines and then Billy Eckstine in their seminal swing-into-bop big bands.

His fluency was attracting attention even then, and his development of a new approach to both rhythmic accents and established melodic-harmonic relationships was bearing fruit. He realized that new and radically different sounding melody lines could be created by avoiding the more obvious notes, and developed his use of the upper 'dissonant' intervals beyond the octave. The effect of these experiments was electrifying. His raw materials were ordinary blues and standard AABA tunes, but he transformed them in spectacular fashion. His work with Dizzy Gillespie in 1945–46 and his own recordings of the period formed a benchmark for bebop and seeded the central directions that jazz would explore in the next two decades.

Saxophone genius Charlie Parker (third from left) performs among other jazz greats at an All-Stars event organized by Metronome *magazine.*

Bird with Strings

He told several people, including the composer Edgar Varese, that he had ambitions to work with more complex musical forms, but never did so. The nearest he got was recording with strings in 1949–52 – sessions that have divided listeners ever since, although they did give him the bestselling 'single' of his career, 'Just Friends'.

Parker had become addicted to heroin sometime in the 1930s and his reliance on the drug is inextricably interwoven with his musical career. An infamous episode in California led to his incarceration in the rehabilitation centre at Camarillo in 1947 (memorialized in his 'Relaxin' at Camarillo'), and tales of his addiction and his heavy drinking are endless. He was eventually banned from Birdland, the New York jazz club named in his honour, and the excesses of his life took their predictable toll.

Bird Lives!

Prematurely worn out, Parker died on 12 March 1955 while watching Tommy Dorsey's television show in the Manhattan apartment of Baroness Pannonica de Keonigswarter (known as Nica), a rebellious member of the Rothschild family who became a celebrated patroness of jazzmen. Graffiti proclaiming 'Bird Lives!' began to appear in the streets of New York's Greenwich Village almost immediately, posted by anonymous fans, and the legend continued to grow.

He made his great musical discoveries early and never recaptured the glories of his best work of the 1940s, but he was the supreme creative figure of his era and remained the major influence on a generation of jazz players. His astringent and penetrating sonority became the prevailing model and improvisers everywhere studied and practised every nuance of his inventions, just as he had pored over Lester Young's recordings in the late 1930s. His stylistic pre-eminence would only really be challenged with the emergence of modal jazz and free jazz in the late 1950s.

Parker (left) shares a joke with bebop collaborator Dizzy Gillespie in New York, 1949.

A-Z of Artists

Charlie Barnet (Various saxophones, 1913–91)

Charlie Barnet led a successful big band from 1933 until the late 1940s and was one of the earliest white bandleaders to employ black musicians, beginning with Benny Carter as a guest soloist and arranger in 1934. He introduced singer Lena Horne as an unknown in 1941 and featured many notable musicians in his line-ups. His style was based on an energized Basie-like riff formula, but he was also an undisguised admirer of Duke Ellington, and attempted to graft elements of the Ellington band's sophisticated harmonies into his own band arrangements.

He is best remembered for Billy May's arrangement of the much-covered 'Cherokee' in 1939, but enjoyed a number of hits with other riff-based favourites, including 'Pompton Turnpike' and 'Redskin Rhumba', both from 1940. Like Harry James, he attempted to move into acting, and was also involved in the restaurant business, but continued to perform intermittently until the 1970s.

Key Tracks

'Skyline' Charlie Barnet
'Flying Home' Charlie Barnet
'Mambo Rincon' Mario Bauzá
'Sleep' Earl Bostic
'Cherokee' Earl Bostic

Mario Bauzá (Trumpet, 1911–93)

Mario Bauzá takes a large amount of credit for bringing music from his native Cuba into jazz. He worked with Noble Sissle and Chick Webb in New York in the 1930s before teaming up with Machito. While with Cab Calloway in 1939–40 he sparked Dizzy Gillespie's interest in Cuban music, which eventually led to 'Cubop'. He was musical director of Machito's Afro-Cubans for 35 years (1940–75), after which he formed his own group.

Earl Bostic (Alto saxophone, 1913–65)

Earl Bostic was a soulful alto saxophonist from Tulsa who won a wide following in the late 1940s and 1950s for his accessible but technically accomplished style. He served a big band apprenticeship as a player and arranger, but then reinvented himself in more populist mode and made a series of bestselling records in the wake of his big 1951 hit 'Flamingo'. His bands nurtured future stars, including John Coltrane, Benny Golson and Stanley Turrentine.

Earl Bostic, whose bands included future stars such as John Coltrane.

A-Z of Artists

Big Sid Catlett (Drums, 1910–51)

Catlett was one of the most well-respected and versatile jazz drummers of the 1930s and 1940s. He played in a variety of ensembles under such luminaries as Benny Carter, Fletcher Henderson, Benny Goodman and Duke Ellington, before going on to join Louis Armstrong's All-Stars. Catlett's remarkable adaptability enabled him to play in a wide range of styles and he also successfully bridged the gap into bebop, contributing to an early Charlie Parker–Dizzy Gillespie session.

George Chisholm (Trombone, 1915–97)

Scottish-born George Chisholm made his name as a top-class traditional jazz trombone player, but also played piano and several other brass instruments. He started out in Glasgow dance bands before moving to London, where he became an accomplished bandleader and arranger, and a successful television personality in comedy shows in the 1960s. Notable jazz associations included the RAF's famous wartime band the Squadronaires, Kenny Baker's Dozen, the Alex Welsh Band, and his own Gentlemen of Jazz.

Key Tracks

'Rose Room' Big Sid Catlett
'Jazz Me Blues' George Chisholm
'No Smoking' George Chisholm
'Get Out Of Town' Kenny Clarke
'Sonor' Kenny Clarke

Kenny Clarke (Drums, 1914–85)

Kenny 'Klook' Clarke was a native of Pittsburgh, but made his primary contribution to jazz in New York in the early flowerings of bebop. Clarke, who adopted the Muslim faith as Liaquat Ali Salaam in 1946, is widely credited with developing the new rhythmic concepts that fuelled bebop. His work with Dizzy Gillespie and especially Thelonious Monk at Minton's in Harlem in the early 1940s laid the foundation for the move away from the persistently stated two- and four-beat emphasis on the bass drum.

Swing Era drummers had already experimented with a lighter and more fluid approach to rhythmic accents, but Clarke developed that concept to new heights, using crisp punctuations on bass drum – known as 'dropping bombs' – to accent his rolling ride cymbal. He was drafted to serve in Europe in 1943–46, and eventually settled in Paris in 1956, where his many associations included the acclaimed Kenny Clarke-Francy Boland Big Band.

Drummers such as Kenny Clarke embellished the 4/4 beat of swing to create new rhythms.

A-Z of Artists

Nat 'King' Cole (Piano, vocals, 1917–65)

Nat 'King' Cole (real name Coles) was one of the few jazz artists to become a household name as a popular singer, and was one of the first black American artists to have his own radio show (1948–49), and later television show (1956–57). He was born into a musical family in Alabama, but moved to Chicago at the age of four, where he learned piano by ear, before studying music formally as a teenager.

He formed a trio with Oscar Moore (guitar) and Wesley Prince (drums) that became the model for many subsequent groups, including Oscar Peterson's trio. However, a vocal hit with 'Straighten Up And Fly Right' in 1943 set him on a different career path as a sophisticated pop singer. His fame as a vocalist and his later celebrity have tended to overshadow the fact that he was also a very fine and influential jazz pianist in trio and quartet settings.

Buddy DeFranco (Clarinet, b. 1923)

Buddy DeFranco (Boniface Ferdinand Leonardo) became the leading clarinet player of the post-Swing Era. His liquid sonority and flowing improvisations drew on elements from both swing and bebop, but without settling fully in either camp. He served a big-band apprenticeship with Gene Krupa, Charlie Barnet and Tommy Dorsey in the mid-1940s, but is best known for his work in smaller groups with vibist Terry Gibbs, bands led by George Shearing and Count Basie, and for leading his own groups.

Key Tracks

'Sweet Lorraine' Nat 'King' Cole
'Straighten Up And Fly Right'
   Nat 'King' Cole
'Yesterdays' Buddy DeFranco
'A Cottage For Sale' Billy Eckstine
'Prisoner Of Love' Billy Eckstine

Billy Eckstine (Vocals, 1914–93)

Billy Eckstine's smooth baritone voice and suave manner brought his music to a wide audience. He joined pianist Earl Hines in Chicago in 1939 and then led a big band from 1944–47 that many see as the cradle of bebop, although few recordings survive. He was one of the few black singers to be featured on national radio, largely thanks to his beguiling romantic ballads. He remained a draw on the cabaret circuit in later years.

Pianist and vocalist Nat King Cole (left) larks about with singer Billy Eckstine.

A-Z of Artists

Dexter Gordon (Tenor and soprano saxophone, 1923–90)

Dexter Gordon is widely credited as the leading figure in the evolution of bebop on his instrument, the tenor saxophone. The Los Angeles native was influenced initially by stars of the Swing Era, in particular Lester Young, and went on to adapt many of Charlie Parker's alto saxophone innovations to the tenor. He was a notable exponent of the so-called 'chase' form, in which two tenors 'duel' for supremacy; he recorded a famous example with Wardell Gray as 'The Chase' (1947) and was also an inspired interpreter of ballads.

His career took a disastrous drug-induced dip in the 1950s, but he relocated to Europe and returned to music with renewed vigour in the 1960s, in a series of acclaimed recordings for Blue Note Records. He made a triumphal return to America in 1977, and went on to star in Bertrand Tavernier's film *Round Midnight* (1986).

Key Tracks

'Body And Soul' Dexter Gordon
'Dexter Rides Again' Dexter Gordon
'The Man I Love' Wardell Gray
'Dell's Bells' Wardell Gray
'One For Pres' Wardell Gray

Wardell Gray (Tenor saxophone, 1921–55)

Wardell Gray died in mysterious, drug-related circumstances without fulfilling his immense potential. His control and invention at fast tempos and fluent, swinging style on the tenor saxophone adapted readily to both swing and bebop settings, while his ballad playing was strong in both emotion and tonal warmth. His sadly underweight recorded legacy is largely derived from live club dates and jam sessions, plus the two volumes of studio recordings issued by Prestige as *Wardell Gray Memorial*. Singer Annie Ross (and later Joni Mitchell) made vocalese hits based on his solos.

Saxophonists Wardell Gray (left) and Dexter Gordon act out their 1947 hit 'The Chase'.

A-Z of Artists

Harry James (Trumpet, 1916–83)

Harry James grew up in a circus and went on to become a media celebrity as a bandleader, a fame that only intensified when he married actress Betty Grable in 1943. James made his initial reputation as a formidable trumpet player with Benny Goodman's band before forming his own group in 1938, but lost some of his credibility with jazz fans when he began to work in a more populist, romantic ballad style in the 1940s.

His playing was admired by his major influences, Louis Armstrong and Bunk Johnson, and his combination of musical invention with bravura technique remained highly impressive throughout his career. He returned to more directly jazz-oriented band arrangements in the 1950s and continued to lead big bands. An inveterate womanizer and compulsive gambler, he worked in Las Vegas for many years from 1963, where his proceeds went straight back into the casinos.

J.J. Johnson (Trombone, arranger, composer, 1924–2001)

J.J. (James Louis) Johnson was the premier bebop trombonist. His speed of execution and fluent, highly inventive approach to both melody and rhythm essentially devised a new language for an instrument that was not obviously made to suit the wide intervals and rapid articulation of the style. He took up trombone in high school in Indianapolis, and honed his craft in swing bands before turning to bebop in the mid-1940s.

'Young Harry says to me, "Pops, I don't have to tell you. You and Louis, only men who can play this horn." That was real nice of young Harry, but he play real good trumpet himself. I told him so.'

Bunk Johnson

He worked with virtually all the great jazz names of the bebop era, including Dizzy Gillespie and Charlie Parker. He was part of Miles Davis's so-called 'Birth Of The Cool' project in 1949–50 and the later 'third stream' experiments initiated by John Lewis and Gunther Schuller in the late 1950s. He co-led a very successful group with Danish trombonist Kai Winding (1954–56). He was a fine composer of film and television music as well as jazz.

J.J. Johnson adapted his trombone style to play bebop music with the likes of Dizzy Gillespie.

A-Z of Artists

Louis Jordan (Alto saxophone, vocals, bandleader, 1908–75)

Louis Jordan & his Tympany Five were major stars in the 1940s, providing energized recordings and exciting live shows. The alto saxophonist began by playing in swing bands, including Chick Webb's, but in 1938 he gambled on the success of his own personality, fronting a small group playing in a more overtly entertaining style. Labelled 'jump blues', this was a precursor of both R&B and rock'n'roll.

He reeled off a succession of jukebox hits through the 1940s, often with novelty titles and lyrics, including 'Five Guys Named Mo', 'Choo Choo Ch'Boogie', 'Ain't Nobody Here But Us Chickens' and 'Saturday Night Fish Fry'. Their appeal, based on melodic good humour and the comic complications of romance, crossed racial boundaries, and his popularity lasted until the early 1950s. Eclipsed by the rise of rock'n'roll, he reverted to more jazz-oriented settings and continued to perform on the cabaret circuit in later years.

Stan Kenton (Piano, arranger, composer, 1911–79)

Stan Kenton pushed big-band jazz in new directions throughout his career, and in the process divided critical opinion more radically than any other bandleader. He formed his first band in 1940, which became the Artistry in Rhythm Orchestra in 1942. Imaginative arrangements and excellent soloists ensured the band's success. It gave way to the more ambitious Progressive Jazz Orchestra in 1947 and the even more overblown, 43-piece Innovations in Modern Music Orchestra in 1950.

Key Tracks

'Is You Is Or Is You Ain't My Baby?' Louis Jordan
'Let The Good Times Roll' Louis Jordan
'Artistry In Rhythm' Stan Kenton
'The Peanut Vendor' Stan Kenton
'Intermission Riff' Stan Kenton

The latter band often featured startling arrangements (notably those by the iconoclastic Bob Graettinger), but fell foul of economic feasibility. Kenton led more standard-sized big bands throughout the 1950s, featuring a galaxy of star players. His expanded groups of the 1960s included the symphonically conceived Los Angeles Neophonic Orchestra. Although uneven in their output, Kenton's bands made a unique contribution to big-band history, and he was also influential as a jazz educator.

Louis Jordan combined elements of jazz and blues to create a feel-good jump-blues sound.

A-Z of Artists

Barney Kessel (Guitar, 1923–2004)

Barney Kessel took inspiration from his fellow Oklahoman, guitarist Charlie Christian, and developed an electric-guitar style that straddled swing and bop in effective fashion. He was featured in the Oscar-nominated short film *Jammin' The Blues* (1944), and recorded with Charlie Parker in 1947. A stint with the Oscar Peterson Trio in 1952–53 led to recordings as a leader from 1953 onwards. Kessel formed Great Guitars with Herb Ellis and Charlie Byrd in 1973; they toured and recorded until his debilitating stroke in 1992.

Machito (Vocals, maracas, c. 1912–84)

Frank Raul Grillo was born in Florida of Cuban extraction and took the name Machito in 1940 when his brother-in-law, trumpet player Mario Bauzá, reorganized his year-old band the Afro-Cubans. Their arrangements clothed Cuban melodies and rhythms in jazz harmonies and instrumental voicings. They were highly influential in the emergence of Afro-Cuban jazz (sometimes known as 'Cubop') in the late 1940s, in the mambo craze of the 1950s and the development of modern salsa and Latin jazz.

Glenn Miller (Trombone, 1904–44)

Glenn Miller was a trombonist of modest accomplishments, but he became one of the most famous big-band leaders in jazz. Although disdained by jazz purists, tunes such as 'In The Mood', 'String Of Pearls' and 'Tuxedo Junction' have remained enduringly popular. Miller's bands played precisely executed riff-based swing tunes and very slow ballads; his signature sound was built on a lead clarinet melody doubled an octave below by tenor saxophone, with the other saxophones, muted trumpets, and trombones all adding soft-focus colour and harmony.

Miller favoured solid, well-disciplined players who could deliver the exact sound that he required on the arrangements, rather than flamboyant jazz soloists. His catchy melodies, intricate but easy-on-the-ear harmonies and swinging rhythms caught the public imagination; his disappearance in a light aircraft over the English Channel *en route* to a concert scheduled for his Allied Expeditionary Force Orchestra only added to the mystique.

Key Tracks

'I Wanna Be Loved By You' Barney Kessel
'Tanga' Machito
'Relax And Mambo' Machito
'In The Mood' Glenn Miller
'Moonlight Serenade' Glenn Miller

Machito, whose band the Afro-Cubans was influential in the 1940s Cubop movement.

A-Z of Artists

James Moody (Tenor and alto saxophone, flute, b. 1925)

James Moody was one of the strongest performers to double on flute in jazz, and was a resourceful and inventive improviser on all his horns. He joined Dizzy Gillespie from the US Air Force in 1946. A recording of 'I'm In The Mood For Love' (1949), made while living in Europe from 1948–51, brought him to a wider audience. He led his own bands in the US from the early 1950s, including a popular septet featuring vocalist Eddie Jefferson (1953–62), in which he often sang a passage of the lyrics in falsetto. Moody continues to tour and record.

Fats Navarro (Trumpet, 1923–50)

Theodore 'Fats' Navarro died prematurely and left a limited recorded legacy, most of it as a sideman. Nonetheless, he stood alongside Dizzy Gillespie and Miles Davis as one of the most significant trumpeters in bebop. He took over Gillespie's chair in Billy Eckstine's seminal big band in 1945, and enjoyed a brief but creative relationship with pianist and arranger Tadd Dameron in 1948.

Key Tracks

'Wail Moody, Wail' James Moody
'Move' Fats Navarro
'Goin' To Minton's' Fats Navarro
'El Loco Blues' Chico O'Farrill

Although curtailed, his career saw him work with most of the major bebop artists, including Coleman Hawkins, Dexter Gordon, Bud Powell and Charlie Parker. His conservative approach to rhythm was balanced by carefully sculpted melody lines and a wealth of harmonic invention, while his burnished tone had a richness unusual among the bebop speed merchants. His recordings for Blue Note as a sideman were gathered in two volumes as *The Fabulous Fats Navarro* (1947). He died of tuberculosis, exacerbated by his heroin addiction.

Chico O'Farrill (Trumpet, composer, arranger, 1921–2001)

Arturo 'Chico' O'Farrill arrived in New York from Havana in 1948 with a self-confessed low opinion of his native Cuban music by comparison with jazz, but found inspiration in the developing Afro-Cuban jazz movement led by Dizzy Gillespie, Machito and Mario Bauzá. He became a key figure in creating what he called the 'very delicate marriage' of Cuban music with jazz. His 'Afro-Cuban Jazz Suite' (1950) is a watershed work and launched a long and successful career.

James Moody was one of the first artists to gain kudos for the flute as a jazz instrument.

A-Z of Artists

Sy Oliver (Trumpet, vocals, arranger, composer, 1910–88)

Sy (Melvin James) Oliver was one of the finest of all big-band arrangers, and a capable instrumentalist and singer as well. His major associations included the bands of Jimmie Lunceford, Benny Goodman and Tommy Dorsey, and he also led his own bands at various times, from the mid-1940s into the 1980s. He worked as music director and arranger for several record companies, as well as filling that role for the New York Jazz Repertory Orchestra in the mid-1970s.

Chano Pozo (Drums, percussion, 1915–48)

Cuban percussionist Chano Pozo was Dizzy Gillespie's principal collaborator in melding Cuban music with jazz (a.k.a. 'Cubop'). Their historic 1947 recordings 'Manteca' and 'Cubana Be, Cubana Bop' (co-written with George Russell) were the first to integrate real Afro-Cuban polyrhythms within a bop idiom. Their association proved brief; Pozo was shot dead in a bar in Harlem in mysterious circumstances shortly after the recordings were made, but the Afro-Cuban fusion sound remained a significant element in Gillespie's music throughout his career.

Buddy Rich (Drums, 1917–87)

Bernard 'Buddy' Rich was a powerhouse drummer with a phenomenal technique, but he was also capable of great delicacy when required. He grew up in the family vaudeville act before joining Joe Marsala's band in 1937. It was the beginning of a series of associations with major Swing Era bandleaders such as Harry James, Artie Shaw, Tommy Dorsey, Benny Carter and – as a deputy for Jo Jones – Count Basie.

Popular Melody

Dizzy Gillespie – 'Manteca' (1947)

He formed his own band in 1945 and also recorded with major bebop artists Charlie Parker, Dizzy Gillespie and Bud Powell. He worked with James again in the 1950s and 1960s, led a small group, and tried unsuccessfully to establish a career as a singer. He formed a new and much more successful big band of his own from the mid-1960s until 1974, then led a small group and ran his own club. Another third big band followed, and Rich enjoyed a high profile, through television appearances, until his death.

Buddy Rich was a virtuoso drummer, equally adept at playing swing and bebop styles.

A-Z of Artists

Max Roach (Drums, b. 1924)

Along with Kenny Clarke, Max Roach shares the credit for inventing bebop drumming. When Clarke found himself drafted in 1943, it was Roach who emerged as the leading activist in the search for a drum style to suit the emerging melodic and harmonic complexities of the new music. He developed an approach that was both powerful and flexible enough to match the invention of Charlie Parker or Dizzy Gillespie, while at the same time elevating the drummer to equal status with the front-line soloists for the first time in jazz.

He founded Debut Records with Charles Mingus in 1952 and went on to establish himself as a major bandleader in his own right, beginning in 1954 with a famous group co-led with trumpeter Clifford Brown. He has remained a creative force through decades of stylistic shifts in jazz and has continued to absorb new influences into his ever-evolving music.

George Russell (Composer, arranger, b. 1923)

Cincinnati-born George Russell is one of a small number of jazz musicians whose primary reputation was earned as a composer and theoretician rather than as an instrumentalist. Initially a student of drums and later a pianist, Russell ultimately limited his onstage contribution to conducting, albeit in the style of a consummate showman. He framed the basic structure of his lifelong work on *The Lydian Chromatic Concept Of Tonal Organization* while hospitalized in 1945–46, and published the first version of that modally based theory in 1953, with several subsequent revisions. Its influence has been vast.

Key Tracks

'Daahoud' Max Roach
'Driva Man' Max Roach
'Cubana Be' George Russell
'Lydiot' George Russell
'Ezz-Thetic' George Russell

Russell composed and arranged for Dizzy Gillespie, Buddy DeFranco and Lee Konitz in the late 1940s, and began to record as a leader in 1956. His small-ensemble recordings of 1960–62 were followed by equally impressive big-band projects. He spent 1963–69 in Europe, mentoring Scandinavian musicians, and then accepted a professorship at the New England Conservatory. He won a prestigious MacArthur Fellowship in 1989.

Pioneering bebop drummer Max Roach reflects between takes.

A-Z of Artists

Lennie Tristano (Piano, 1919–78)

Lennie Tristano began his career in his native Chicago, but later focused much of his time and energy on teaching. He was born weak-sighted and was blind from the age of 10. He gathered a group of important acolytes around him during the late 1940s in New York, including saxophonists Lee Konitz and Warne Marsh and guitarist Billy Bauer, and ran a school of jazz in the city from 1951–56. His musical concept offered an alternative to the prevailing bop orthodoxy of the day, and was an early explorer both of free jazz and of creating multitracked recordings by overdubbing. His own music never found a wide audience and much of it was only released posthumously, but his students ensured that his influence was a significant one.

'Now, take a group like Lennie Tristano's, which added on to that [Dixieland] feeling, made it atonal, the chord progression more intriguing and challenging.'

Dave Brubeck

Sarah Vaughan (Vocals, 1924–90)

Sarah Vaughan began her career singing in jazz bands led by Earl Hines and Billy Eckstine, but achieved her greatest fame singing ballads in more commercial settings from the late 1940s onwards. She continued to record until 1967, when she took a five-year break. Her striking control and wide vocal range established her as a major international star, and she left an extensive – if sometimes infuriatingly inconsistent – recorded legacy.

Ben Webster (Tenor saxophone, 1909–73)

Ben Webster served an initial apprenticeship in 'territory' bands in the Southwest before moving to New York in 1934. He recorded with Billie Holiday and worked with a succession of notable bandleaders before joining Duke Ellington in 1940. He was a key member of Ellington's legendary band of the time. Webster led his own small groups from 1943 and established a reputation for his warm, lyrical approach to ballad playing. He rejoined Ellington in 1948, but problems with alcohol forced him to leave music entirely from 1950–52. He returned to tour with Norman Granz's Jazz at the Philharmonic and recorded extensively as both leader and accompanist. He settled permanently in Europe from 1964, where he remained active on the club and festival circuit.

Sarah Vaughan's extensive vocal range ensured her international success.

The Fifties

The economic prosperity of America in the 1950s echoed that of the Roaring Twenties. The relief at finally being able to leave the misery of the Great Depression and the Second World War behind led to a consumerist society that revelled in its automobiles, designer products, low-cost housing and modern kitchen appliances – the American Dream had taken hold.

Television replaced radio as the dominant form of mass media, with a wealth of programmes aimed at a variety of audiences. It was the Golden Age of Hollywood, with glamorous movie stars and hugely successful movies offering a new breed of escapism. The baby boom following the Second World War led to the rise of teenage culture.

Key Artists

Miles Davis
Bill Evans
Thelonious Monk
Gerry Mulligan

Rock'n'roll ripped through the airwaves triggering a musical revolution and overshadowed jazz, which thrived in bohemian circles. As if in contrast to the frantic sounds of rock'n'roll, jazz became more refined; the Cool Jazz style, epitomized by the music of Miles Davis and Dave Brubeck, gained popularity.

As the Cold War intensified, the US undertook more research into nuclear weaponry. The Korean War, which lasted from 1950–53, claimed many thousands of American lives. There was a constant suspicion of Communism and Soviet espionage infiltrating American culture, which gave an underlying feeling of fear and vulnerability to this otherwise glorious decade.

By the 1950s jazz-orientated vocalists such as Hollywood legend Frank Sinatra were now international stars, crossing over to pop audiences with ease.

Rock'n'Roll Revolution

The 1950s was a period of sharp social and political contrasts. The decade is often regarded as a conservative one, but the solidification of middle-class values took place under the looming shadow of the Cold War in America and the physical separation of East and West in Europe. The threat of atomic weapons loomed large, and the 'space race' added further tensions to fraught international relations.

It was also a period of intensifying campaigns to secure civil rights for the African-American population, and the seeds were sowed for the removal of segregationist legislation during the 1960s. That campaign was directly reflected in the music of several major jazz musicians, including Sonny Rollins (b. 1930), Max Roach (b. 1924) and Charles Mingus (1922–79). In Europe, wartime austerity carried on well into the 1950s, and the domination of US culture on a global basis became increasingly apparent – transmitted through media including films, music, Broadway musicals, radio and eventually television.

'In New Orleans ... there was the African influence ... from Western Europe came the harmonic sense, the tonal structure, the instruments employed. **Dave Brubeck**

Jazz faced a major new competitor in the quest for listeners – one that was to dominate almost from the outset. Rock'n'roll exploded on to the music scene – the convenient launch point is usually taken to be Bill Haley's 'Rock Around The Clock' in 1954, but the groundwork had already been laid by jazz, blues, country, R&B and gospel music, all of which fed into the new teen-oriented form (the teenager as a distinct – and increasingly marketable – entity was also a new 'invention' of the decade).

Jazz had enjoyed a brief tenure as the principal popular music of America from the 1920s to the early 1940s, but would never regain that position. In the 1950s, though, hard-bop artists enjoyed wide popularity within African-American communities, and jazz was still a mainstay of the neighbourhood jukeboxes and clubs. In Europe, bop began to generate its own adherents, led by the likes of John Dankworth, Ronnie Scott and Tubby Hayes in England; the divisive arguments of the 1940s in America were replicated on the jazz scenes there. As in Hitler's Germany, jazz also came to be seen as an underground symbol of freedom within the Communist bloc, and spawned a clandestine music scene in later decades.

African-American jazz artists such as Charles Mingus promoted civil rights in their music.

Hard Bop Takes Centre Stage

Hard bop became the 'mainstream' jazz form of the 1950s. It grew out of the new direction pioneered by the bebop artists of the late 1940s, but introduced an earthier feel that drew more on blues and gospel. Art Blakey (1919–90) and Horace Silver (b. 1928) led the way, while Jimmy Smith (1925–2005) laid the ground rules for the related form of soul jazz, and paved the way for an eruption of Hammond organ trios.

The music associated with hard bop draws on the rhythmic and harmonic principles laid down in bebop, but with simpler motifs, a greater rigidity in the theme-solos-theme structure and a heavier reliance on 'running' the chord changes. The music had a heavier feel in both instrumental expression and rhythm than the airier registers of bebop, and its more obvious use of blues, gospel and R&B antecedents prompted the 'soul' and 'funk' tags, which quickly became attached to the music.

A Complex Mosaic

By the end of the 1950s, the perceived limitations of hard-bop were pushing some musicians into more experimental directions. The emergence of Cecil Taylor (b. 1929) and Ornette Coleman (b. 1930) in New York in 1959 were crucial turning points in the move towards free jazz in the 1960s, but bop continued to thrive in the hands of young musicians such as Lee Morgan (1938–72). If hard bop was the signature jazz sound of the decade, it was only part of an increasingly complex mosaic within the broad parameters of the music. Louis Armstrong (1901–71) consolidated his position as the most famous of all jazz names with his All-Stars, while traditional jazz still thrived through musicians like Al Hirt, Pete Fountain and many others.

Popular Melody

Horace Silver – 'The Preacher' (1955)

The developments in popular music since the late 1930s had installed singers as the main focus of teenage devotion; jazz-oriented singers such as Frank Sinatra (1915–98), Ella Fitzgerald (1917–96), Sarah Vaughan (1924–90) and Nat 'King' Cole (1917–65). The major names in modern jazz were all musicians who had launched their careers in bebop, but had moved off in diverse directions. They included Miles Davis (1926–91), Thelonious Monk (1917–82), Dizzy Gillespie (1917–93) and Charles Mingus – all of whom helped to shape the development of jazz.

Art Blakey helped to form the new hard-bop sound.

Playing it Cool

Modal jazz was well established by the end of the decade, reflected in the success of Miles Davis's album *Kind Of Blue* (1959). Cool jazz was also a key contributor to the mix. Often seen as a largely white reaction to the mainly black hard-bop mainstream, cool jazz grew out of the arranging experiments of Gerry Mulligan (1927–96) and Gil Evans (1912–88), exemplified in Miles Davis's Nonet recordings of 1949–50 (later dubbed the 'Birth Of The Cool' on their LP release).

As the name implies, cool jazz adopted a less frenetic and more arrangement-oriented approach than hard bop, although the forms are clearly related; indeed, they are effectively a parallel development from the same harmonic and rhythmic foundations in bebop. Mulligan's subsequent quartet in Los Angeles with trumpeter Chet Baker (1929–88) proved very popular, and the West Coast became the centre of the cool movement in the work of artists such as Shorty Rogers, Bud Shank, Shelly Manne, Chico Hamilton and Teddy Edwards. Major names like Dave Brubeck (b. 1920), Stan Getz (1927–91) and Art Pepper (1925–82) often reflected a cooler approach, while Lennie Tristano (1919–78) acolytes Lee Konitz and Warne Marsh also explored related ground.

Popular Melody

Dave Brubeck Quartet – 'Take Five' (1959)

The Advent of the LP

The arrival the long-playing (LP) record was a significant development in itself. Up until the early 1950s, all recordings had been made under the time limitations of 78-rpm records. In practice, jazz musicians often played at very extended lengths in live performance – especially in club sets or jam sessions.

Broadcasts permitted the players to stretch out, but it was only with the advent of the longer playing time of the LP that they were able to begin reflecting their live work more accurately in the recording studio. That could be a mixed blessing, and many 1950s recordings were little more than loose blowing sessions, but it did allow a more faithful record of a musician's style and abilities to be preserved in the studio environment. The 1950s, then, turned out to be a complex decade, both within jazz and in the wider world, rather than – as they are sometimes depicted – simply the dull, hidebound prelude to the new freedoms and excesses of the 1960s.

Miles Davis's 1959 Kind Of Blue *is considered the definitive jazz album and a acclaimed standard of excellence.*

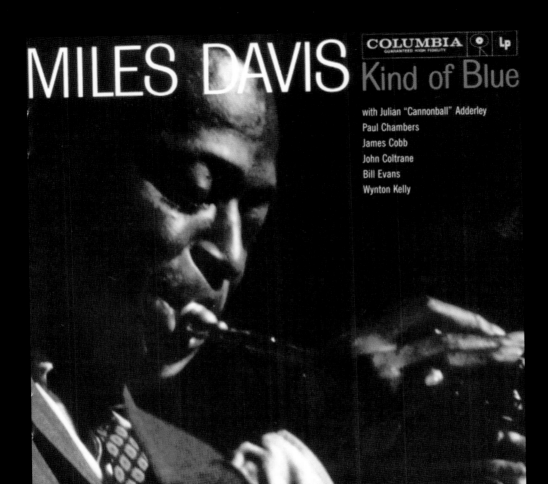

MILES DAVIS

COLUMBIA
GUARANTEED HIGH FIDELITY

lp

Kind of Blue

with Julian "Cannonball" Adderley
Paul Chambers
James Cobb
John Coltrane
Bill Evans
Wynton Kelly

Key Artist: Miles Davis

The history of post-war jazz tracked the musical development of Miles Dewey Davis III so closely that it is tempting to see the trumpeter as the orchestrator of each of the most significant stylistic shifts of the era. With the notable exception of free jazz, Miles seemed to trigger a new seismic shift in the music with each passing decade. The reality is inevitably less simple, but there is no question that if Miles did not initiate successive revolutions, he was consistently in the frontline of their development and popularization.

Born into a black, bourgeois family in Alton, Illinois in 1926, Miles was brought up in St Louis and first played music professionally in that city. He moved to New York in 1944, in time to catch the flowering of bebop, and played with Charlie Parker and Dizzy Gillespie in the city's clubs – but the frenetic style of the new music was not his real forte.

Miles Ahead

A lateral shift into a development that had been bubbling under the work of arrangers such as Gil Evans and Gerry Mulligan came with Miles's 1949–50 sessions, later dubbed the 'Birth Of The Cool', which paved the way for cool jazz. That new style quickly came to be seen, despite Miles, as a largely white response to bebop.

'Don't play what's there, play what's not there.'

Miles Davis

In 1954 Davis kicked his heroin addiction and re-launched his flagging career. His use of a Harmon Mute with its stem removed gave him a lyrical, instantly recognizable sound, and perhaps helped him to work around the fact that, by jazz standards, he was not a dazzling virtuoso. The latter half of the 1950s witnessed outstanding peaks of Davis's achievement. In those years, he led his great quintet with saxophonist John Coltrane and also made a series of classic records with Gil Evans, including *Miles Ahead* (1957), *Porgy And Bess* (1958) and *Sketches Of Spain* (1959–60).

Above: Miles Davis (far right) with Sidney Bechet (far left) at the 1949 Jazz Fair in Paris, France.

Mastering the Modes

The influence of George Russell led Davis towards a modal theory of jazz, in which improvisation was based on a set of scales (modes were originally part of early Greek music) rather than on the chord-based structures of bop. Miles brought these ideas to a wide audience, notably in *Milestones* (1958) and the classic *Kind Of Blue* (1959).

Typically, though, a new decade brought another change of direction. Davis's classic 1960s quintet with saxophonist Wayne Shorter, pianist Herbie Hancock and the rhythm section of Ron Carter and Tony Williams was one of the great units in jazz history. In 1969, he recorded *In A Silent Way* with an electrically-enhanced line-up, followed by the dense *Bitches Brew* (1969), generally regarded as the cornerstone of the jazz-rock wave of the 1970s. Many older jazz fans parted company with his music at this point, but Miles was unrepentant in seeking a new, rock-oriented audience.The textural mass of his music grew increasingly dense with guitars and keyboards, and he himself became progressively more distant from his audience, a move exacerbated by poor health and drug use. He was in the habit of playing with his back to the house, using a trumpet fitted with a modified wah-wah pedal.

Back in Business

He stopped playing altogether throughout 1975–80, but resumed his performing and recording career with a series of pop-funk-oriented bands in the 1980s. Out-of-character reunions in the summer of 1991 with some of his eminent former sidemen at Montreux and in France suggested he was aware that his death in September was imminent.

For four decades Miles had launched the careers of musicians including John Coltrane and Bill Evans in the 1950s, Ron Carter, Wayne Shorter and Herbie Hancock in the 1960s, John McLaughlin, Chick Corea, Jack DeJohnette and Dave Holland in the 1970s, and John Scofield, Mike Stern and Kenny Garrett in the 1980s. He was always open to experiments and brought together diverse influences, ranging from Stockhausen's electronic textures to soul, funk, hip hop and ethnic instruments. The connecting thread in all of this was Miles himself. His own sound and approach remained largely a constant at the centre of all these changing musical contexts. The abrasive personality, menacing aloofness, foul language and arrogant demeanour that saw him dubbed the 'Prince of Darkness' seemed only to add to his charisma.

Next Page: The classic quintet of the 1960s: (l–r) Herbie Hancock, Miles Davis, Ron Carter, Wayne Shorter, Tony Williams.

Key Artist: Bill Evans

Bill Evans was one of the most lyrical and romantic of all jazz pianists. His distinctive lightness of touch and singing tone on the piano shone most brightly in his favoured trio settings with compatible bass players and drummers, including famous line-ups that featured Scott LaFaro and Paul Motian, and later Eddie Gomez and Marty Morrell.

Evans was born in Plainfield, New Jersey in 1929 and studied classical piano (and also violin) from the age of six (the trademark hunched position that he later adopted at the keyboard would doubtless have horrified his teacher!). He turned to jazz in his teens and began working professionally in New York in the early 1950s. He came to wider notice through associations with George Russell, Cannonball Adderley and – most significantly – the Miles Davis Sextet of the late 1950s.

Rethinking the Piano Trio

Evans' contributions as pianist or composer to all but one track on the classic *Kind Of Blue* was as crucial as anyone's to the success of that famous session. His own recording career as a leader began with *New Jazz Conceptions* (1956). His influences included Bud Powell and Horace Silver, but while his style remained rooted in bop, he developed his approach in an individual fashion that laid heavy stress on the lyrical facets of his music and on original harmonic thinking.

'He changed forever the way the piano was approached. He opened up so many different possibilities in terms of harmony and rhythm.... He was creating all the time.'

Joe La Barbera

His famous trio with bassist Scott LaFaro and drummer Paul Motian brought a new lustre to one of jazz's most established formats, but the tragic death of LaFaro in a road accident in 1961 brought the group to a premature end. The live recordings that they made at the Village Vanguard in New York are among the highest accomplishments of the trio repertoire in jazz. LaFaro was well-equipped to adopt the kind of interactive accompanying role that Evans favoured, and set a benchmark that the pianist always sought to emulate in his choice of bassists. Later incumbents of that key position included Gary Peacock and Eddie Gomez.

Bill Evans played in a small group in the 1970s, a period in which he also experimented with the sound of a Fender Rhodes electric piano.

A Pervasive Influence

The pianist's refined sense of melodic inflection and harmonic subtlety proved very influential, not only on his peers but also on a subsequent generation of great jazz pianists, including Herbie Hancock, Chick Corea and Keith Jarrett. That influence remains equally pervasive today. If the trio was his principal vehicle, Evans also explored the use of overdubbing to create multitracked 'solo' piano recordings, as on *Conversations With Myself* (1963). He recorded duo albums with guitarist Jim Hall and singer Tony Bennett, as well as with Eddie Gomez, and sometimes worked with horn players added to his trio. He also recorded with a symphony orchestra in 1965.

Making the Piano Sing

Evans' ability to radically remake standard tunes by the most deft and subtle of alterations was legendary, and his own compositions have stood the test of time. His best-known originals include 'Blue In Green' (jointly credited to Miles Davis), 'Waltz For Debby', 'Comrad Conrad', 'Peace Piece', 'Detour Ahead', 'Funkallero', 'Interplay', 'NYC's No Lark' (an anagram of the name of pianist Sonny Clark, and a tribute to his memory), 'Laurie', 'Re: Person I Knew' (another anagram, of producer Orrin Keepnews), 'Song For Helen', 'Time Remembered' and 'We Will Meet Again'.

He experimented with a Fender Rhodes electric piano in the 1970s, but his music is inextricably welded to the sonority of the acoustic piano, and his ability to make that instrument sing lay at the heart of his achievement. He acquired a heroin addiction while serving in the US Army, and was plagued with drug problems and ill-health at various times in his career. He died in New York in September 1980, having done much to redefine the art of the piano trio.

Pianist Bill Evans, whose classical training gave him a romantic sensitivity unusual in jazz performers.

Key Artist: Thelonious Monk

Thelonious Monk was one of the most original and idiosyncratic figures in jazz history. Almost from the start of his long career, the pianist and composer pursued a singular but relentlessly focused path through jazz, playing his own music in his own instantly identifiable way, with a seeming disregard for popular acceptance that was extreme even by jazz standards.

Thelonious Sphere Monk Jr was born in Rocky Mount, North Carolina on 10 October 1917, but lived in New York from the age of six. The Harlem stride pianists of the 1920s became a sublimated but palpable influence on his rhythmic style. His idiosyncratic approach extended to every element of his music. His angular melodies, unconventional dissonant harmonies and oblique rhythmic patterns all bore his stamp, as did his touch at the keyboard (not to mention his penchant for using his elbow and forearm to crash out huge clusters of notes, or breaking into a little dance around the instrument).

A Unique Artistic Vision

Monk recycled his compositions endlessly in concert and on records, often in rather rigidly demarcated fashion. He was an introverted, eccentric figure in the colourful world of jazz, but he had a unique artistic vision and a single-minded determination to realize that vision. He was at the centre of the group of musicians who forged the framework for bebop at Minton's Playhouse in the mid-1940s, but even there his highly individual style placed him a little to the side of the central flow of the music (Bud Powell, a friend of Monk's, provided the more canonical example of the bebop pianist).

'He'll come in [Minton's] any time and play for hours with only a dim light and the funny thing is he'll never play a complete tune. You never know what he's playing.'

Teddy Hill

He worked with Coleman Hawkins, Lucky Millinder, Cootie Williams and Dizzy Gillespie in the mid-1940s, and began recording as a leader for Blue Note Records in 1947. His recordings for that label (until 1952), Prestige (1952–54) and Riverside (1954–60) comprise the bulk of his classic music. He signed to Columbia in 1960 and recorded in solo and big-band settings with the label – as well as in the familiar quartet format – but added only 11 new compositions in that time, preferring to

---

Above Right: A US Post Office stamp featuring Thelonious Monk, from the Jazz Series. Below Right: Innovative bebop pianist Thelonious Monk.

rework his classic canon of the 1950s until his departure from the label, and start of total withdrawal, in 1969.

No Compromises Accepted

Monk's music rarely diverged from the structures of the standard 12-bar and 32-bar forms that dominated the era, but they were recast in strange new harmonies and rhythms. He brooked no compromises with his music, and many musicians baulked at the discipline his music required, although others – John Coltrane, Clark Terry, Steve Lacy and Charlie Rouse among them – embraced its spiky demands. Many of his tunes have entered the jazz repertoire, including ''Round Midnight', 'Blue Monk', 'In Walked Bud', 'Rhythm-A-Ning', 'Misterioso', 'Straight No Chaser', 'Well You Needn't' and 'Evidence'.

Monk was featured on the cover of *Time* magazine in 1964 and his increased profile led to his making a tour of Europe in 1961. It had been a long time coming, but he went on to tour abroad regularly throughout the 1960s, mainly with his quartet but also with a nine-piece group in 1969; there are numerous live recordings from Europe and Japan as well as America in that decade.

A Timeless Legacy

His public appearances became increasingly rare in the early 1970s. He made his final studio recordings in London in 1971, and played his last concert at the Newport in New York jazz festival in 1976. His often troubled psychological state and bizarre personal life were overseen by three protective women – his mother, his wife Nellie and his patron the Baroness Pannonica de Koenigswarter. He retired to the Baroness's home in Weehawken, New Jersey in 1976, and there he lived the rest of his life in self-imposed seclusion. He died of a cerebral haemorrhage in February 1982, leaving behind a mysterious, near-mythic reputation and a timeless, unique and endlessly challenging contribution to jazz.

Next Page: Monk at New York's Carnegie Hall in his last live appearance, 1976.

Key Artist: Gerry Mulligan

Gerry Mulligan was the leading exponent of the baritone saxophone in jazz, and one of the key instigators of the style that came to be known as cool jazz. Along with trumpeter Chet Baker, Mulligan came to exemplify the cool ethos in the 1950s; he returned to the roots of that style with his Re-Birth Of The Cool (1992).

The title and the concept echoed the groundbreaking Nonet sessions of 1949–50, which were led by Miles Davis but fuelled by the arrangements of Mulligan and Gil Evans. The use of French horn and the

intricate weave of timbre and texture in the music foreshadowed the later developments of the 'third stream' (the movement's main progenitors, pianist John Lewis and composer Gunther Schuller, were both involved in the sessions), as well as the cool school.

Birth of the Cool

Mulligan was born in New York City in April 1927 and grew up in Philadelphia. He began arranging music in his teens, inspired by the example of the great swing band arrangers such as Duke Ellington, Jimmy Mundy, Fletcher Henderson, Sy Oliver and Gil Evans.

Mulligan wrote arrangements for the Claude Thornhill band in New York in 1946, and was introduced to the textural possibilities of twentieth-century classical music by Evans and drummer Gene Krupa, a devotee of Ravel. Mulligan was an eager learner and quickly began to develop a style that built on his roots in swing but displayed a more contemporary idiom and personal voice.

'Mulligan's main contribution was to bring jazz dynamics down to the dynamic range of a string bass – and then to use counterpoint in a natural, unschooled way.'

John Graas

The 'Birth Of The Cool' recordings of 1949–50 featured his compositions ('Jeru', 'Venus De Milo', 'Rocker') and arrangements. The clarity, control, swing, and rhythmic and harmonic invention of the music were all less frenetic than the bop model, and the cooler approach was ideal for Mulligan.

Above: Baritone saxophonist Gerry Mulligan was an important figure in cool jazz, as well as a gifted composer and arranger. Right: A performance at the 1955 Newport Jazz Festival featuring (l–r) Percy Heath, Miles Davis and Mulligan.

Quartet and Big Band

Mulligan formed the first of his 'pianoless' quartets in Los Angeles in 1951, featuring Chet Baker's romantic trumpet. The contrapuntal possibilities of two (or more) horns, bass and drums would preoccupy him throughout the 1950s. His collaborators included trumpeters Jon Eardley and Art Farmer, valve trombonist Bob Brookmeyer and saxophonist Zoot Sims.

Mulligan began touring with his Concert Jazz Band in 1960, and continued to work on and off in that format throughout the rest of his career. While he made his greatest impact with his smaller groups, where improvisation was the primary element of the music, the large ensemble lent itself well to his particular style of writing and arranging. He revelled in the greater textural possibilities that the big band offered, and he went on to experiment with composing for orchestral ensembles as well, albeit less successfully.

Exploring the Big Horn

Mulligan's interest in musical textures extended to his choice of instrument. He began playing tenor saxophone but was seduced very quickly by the deeper sonorities and extended textural possibilities offered by the baritone register. Although he also played soprano saxophone and piano, he was best known for his finely burnished sound on baritone saxophone, and was one of the small group of players who have evolved a genuinely distinctive soloist's voice on that instrument.

The stamp of the Swing Era never left Mulligan's music, both as player and writer. He favoured a lightly textured, flowing style that relied on grace rather than volume, with a special liking for the whispered effects that can be achieved by players who understand the virtues of playing *pianissimo*, but without any sacrifice of intensity.

Given his close link with the cool approach, it is a useful corrective to the typecasting impulse to remember that he also collaborated with the likes of Thelonious Monk and Charles Mingus, and proved himself adaptable to the demands of these two idiosyncratic giants. Despite a long illness, he continued to perform until shortly before his death in January 1996.

Next Page: Mulligan with his band at the Capital Jazz Festival in 1982.

A-Z of Artists

Gene Ammons (Tenor saxophone, 1925–74)

The son of pianist Albert Ammons, Gene was equally at home in jazz and R&B settings. He was a prolific recording artist and his hard-hitting, emotionally direct blowing in a blues and funk vein also featured in a popular two-tenor band, co-led by Sonny Stitt. His work in a soul-jazz idiom with organists such as Jack McDuff and Johnny Smith added to his popularity. He served a harsh prison sentence for marijuana possession from 1962–69, resuming his recording career upon his release.

Chet Baker (Trumpet, 1929–88)

Chet Baker was an icon of cool at the height of his fame in the 1950s. His recording of 'My Funny Valentine' with Gerry Mulligan in 1952 established him as a star of the emerging cool jazz genre; his boyish, film-star looks (later ravaged by drug abuse) and a light, seductively lyrical trumpet style assured his popularity for much of the decade. Baker was born in Yale, Oklahoma but moved to Los Angeles at a young age. He led his own quartet on the West Coast from 1953.

Drugs, imprisonment in both the US and Europe, and poor health took a heavy toll from the late 1950s; he also lost some teeth in an assault in 1968, which kept him off the stage until 1973. He worked mainly in Europe from 1975, where he was in demand as a soloist in both small group and orchestral settings, and remained an artful improviser throughout the many vicissitudes of his career. He died after falling from a hotel window in Amsterdam.

'I think we were all secretly happy at the success of Chet Baker, a guy who uses about one octave in a dynamic range of ppp to mf.'

John Graas

Chris Barber (Trombone, b. 1930)

Chris Barber has been a key figure on the British traditional jazz scene since he broke away from Ken Colyer's band to lead his own group in 1954. The band was one of the leading names in the so-called 'trad boom' of the late 1950s. It became the Chris Barber Jazz & Blues Band – with the addition of electric guitar – in 1968, and brought fresh arrangements and cogent soloing to their venerable traditional jazz and blues repertoire. Barber now tours with his Big Band.

Gene Ammons, big-toned tenor saxophonist and son of boogie-woogie great Albert Ammons.

A–Z of Artists

Acker Bilk (Clarinet, b. 1929)

Acker Bilk was born in Somerset, England. He took up clarinet in the Army and formed his first band in 1950. His Paramount Jazz Band adopted trademark uniforms of striped waistcoats and bowler hats and was very successful in the UK's trad boom of the late 1950s. Bilk enjoyed a major pop hit with his own 'Stranger On The Shore' in 1961 and remained a popular draw on the international traditional jazz circuit in subsequent decades.

Art Blakey (Drums, 1919–90)

Art Blakey (also later known as Buhaina after he converted to Islam) led the quintessential hard bop group the Jazz Messengers across four decades from the late 1940s, and was a fervent advocate of

'If Art Blakey's old-fashioned, I'm white.'

Miles Davis

the music he loved. He formed his first band in his native Pittsburgh, but moved to New York and played in Billy Eckstine's seminal big band in 1944–47, before relaunching his career as a bandleader with the Seventeen Messengers. The band had a horns-plus-rhythm set-up in quintet and sextet forms and defined hard bop, spicing bebop with the earthy urgency of blues, gospel and R&B. Blakey's propulsive drumming drove a band whose changing personnel – including trumpeters Lee Morgan, Freddie Hubbard and Wynton Marsalis, saxophonist Wayne Shorter, trombonist Curtis Fuller and pianist Bobby Timmons – was remarkable.

Clifford Brown (Trumpet, 1930–56)

The tragic death of Clifford Brown in a road accident robbed jazz of one of its brightest young stars. He took up the trumpet at the age of 13, drawing on the influence of bebop stars Dizzy Gillespie and Fats Navarro. The latter's rich sonority and melodic lyricism made a particularly telling impact on the development of Brown's own style. He recorded with Lou Donaldson, J.J. Johnson and Art Blakey for Blue Note, and cut his own sessions for Pacific Jazz, but his best-known work was recorded in 1954–56, with the quintet he co-led with drummer Max Roach. His technical virtuosity and improvisational flair marked him out as a potential giant. He contributed several much-played compositions to the jazz repertoire, notably 'Joy Spring' and 'Daahoud'.

Trumpet star Clifford Brown, who died tragically young in 1956.

A-Z of Artists

Dave Brubeck (Piano, b. 1920)

The Dave Brubeck Quartet was one of the most successful jazz groups of all time; Brubeck's fascination with unusual time signatures brought major hits with 'Take Five' (written by saxophonist Paul Desmond) and 'Blue Rondo À La Turk' in 1959. His recording of 'Dialogues For Jazz Combo And Orchestra', composed by his brother Howard, appeared the same year, and the writing of large-scale works became increasingly central to Brubeck's compositions. He has continued to tour with small groups.

Ken Colyer (Cornet, trumpet, guitar, 1928–88)

Ken Colyer was a key figure in the UK revivalist movement. He took an infamously purist stance on the New Orleans style of ensemble playing, brooking no departures from orthodoxy. He co-founded the influential Crane River Band in 1949 and formed his own Jazzmen after a visit to New Orleans in 1953, but was ousted when Chris Barber assumed leadership the following year. Colyer formed an influential new band, and then continued to lead his own groups.

Gil Evans (Arranger, composer, piano, 1912–88)

Gil Evans (born Ian Green) achieved fame through his work with Miles Davis on the seminal recordings *Miles Ahead* (1957), *Porgy And Bess* (1959) and *Sketches Of Spain* (1960). His own output was relatively small, but his influence was much larger. His greatest gift lay in arranging – or more accurately, re-composing – the music of others, elaborately cloaked in his own distinctive manipulations of timbre, colour, texture and shape.

Key Tracks

'Take Five' Dave Brubeck
'The Duke' Dave Brubeck
'Dr Jazz' Ken Colyer
'After You've Gone' Ken Colyer
'Ella Speed' Gil Evans

Working with Claude Thornhill in the 1940s allowed him to experiment with unusual instrumentation and distinctive ideas, which came to fruition in the projects with Miles, including his contribution to the 'Birth of the Cool' sessions (1949–50). His own recordings included *Out Of The Cool* (1960) and *The Individualism Of Gil Evans* (1964). His orchestra became an attraction on the international circuit from the mid-1970s; his later music was notably more improvisational in content and allowed the players considerable freedom within looser, sometimes electric and rock-referent structures.

Gil Evans (right) and Miles Davis, who worked together on the 1949–50 Nonet 'Birth Of The Cool' sessions, among various other projects.

A-Z of Artists

João Gilberto (Vocals, guitar, b. 1931)

João Gilberto came to the notice of the wider jazz public in the wake of saxophonist's Stan Getz's successful *Jazz Samba* (1962). Gilberto had earlier been working with composer Antonio Carlos Jobim on a development of the samba known as 'bossa nova', and Getz translated that form into a popular success. The subsequent *Getz/Gilberto* (1963) album included vocals by his companion, Astrud Gilberto, and spawned a famous hit version of 'The Girl From Ipanema'. Gilberto is a successful international performing artist as well as composer.

Jimmy Giuffre (Clarinet, baritone, tenor and soprano saxophones, b. 1921)

Giuffre composed 'Four Brothers' for Woody Herman's saxophone section in 1947 and later joined the Second Herd. He formed a trio with Jim Hall (guitar) and Ralph Peña (bass) in 1957, then replaced bass with Bob Brookmeyer's trombone in 1958. A later trio with Paul Bley (piano) and Steve Swallow (bass) in 1961–62 was influential in the rise of free jazz. He remained open to new directions and experimented with electric instruments in the 1980s.

Popular Melody

Woody Herman – 'Four Brothers' (1947)

Eddie Harris (Tenor saxophone, vocals, 1934–96)

Eddie Harris was one of the few jazz musicians to achieve the distinction of a million-selling hit single with his version of the theme from the film *Exodus* (1960). A funky, hard-blowing saxophonist from Chicago, he pioneered the use of electronics with tenor saxophone through the Varitone signal processor and similar devices from the mid-1960s. Harris also played several other instruments and sang; he had an expressive sound and polished technique in straight and exploratory jazz, as well as in crossover settings.

Roy Haynes (Drums, b. 1925)

Roy Haynes is a major jazz drummer taking in most genres of the music. He spent three years with Charlie Parker (1949–52) and five with Sarah Vaughan (1953–58), and by the mid-1960s had also worked with Bud Powell, Miles Davis, Thelonious Monk, Eric Dolphy and John Coltrane. Later associations include Gary Burton, Chick Corea and Pat Metheny. He has continued to lead his own groups.

João Gilberto's vocalist collaborator Astrud Gilberto performs with two other important figures in the bossa nova movement, Antonio Carlos Jobim (centre) and Stan Getz.

A-Z of Artists

Jimmy Heath (Tenor and soprano saxophone, flute, b. 1926)

Jimmy Heath's early devotion to Charlie Parker saw him nicknamed 'Little Bird', but he switched from alto to tenor saxophone and developed his own voice. He honed his writing skills with the Dizzy Gillespie Orchestra throughout 1949–50. He spent 1955–59 in prison, but rebuilt his career with a series of recordings for Riverside. Later, he performed with bassist Percy Heath and drummer Albert 'Tootie' Heath in the Heath Brothers. He remains an influential jazz arranger and educator.

Milt Jackson (Vibraphone, 1923–99)

Milt Jackson diverged from his two great predecessors on vibes, Lionel Hampton and Red Norvo, by developing a linear, rhythmically inflected approach rooted in bebop rather than swing. He preferred the slightly larger vibraharp to the more familiar vibraphone, and adjusted the oscillator to give a trademark rich, warm sound.

He recorded as a leader and worked with many major names, including Coleman Hawkins, John Coltrane, Oscar Peterson and Ray Charles, but was best known as part of the long-running Modern Jazz Quartet, one of the most successful groups in jazz history. That band began as the Milt Jackson Quartet but ran as the MJQ from 1952–74, and occasionally thereafter. Jackson was a gifted soloist, steeped in the earthy pragmatism of gospel and blues; his playing provided a counterweight to the intricate classicism of pianist John Lewis's compositions and arrangements for the group, but without upsetting the balance of the music.

Key Tracks

'Gingerbread Boy' Jimmy Heath
'Bags' Groove' Milt Jackson
'Every Time We Say Goodbye' Milt Jackson
'Poinciana' Ahmad Jamal

Ahmad Jamal (Piano, b. 1930)

Ahmad Jamal made his name with his very successful trio of the late 1950s and had a hit with his version of 'Poinciana' in 1958. His light touch and use of space has led some to hear too much of the cocktail lounge in his playing, but he is an inventive and influential musician and composer. He experimented with more avant-garde approaches after a break from performing in the early 1960s, and later with electric instruments and symphonic settings; however, he has mostly worked in trios.

Milt Jackson (right) and Percy Heath perform in the long-lived Modern Jazz Quartet.

A-Z of Artists

Antonio Carlos Jobim (Composer, piano, guitar, 1927–94)

Jobim was the best known of the Brazilian composers who made an impact on jazz. His international reputation blossomed due to his songs in the film *Black Orpheus* (1959) and with João Gilberto he sparked a bossa nova craze, boosted by Stan Getz and Charlie Byrd's *Jazz Samba* (1962). He led his own band on international tours, and his songs – including 'Girl From Ipamena', 'Desifinado' and 'One Note Stand' – with original lyrics in Portuguese and light, sophisticated harmonies, remain jazz staples.

Quincy Jones (Trumpet, arranger, b. 1933)

Quincy Jones started out as a trumpet player but first achieved public acclaim as an arranger and subsequently went on to earn an even greater reputation as a record producer for artists including Aretha Franklin and Michael Jackson. He began arranging with Lionel Hampton in 1951 and toured as music director of Dizzy Gillespie's big band in 1956. He wrote for Ray Charles and Frank Sinatra among many others, and produced USA For Africa's 'We Are The World' (1985). He is also a successful film composer and record-company executive.

Key Tracks

'Girl From Ipanema' Antonio Carlos Jobim
'Soul Bossa Nova' Quincy Jones
'Blinks' Steve Lacy

Steve Lacy (Soprano saxophone, 1934–2004)

Steve Lacy began his career in Dixieland jazz, sitting in with Henry 'Red' Allen, among others, at New York's Café Metronome. However, he quickly shifted tack and became one of the leading figures in the jazz avant-garde. Soprano saxophone is now widely played, but Lacy concentrated on the then-neglected horn from the outset.

He worked with Cecil Taylor and Thelonious Monk in the late 1950s and Monk's music remained a constant artistic preoccupation, including in later projects with trombonist Roswell Rudd and pianist Mal Waldron. Lacy also began a long musical relationship with Gil Evans at that time and became involved with free jazz in the early 1960s. He began to perform in Europe in 1965 and lived in France from 1970–2002, where he continued to pursue new and experimental musical ideas. These included his long-running sextet; electronic music; projects involving his wife (singer Irène Aebi); collaborations with poets, dancers and visual artists; and an ambitious improvisational 'opera', *The Cry*.

Trumpeter Quincy Jones is also a successful composer, arranger and record producer.

A-Z of Artists

John Lewis (Piano, 1920–2001)

John Lewis was an important pianist, composer and educator, but was best known as the musical director of the most successful jazz group of the era, the Modern Jazz Quartet. Over five decades, Lewis was the architect of the group's characteristic fusion of jazz and classical music. The MJQ's light, spacious, swinging arrangements established them as an international concert draw, while Lewis's compositions amounted to a substantial canon.

His work away from the group was also significant. He worked with Dizzy Gillespie, Charlie Parker and Miles Davis (on the 'Birth Of The Cool' sessions) in the late 1940s and co-founded the jazz-classical fusion movement known as 'third stream' with Gunther Schuller in the late 1950s. He was musical director of the Monterey Jazz Festival from 1958–82, and was leader and director of two ensembles: Orchestra USA (1962–65) and the American Jazz Orchestra (1985–92). Lewis's acclaimed solo album, *Evolution II* (2001), was issued shortly before his death.

Key Tracks

'Afternoon In Paris' John Lewis
'Django' John Lewis
'Fat Tuesday' Humphrey Lyttelton
'Soul' Jackie McLean

Humphrey Lyttelton (Trumpet, clarinet, b. 1921)

Humphrey Lyttelton acquired a passion for jazz as a schoolboy at Eton and developed it in the Grenadier Guards – not a standard jazz background. His professional career began with George Webb's Dixielanders in 1947. He led his own bands from 1948, and courted controversy in the 1950s by bringing bop musicians into his group, to the immense chagrin of traditional purists. His contribution to British jazz as a player, composer, bandleader, historian, broadcaster and writer has been a substantial one.

Jackie McLean (Alto saxophone, 1931–2006)

Jackie McLean worked with Sonny Rollins and practised with Bud Powell as a teenager. His invention and passionate delivery on alto saxophone attracted collaborations with Miles Davis (1951–52), Charles Mingus (1956, 1958–59) and Art Blakey (1956–57). He recorded a series of albums for Prestige and acted in Jack Gelber's play *The Connection* (1959–61). His powerful recordings for Blue Note in the early 1960s were more experimental. He became an eminent jazz educator in later decades.

Humphrey Lyttelton, a self-taught trumpeter, is one of Britain's leading Dixieland revivalists.

A-Z of Artists

Charles Mingus (Bass, piano, composer, 1922–79)

Charles Mingus had a tempestuous, multi-faceted personality, which is reflected in the almost schizophrenic extremes of his music and the sheer magnitude of his creative aspirations. Early work with Lionel Hampton and Red Norvo brought him in 1951 from California to York, where he worked with Miles Davis, Duke Ellington, Charlie Parker and others.

Mingus formed Debut Records with Max Roach and issued some of his early Jazz Workshop recordings on the label (along with the famous concert from Massey Hall in 1953 with Parker, Gillespie, Powell and Roach). His radical style of ensemble improvisation and his enduring compositions are captured in groundbreaking discs such as *Pithecanthropus Erectus* (1956), *Ah Um* (1959) and the big band album *The Black Saint and the Sinner Lady* (1963). His large-scale work *Epitaph* was only performed in complete form in 1989, a decade after his death.

'I believe in using the entire piano as a single instrument, capable of expressing every possible musical idea. I have no one style. I play as I feel.'

Oscar Peterson

Art Pepper (Alto and tenor saxophones, 1925–82)

Art Pepper was a soloist with Stan Kenton (1947–52) and took part in trumpeter Shorty Rogers's first so-called West Coast jazz recordings in 1951. He made a series of classic records for the California-based Contemporary label (1957–60), but was imprisoned at various times for heroin-related offences, culminating in three years' voluntary rehabilitation in Synanon from 1969. He played with the Don Ellis Orchestra in 1975 and enjoyed a triumphant finale to his career as a leader from 1977.

Oscar Peterson (Piano, b. 1925)

Canadian pianist Oscar Peterson made his name on 'Jazz At The Philharmonic' (JATP) tours in the early 1950s, and formed his own trio in 1952. His most famous line-up (1953–58) featured Herb Ellis (guitar) and Ray Brown (bass); he replaced the guitar with more conventional drums from 1958. His extravagant improvisations combined pre-bop and bop elements. He was a virtuoso technician until illness restricted his playing in the 1990s; he recorded voluminously, produced most often by his champion, JATP founder Norman Granz.

Oscar Peterson puts his all into a solo during a 1957 performance.

A-Z of Artists

Oscar Pettiford (Bass, cello, composer, 1922–60)

Oscar Pettiford was the first bass player to develop the new melodic and rhythmic concepts of bebop on his instrument and was an accomplished cellist and composer. He was of mixed African-American and Native American extraction and had a famously irascible temperament, frequently falling out with his many collaborators. He worked with Duke Ellington and Woody Herman, and led his own small groups and a big band (1956–57). He spent his final two years in Europe.

Bud Powell (Piano, 1924–66)

Bud Powell was the pre-eminent bebop pianist. His spare chords and asymmetric accents in the left hand combined with fluid linear inventions in the right hand to establish the foundation of the standard approach to bop piano playing. The mental instability and introverted character that dogged his life are often ascribed to a beating by the police in 1945 but may have preceded it.

He was part of Dizzy Gillespie's seminal bebop quintet in 1945, recorded with Charlie Parker in 1947 and made a series of classic trio recordings from 1949–56 that are his primary legacy. He also took part in the famous Massey Hall concert in 1953 with Parker, Gillespie, Mingus and Roach. He moved to Paris, France in 1959 and continued to perform there (albeit erratically) until 1964, when he made an unsuccessful return to the US. His troubled life in Paris was the major inspiration for the film *Round Midnight* (1986).

Key Tracks

'Bohemia After Dark' Oscar Pettiford
'Dance Of The Infidels' Bud Powell
'Cumbia and Jazz Fusion'
   The Dannie Richmond Quintet

Dannie Richmond (Drums, 1935–88)

Dannie Richmond's career is inextricably linked with that of Charles Mingus. He played saxophone and piano before taking up drums in 1956, working closely with Mingus until 1979. Richmond's energetic, versatile style was also well-suited to jazz rock; he played with the UK band Mark-Almond (1970–73) and worked with Joe Cocker and Elton John. He co-founded Mingus Dynasty in 1979, and played with bassist Cameron Brown, saxophonist George Adams and pianist Don Pullen until his death.

Highly influential bebop pianist Bud Powell takes a break.

A-Z of Artists

Sonny Rollins (Tenor and soprano saxophone, b. 1930)

Sonny Rollins stands alongside John Coltrane as the major bop-rooted stylist on tenor saxophone. He cut his teeth in New York with bop giants including Charlie Parker, Bud Powell, Thelonious Monk and Miles Davis. He was a member of the Clifford Brown–Max Roach Quintet (1955–57), and has led his own bands since then. His late 1950s recordings confirmed his standing as one of the great talents in the music; calypso-based tunes have been a recurring motif since 'St Thomas' (1956).

He stopped performing to recharge creatively between 1959–61, then recorded with an early hero, Coleman Hawkins (1963), and flirted with the emerging free jazz avant-garde (1965–66). He took his long and discursive soloing to its logical conclusion in *The Solo Album* (1985) and experimented with soprano saxophone, also adding various electric instruments to his group. Rollins is capable of a power and invention that few musicians in jazz have been able to match.

Horace Silver (Piano, b. 1928)

Horace Silver stands with Art Blakey as the progenitor of the earthier development of bebop, known as hard bop. His Hartford-based trio was hired by Stan Getz in 1950 and he moved to New York the following year. He began recording for Blue Note in 1952, a relationship that would last for 28 years. He formed a band with Art Blakey that became the latter's Jazz Messengers when the pianist left in 1956.

Like the Jazz Messengers, Silver's quintets became a nursery for new talent as well as a vehicle for his own compositions; many of his tunes became part of the standard jazz repertoire. He incorporated the influence of his father's native Cape Verdean folk music, most famously on 'Song For My Father'. His more experimental music of the 1970s was less well-received, but he returned to hard bop from the early 1980s and remains a successful artist, although increasingly hampered by arthritis.

Key Tracks

'St Thomas' Sonny Rollins
'The Bridge' Sonny Rollins
'Song For My Father' Horace Silver
'Señor Blues' Horace Silver
'The Preacher' Horace Silver

Sonny Rollins, one of the most inventive voices on the saxophone since Charlie Parker.

A-Z of Artists

Zoot Sims (Tenor, soprano and alto saxophones, 1925–85)

John 'Zoot' Sims performed in the family vaudeville act as a child and was a professional musician at 15. His Lester Young-derived tenor sound and artful improvisations were heard to advantage in large and small bands. He worked with Benny Goodman intermittently over four decades, and was part of Woody Herman's famous 'Four Brothers' saxophone section (1947–49). His small groups included stints with Gerry Mulligan (1954–56) and tenor saxophonist Al Cohn, a partnership resumed on many occasions.

Frank Sinatra (Vocals, 1915–98)

Frank Sinatra was best known as a popular singer and film actor but established his jazz credentials early in his career. He combined the smooth, Italian *bel canto* style with a sure sense of swing, toured with Harry James and learned about breath control from Tommy Dorsey (1940–42). He worked with arrangers Billy May, Gordon Jenkins and Nelson Riddle in his classic years (1953–61). Later projects included collaborations with Count Basie (1962–66) and Duke Ellington (1967).

Key Tracks

'If I'm Lucky' Zoot Sims
'I've Got You Under My Skin' Frank Sinatra
'I Get A Kick Out Of You' Frank Sinatra
'The Sermon' Jimmy Smith
'Cherokee' Sonny Stitt

Jimmy Smith (Organ, piano, 1925–2005)

Jimmy Smith, a fluent and inventive jazz improviser, is regarded as the greatest of the soul jazz organists; he essentially defined the form in his recordings for Blue Note in the 1950s. His adoption of the Hammond organ to soul jazz's combination of jazz improvisation over blues-rooted grooves opened up a new field. Smith was the genre's most eminent practitioner, although he spawned dozens of imitators and a generation of younger players.

Sonny Stitt (Alto, tenor and baritone saxophones, 1924–82)

Edward 'Sonny' Stitt was equally proficient on the alto and tenor saxophones. Initially a devotee of Charlie Parker, he developed into a hard-hitting and fluid improviser with a reputation for extreme toughness in 'cutting' contests. He worked with Dizzy Gillespie, Bud Powell, J.J. Johnson and Oscar Peterson, but is best known for his collaborations with fellow tenormen Sonny Rollins, Dexter Gordon, Eddie 'Lockjaw' Davis and Gene Ammons. His prolific discography is uneven, but often brilliant.

Soul jazz organist Jimmy Smith, who recorded extensively for Blue Note in the 1950s.

The Sixties

As the post-war baby boomers began to reach adulthood, the 1960s gave way to great social change. Civil rights became a key issue, with figures such as Martin Luther King and Malcolm X leading peaceful protests with huge followings of educated young men and women. Segregation was finally brought to an end, and the flower power movement championed peace and love as the future of civilization.

Jazz music, along with culture in general, allowed itself more freedom. The end of the 1950s had seen many groundbreaking and forward-thinking records that had encouraged a more open-minded approach to jazz. As the 1960s progressed, music from other cultures, notably Brazil, also began to have a major influence.

Key Artists

Ornette Coleman
John Coltrane
Freddie Hubbard
Sun Ra

The decade was simultaneously punctuated with violent events. The Cuban Missile Crisis of 1962 gave rise to political unrest, while the assassinations of President John Kennedy and his brother Robert, Martin Luther King and Malcolm X tarnished the hippy idealism that was prevalent at the time. The Vietnam War resulted in record numbers of students turning out to protest, and brought home a grim sense of reality through the smoky haze of free love.

The 1960s was also a decade of progress and expanding horizons. The US and the Soviet Union became involved in the 'space race'; Russia won, although the US trumped them by staging the moon landing in 1969. Suddenly, anything seemed possible.

In the 1960s pre-eminent flautist Herbie Mann began to incorporate elements of Brazilian music into his repertoire. His albums of the time helped to popularize the decade's bossa nova craze.

Running Free

The 1960s was as turbulent a time for jazz as it was for the world's socio-political climate. The American civil rights movement, the Vietnam War and advances in technology all worked to change the face of jazz. Several major movements arose during the decade, generating waves of controversy and mass popularity.

Perhaps the most divisive development of the 1960s was the rise of free jazz, the roots of which had been planted several years before. In December 1960 the movement received its name and philosophy from the Atlantic album *Free Jazz: A Collective Improvisation By The Ornette Coleman Double Quartet*. Coleman and seven creative peers improvised with the barest of guidelines, one-upping each other continually until the final climax of a wild, polyphonic performance unlike anything that had been heard before. Free jazz was an artistic translation of the American civil rights struggle. The music they created was a mirror image of the anguish, bitterness, yearning, resistance, sarcasm and faith inside their collective heart. Their jazz raged, or was introspective and lamenting, or was raw, or, perhaps, free.

'Jazz is the only music in which the same note can be played night after night but differently each time.'

Ornette Coleman

A Spiritual Side to Jazz

Coleman was an essential spokesman for the new music, his alto sax a voice crying out for humanity. Cecil Taylor was similarly emotional, intellectual and articulate. Bandleader Sun Ra built a complex fantasy world about himself, claiming to be a visitor from Saturn who was seeking a new home in the cosmos for the black race. Ra appealed to both a sense of tradition and community, operating almost beyond commercial society. John Coltrane (1926–67) and Albert Ayler (1936–70) took a different spiritual tack, actively seeking God through free musical expression.

Coltrane made a lasting impression with his 1964 album *A Love Supreme*, his greatest popular achievement, before heading further into extreme freedom. Many critics hated the new music and labelled it 'anti-jazz'. Although free jazz was a novel, exciting and honest form of music that reflected the turmoil of the era, it never won over the majority of jazz listeners. It has since, however, had a continuing impact on jazz and its major proponents have become revered by critics and honoured with awards.

Saxophonist Albert Ayler, who influenced John Coltrane, led his ensembles through several distinct, ecstatic musical styles.

Blue Notes and Bossas

While free jazz may have barely made a dent in the music market, hard bop was the sound of the times for most jazz listeners. The soulful, blues-drenched, rhythmically rich style was all the rage on jazz radio and in clubs. A dozen record labels capitalized upon hard bop, none with more success than Blue Note.

Founded in the 1930s, Blue Note embraced the hard-bop aesthetic and promoted it with vigour, making stars out of Art Blakey (1919–90), Dexter Gordon (1923–90), Jackie McLean (1932–2006), Horace Silver (b. 1928), Joe Henderson, Lee Morgan (1938–72), Kenny Dorham (1924–72), Wayne Shorter (b. 1933), Herbie Hancock (b. 1940), Freddie Hubbard (b. 1938) and a host of other young jazzmen. Occasionally a top 10 victory was chalked up, as with Lee Morgan's 1964 crossover hit 'The Sidewinder'. For several years Blue Note was the premier label for jazz in the US.

More short-lived was the bossa nova craze. Tenor saxophonist Stan Getz (1927–91), a former member of the Woody Herman Orchestra and star of the 'cool school', collaborated first with guitarist Charlie Byrd and then with the Brazilian musicians João Gilberto (b. 1931) and Antonio Carlos Jobim (1927–94) on a series of albums which brought jazz and Brazilian musical styles together into a captivating new sound. 'The Girl From Ipanema', featuring the warm, distingüe singing of the woman who became known as Astrud Gilberto, was a huge US hit in 1963 and guaranteed the bossa nova a place in jazz history.

Popular Melody

Miles Davis Quintet – 'Footprints' (1966)

Demise of the Cool

The 1960s saw the dwindling of cool jazz. Pianist Lennie Tristano (1919–78), who had built a cult following, spent less time onstage and more time teaching. On the West Coast, cool icons such as Shorty Rogers and Bud Shank were fortunate enough to find work in Hollywood's film and television studios as their sounds went out of vogue. Jimmy Giuffre (b. 1921) and Gerry Mulligan (1927–96), who had made names for themselves in Los Angeles, found more fertile ground in New York City and abandoned much of their cool-jazz interest. Even the Modern Jazz Quartet, mixing hard bop and cool jazz, took frequent hiatuses. One legacy of cool jazz was the so-called 'third stream' of jazz and classical hybrids, in which both Giuffre and the MJQ's John Lewis (1920–2001) took part.

Lee Morgan, one of the stars born with the help of Blue Note records, had a 1964 hit with 'The Sidewinder'.

Miles Davis, Revolutionary

The most prominent of the cool jazz pioneers, Miles Davis (1926–91), was perhaps the key innovator of the 1960s. He ushered in the decade with an extension of the modal jazz studies he had championed in 1959's _Kind Of Blue_. His partnership with arranger Gil Evans (1912–88) continued with the triumphant _Sketches Of Spain_ (1959–60) and the less accomplished _Quiet Nights_ (1962).

In 1963 Davis gathered what would become the greatest rhythm section of his career. Drummer Tony Williams (1945–97) joined pianist Herbie Hancock and bassist Ron Carter (b. 1937) in backing Davis and a series of tenor saxophonists: first George Coleman, then Sam Rivers (b. 1923) and finally Wayne Shorter, whose innovative compositions gave a bold new sound to the quintet. In their repertoire, chords and traditional improvisation were often abandoned altogether. There were no up-front solos in pieces such as Shorter's 'Nefertiti' – only fully composed passages. At other times, the rhythm section would play _ostinatos_ – repetitive patterns over which Davis would improvise. Hancock, Carter and Williams became masters of subtle variation, altering the mood and feeling of tunes over the course of several minutes, while the horns had their say. This kind of play was about as close as Davis ever got to free jazz until his 1970s electric works.

Popular Melody

Horace Silver – 'Song For My Father' (1964)

Jazz Goes Electric

Later in the decade Davis brought in more young musicians and explored the concept of electric jazz. He initially encouraged Chick Corea, Keith Jarrett (b. 1945) and Joe Zawinul (b. 1932) to play electric piano and organ in a brave first step towards what became known as 'fusion', the union of jazz and rock elements. British electric guitarist John McLaughlin (b. 1942) pushed the envelope further outward with his unprecedented performances. Eventually Davis plugged his trumpet into a wah-wah pedal to emulate the guitar of Jimi Hendrix (1942–70). Record producer Teo Macero was also a primary factor in the new sound, manipulating the band's tapes into exhilarating collages of music. In 1969 Davis and his troupe made two groundbreaking albums for Columbia, _In A Silent Way_ and _Bitches Brew_, which announced the arrival of a fresh new form of jazz. As he had 10 years before with _Kind Of Blue_ (1959), Miles Davis had forever altered the course of music.

(l–r) Herbie Hancock, Wayne Shorter and Ron Carter, whose innovative compositions added a bold sound to Miles Davis's quintet.

Key Artist: Ornette Coleman

Since his emergence in the mid-1950s, alto saxophonist and creative composer Ornette Coleman has risen above controversy to become a respected elder statesman of jazz.

Born in 1930 in Fort Worth, Texas, Coleman taught himself the saxophone through trial and error. By avoiding chord structures and set rhythms in favour of melodic experimentation, he developed the new style of 'free jazz'. He dubbed his controversial theory 'harmolodics' – a combination of harmony, motion and melody. Coleman's characteristic tone and his variety of intonation effects often recall a plaintive human voice, touched by the blues.

Breaking New Ground

Coleman received his first saxophone at the age of seven. As he found his way around the horn, Coleman developed notions about music that clashed with traditional practices but remained permanent parts of his artistic philosophy. Four years after beginning his career at the age of 15 with an R&B group, Coleman took to the road and encountered hostility from musicians and audiences who appreciated neither his bebop alterations nor his unkempt appearance. However, bandleaders admired his songwriting abilities and assigned him to refresh their books of blues-related pieces.

'Musicians tell me, if what I'm doing is right, they should never have gone to school.'

Ornette Coleman

In 1956 Coleman found himself unemployed in Los Angeles, where he met some like-minded musicians who were interested in his new concepts. His circle included trumpeters Don Cherry and Bobby Bradford, bassist Don Payne, drummer Billy Higgins and Canadian-born pianist Paul Bley, under whose name they performed at the Hillcrest Club. Recordings of those exciting gigs were released years later by Bley's IAI record label.

In 1958 bassist Red Mitchell brought one of Coleman's compositions to Contemporary Records boss Lester Koenig, who signed Coleman to a contract. Coleman and Cherry had developed a loose, intuitive ensemble sound, evident on several Coleman compositions such as 'When Will The Blues Leave' and

Coleman (centre) performs at Newport in 1977 with Don Cherry (left) and Dewey Redman.

'The Blessing', backed somewhat uneasily by Payne and Higgins. Coleman's second Contemporary release featured another sheaf of originals, including 'Tears Inside' and 'Rejoicing'.

The session's drummer was big-band veteran and LA jazz-club operator Shelly Manne. Open-minded, responsive pianist Walter Norris interpreted Coleman's compositions creatively, but the altoist later remarked that the piano's chordal, tempered nature was incompatible with the melody-driven freedom that he sought.

In 1959 Coleman, Cherry, bassist Charlie Haden and drummer Ed Blackwell moved to New York, where they impressed composer-conductor Leonard Bernstein. Coleman continued to experiment with different ensembles and ideas, few as well-received as his famous quartet. In 1960 he recorded the landmark *Free Jazz: A Collective Improvisation By The Ornette Coleman Double Quartet* for Atlantic Records. It consisted of one long group improvisation, punctuated by a few composed reference points. The performers – Coleman, Cherry, Haden, Blackwell, Higgins, trumpeter Freddie Hubbard, Eric Dolphy on bass clarinet and second bassist Scott LaFaro (who died prematurely in a car accident seven months after the session) – interacted continuously, as individuals and also as an ensemble.

Further Innovations

Following *Free Jazz*, Coleman experimented with a new trio. He took up the violin and trumpet, although these instruments have never been more than ornaments in his overall conception. He dabbled in chamber music, wrote some film scores and arrangements for a posthumous John Coltrane release and often reunited with his former sidemen. Tenorman Dewey Redman became a key associate in that period. In 1966 Coleman controversially began using his 10-year-old son Denardo as his regular drummer. Denardo has since continued to play drums and act as a producer for both his father and his mother, poet-vocalist Jayne Cortez.

In 1972 Coleman premiered his mammoth *Skies Of America*, a concerto grosso in which his ensemble improvised with a symphony orchestra. After collaborating with Yoko Ono and Morocco's Master Musicians of Jajouka, Coleman assembled the electric band Prime Time and recorded *Dancing In Your Head* in 1976. The group included two drummers (one of them often tabla player Badal Roy), two electric guitarists and electric bass. Later, multi-keyboardist David Bryant further widened Prime Time's scope, culminating in *Tone Dialing* (1995).

Since the late 1990s, Coleman has returned to acoustic groups with pianists. He has also led a quartet with two bassists and his son Denardo. Coleman, who remains a unique saxophone melodicist, an inspiring and world-renowned artist and an enduring composer, has also recorded with Pat Metheny, Jerry Garcia (of the Grateful Dead) and an esoteric range of other musicians.

Alto saxophonist and composer Ornette Coleman, one of the chief exponents of free jazz.

Key Artist: John Coltrane

By the time John Coltrane died in 1967 at the age of 40, he had experienced one of the most remarkable careers in music. 'Trane' was a compelling voice who contributed to some of jazz's greatest innovations, from bebop to free jazz, resulting in both controversy and enduring success through critical and popular acclaim.

Coltrane was born in 1926 in Hamlet, North Carolina and began playing alto saxophone in high school. He made his first recordings while in the Army and switched to tenor sax at the encouragement of Eddie 'Cleanhead' Vinson. Work in R&B bands led to bebop gigs and in 1949 Coltrane joined Dizzy Gillespie's big band and septet. He continued to grow musically but became addicted to heroin. Coltrane moved on to the bands of Earl Bostic and Johnny Hodges, before meeting Miles Davis in 1955.

The Davis quintet, which included pianist Red Garland, bassist Paul Chambers and drummer Philly Joe Jones, was among the most popular jazz groups. The band cut several albums for Prestige in the mid-1950s with Davis and Coltrane on the front line; however, Davis fired the tenorman in 1957 because of his drug problems. Coltrane returned home to Philadelphia, overcame his addictions, and returned to jazz a new man. He worked with Thelonious Monk before getting his own contract with Prestige.

'He contributed a whole different kind of openness to the music and added a spiritual essence to the music scene.'

Herbie Hancock

'Sheets of Sound'

By the time Coltrane rejoined Davis in 1958, he had developed a technique of playing lengthy cascades of notes in propulsive harmonic extrapolations of complicated chord changes, termed 'sheets of sound' by writer Ira Gitler. The saxophonist joined Davis, altoman Julian 'Cannonball' Adderley and pianist Bill Evans on the classic *Kind Of Blue*, simplifying the music by using modal scales instead of chords. Coltrane responded with his own harmonically complicated *Giant Steps* (1959–60) for Atlantic Records; the title composition remains a test for any jazz musician. In the 1960s Coltrane began playing the soprano saxophone and scored another hit with *My Favorite Things*.

Above: Pianist McCoy Tyner played in Coltrane's hugely popular quartet of the early 1960s. Right: One of Coltrane's best known albums, 1964's A Love Supreme.

Bassist Jimmy Garrison, pianist McCoy Tyner and drummer Elvin Jones formed the core of Coltrane's early 1960s quartet, which soon became one of the most lauded ensembles in jazz. However, as his career progressed, the artistically restless Coltrane continued to develop his instrumental technique, grounded in what became a deeply spiritual and personal vision. He collaborated with gifted reedman Eric Dolphy, recording dates at New York's Village Vanguard that were later edited into an array of albums, as well as with Duke Ellington, cornettist Don Cherry, vibist Milt Jackson and vocalist Johnny Hartman.

In December 1964 Coltrane's basic quartet recorded *A Love Supreme*. The album-length devotional suite offered jazz more exotic than most fans had ever heard. The public embraced it readily, and it became another of the era's hallmark jazz albums.

Ascending to Freedom

Coltrane moved further into free jazz in June 1965, assembling a large ensemble that included trumpeter Freddie Hubbard and saxophonists Pharoah Sanders and Archie Shepp, and recording *Ascension* (1965), two album-length versions of thematically and harmonically unbridled, dense and extremely high-energy improvisation. A few days later Coltrane and Shepp unveiled their somewhat more muted but nonetheless radical new directions at the Newport Jazz Festival.

Although Jones and Tyner followed Coltrane's fearless explorations through frequent sessions that resulted in albums such as *Transition* (1965) and *Meditations* (1966), they were uncomfortable with some of his more free-form, polyphonic and polyrhythmic directions. In 1965 Alice Coltrane, the saxophonist's second wife, became the pianist, and drummer Rashied Ali emerged as a significant player, especially on duet recordings preserved as *Interstellar Space* (1967). John Coltrane continued to explore intense, abstract, progressive and uncompromising jazz until his death from liver disease in July 1967. He stands as a jazz saint to the modern world, a model of musical devotion, authentic discovery and enduring art.

Next Page: The controversial and endlessly experimental avant-garde saxophonist John Coltrane.

Key Artist: Freddie Hubbard

In the 1960s and early 1970s, trumpeter Freddie Hubbard was the primary alternative to Miles Davis's domination. Hubbard came up in the hard-bop era, blew free jazz with Ornette Coleman and John Coltrane, and established a body of exemplary compositions, recordings and improvisations with the best of the 1960s Blue Note artists: Art Blakey, Herbie Hancock, Wayne Shorter, Andrew Hill, Eric Dolphy, Lee Morgan, Tony Williams, Sam Rivers and many others.

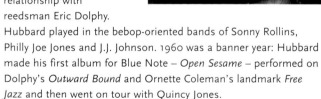

Born in Indianapolis in 1938, Hubbard drew inspiration from the bebop trumpeters of the early 1950s, particularly Clifford Brown. The Montgomery brothers, guitarist Wes, vibist Buddy and bassist Monk, were quick to hire the young trumpeter because of his stylistic resemblance to Brown. At the age of 20 Hubbard moved to New York City, where he roomed and formed a working relationship with reedsman Eric Dolphy. Hubbard played in the bebop-oriented bands of Sonny Rollins, Philly Joe Jones and J.J. Johnson. 1960 was a banner year: Hubbard made his first album for Blue Note – *Open Sesame* – performed on Dolphy's *Outward Bound* and Ornette Coleman's landmark *Free Jazz* and then went on tour with Quincy Jones.

'He had the biggest sound and the most powerful swing out there, on almost any instrument. It was pretty amazing.'

Don Braden

In 1961 Hubbard made another lasting impression with Oliver Nelson on *Blues And The Abstract Truth*, which resulted in the classic 'Stolen Moments'. That same year he joined tenorman Wayne Shorter and trombonist Curtis Fuller on the front line of Art Blakey's Jazz Messengers, the premier hard-bop ensemble. He remained a Messenger for three years, appearing on some of the band's finest recordings.

Above: Trumpeter Freddie Hubbard was inspired by Clifford Brown and played with the Montgomery brothers from a young age.

In 1964 he left the group and contributed to two more enduring sessions, Dolphy's *Out To Lunch* and Herbie Hancock's *Maiden Voyage*. The following year Hubbard ventured deeper into free jazz on John Coltrane's *Ascension*, before joining Max Roach's band.

Rising Star

In 1966 Hubbard took steps to broaden his profile, putting together a quintet that featured alto saxophonist James Spaulding. His next two recordings, *Backlash* – which included his perennially popular composition 'Little Sunflower' (1966) – and *High Blues Pressure* (1967), both for the Atlantic label, garnered more critical acclaim for Hubbard. His subsequent albums included the politically themed, abstract electronic composition *Sing Me A Song Of Songmy* (1971), and in 1970 he broke new ground on producer Creed Taylor's CTI label. Taylor was a master at reshaping jazz with more popular flourishes such as electric instruments and strings, and Hubbard benefitted greatly from his touch. The soulful albums *Red Clay* (1970), *Straight Life* (1970) and *First Light* (1972) all propelled Hubbard to the top of the jazz record and radio charts.

His triumphs on CTI collapsed when Hubbard signed with Columbia Records in 1972. The label pushed the 'contemporary' angle, dragging the trumpeter into one shallow, poorly conceived session after another. By the mid-1970s Hubbard seemed destined for has-been status. Herbie Hancock helped to rescue Hubbard's career by hiring him for the VSOP repertory group in 1977. The quintet revisited the musicians' 1960s Blue Note accomplishments and proved that an acoustic setting was where Hubbard shone the brightest.

Welcome Return

Rejuvenated as a player and composer, Freddie Hubbard resumed his climb up the jazz echelon with a triumphant appearance at the 1980 North Sea Jazz Festival in Holland. New records for Pablo, Prestige and Enja led fans to embrace the trumpeter once more, although his stardom was still long past. In 1985 he signed back with the rejuvenated Blue Note, working with the brilliant trumpeter Woody Shaw on a few projects. Unfortunately, Hubbard soon became plagued by lip trouble that ruined his embouchure and required surgery. It took him several more years to return to a point where he could play comfortably again, but he remains on the scene and has recorded with David Weiss's New Jazz Composers Octet.

Next Page: Pianist Herbie Hancock (left), shown here with Ron Carter, helped to resurrect Hubbard's career in the late 1970s.

Key Artist: Sun Ra

From the 1950s through to the 1990s there was rarely a stranger experience for jazz audiences than witnessing the stage shows of Sun Ra and his Solar-Myth Arkestra. The mysterious, robed keyboardist and his exotic big band blended theatrics with pure jazz and free exploration, crafting a unique brand of 'space jazz' that reflected the mid-century's curiosity about exploring the unknown universe.

Although Sun Ra claimed to have come to Earth from Saturn, he was in fact born Herman 'Sonny' Blount in Birmingham, Alabama in 1914. He was mostly self-taught as a pianist and performed with his own bands from the age of 20. Later, at Alabama State College, Blount proved to be such an exceptional student that he was permitted to teach from time to time.

'The outer space beings are my brothers. They sent me here. They already know my music.'

Sun Ra

Acclaimed as a creative, knowledgeable pianist, young Blount was also an inventive arranger. In 1946 he was hired by bandleader Fletcher Henderson, but his arrangements were so difficult and unusual that the musicians' complaints got him fired within a year. Around this time, Blount had been discussing Egyptian cosmology and science fiction with record producer Alton Abraham. The pair decided to put together a band that combined jazz, mythology, black pride and pulp science fiction. At the helm would be Blount, who assumed the persona of 'Sun Ra, Traveler of the Spaceways'. They built up a fantastic backstory for Ra as a sojourner from Saturn who searched the galaxy to find a new home for the mistreated black race on Earth.

Space is the Place

By the mid-1950s Sun Ra was leading the first incarnation of his big band, called the Arkestra (sometimes augmented with spacy appellations such as 'Solar-Myth' or 'Myth-Science'). Blount's expansive knowledge of jazz history, from Jelly Roll Morton to the modern day, was filtered into his arrangements and compositions for the Arkestra. The band boasted several excellent musicians, among them trombonist Julian Priester, bassist Ronnie Boykins and saxophonists John Gilmore, Marshall Allen and Pat Patrick. Sun Ra used a number of keyboards, including Wurlitzer organ,

Eccentric keyboard player Sun Ra was the pioneer of a unique brand of 'space jazz' in the 1960s.

clavinet and Moog synthesizer. The Arkestra's unusual sonic palette added to the other-worldliness of its music. Ra was a strict enforcer of rules, leading the band as a sort of commune and counselling its members against drug abuse and other unwelcome excesses.

The Arkestra debuted on record in 1957 with *Jazz By Sun Ra* (reissued on Delmark as *Sun Song*). The combination of straight jazz, heavy percussion and far-reaching improvisation heralded a new direction for jazz, but the album received scant distribution and little notice. That same year Ra formed his own record label, Saturn, which issued new Arkestra albums in haphazard form with hand-painted covers and unreliable sound quality. Saturn was one of the earliest labels run completely by musicians, and the enterprise endured even after Ra's death.

Other Worlds of Sound

However, taut musicianship and consistently interesting music were not sufficient for the Arkestra to be taken seriously by many audiences or music critics, due in part to its outlandish stage costumes and cosmic pretensions. Still, Sun Ra became one of the most recognized, if begrudgingly respected, performers in modern jazz. The psychedelic era was a boon to the bandleader, whose spacey aesthetic was easy for the hippie generation to embrace. In 1972 the band made the movie *Space Is The Place*, based upon Sun Ra's invented mythology.

In the 1980s Sun Ra began to back away from writing original material, preferring to interpret past masters such as Duke Ellington and Fletcher Henderson. In the 1990s he became wheelchair-bound following a series of strokes and died on 30 May 1993, having schooled a further generation of players (including violinist Billy Bang and trombonist Craig Harris). After his death, Evidence Records initiated a reissue programme of Sun Ra's Saturn recordings.

Left: Duke Ellington (centre), a key influence on Sun Ra's later compositions, 1969.

A-Z of Artists

Muhal Richard Abrams (Piano, b. 1930)

Muhal Richard Abrams was one of the principal architects of free jazz in Chicago. After playing with Eddie Harris and the MJT+3, Abrams founded his Experimental Band in 1961 to explore original composition and new directions. In 1965 he founded the Association for the Advancement of Creative Musicians (AACM), which emphasizes creativity, professionalism and social responsibility. Abrams is a gifted composer and bandleader, having recorded many excellent albums with some of Chicago's – and later New York's – finest musicians.

Cannonball Adderley (Alto saxophone, 1928–75)

Julian 'Cannonball' Adderley and his brother, trumpeter Nat, presided over one of the 1960s' hippest hard-bop outfits with pianist Joe Zawinul. Adderley had been employed as a Florida school band director when he was overheard at a New York gig and was encouraged by musicans. Besides his own popular groups, Adderley recorded impressively with Miles Davis, John Coltrane, Bill Evans and Gil Evans' Orchestra.

Key Tracks

'Levels And Degrees Of Light' Muhal Richard Abrams
'Mery, Mercy, Mercy' Cannonball Adderley
'Ghosts' Albert Ayler
'The Truth Is Marching In' Albert Ayler
'Silent Spring' Carla Bley

Albert Ayler (Various saxophones, 1936–70)

Albert Ayler was one of the most controversial free-jazz performers. Eccentric and tirelessly inventive, he shifted ensemble roles in his music so that drummers and bassists were on equal ground with the horns. Ayler influenced John Coltrane and many younger saxophonists, and his recordings gradually moved from free jazz towards rock and soul themes. *Spiritual Unity* (1964) remains one of his most acclaimed albums. Ayler died in mysterious circumstances at the age of 34.

Carla Bley (Piano, organ, arranger, b. 1938)

Self-taught, Carla Bley is as respected for her compositions and arrangements as for her excellent piano and organ playing. In the 1950s she was briefly married to pianist Paul Bley, who championed her works. In 1965, with her second husband, trumpeter Michael Mantler, Bley co-founded the Jazz Composers Orchestra Association to encourage the creation and distribution of new music in New York. Bley continues to lead a big band and smaller ensembles, often featuring electric bassist Steve Swallow.

(l–r) Joe Zawinul, Nat Adderley, Sam Jones, Cannonball Adderley and Louis Hayes perform on BBC2's Jazz 625 in 1964.

A-Z of Artists

Paul Bley (Piano, synthesizer, b. 1932)

Paul Bley came from Montreal to New York in the early 1950s and worked with Jackie McLean. Later, in Los Angeles, he pioneered free jazz with Ornette Coleman. Bley helped to popularize the new Moog synthesizer in the early 1970s and has collaborated with Gary Burton, Barre Phillips, Evan Parker, Pat Metheny, Jaco Pastorius, and many others.

Gary Burton (Vibraphone, b. 1943)

Gary Burton is one of the most impressive vibists in jazz, at times using four mallets in order to harmonize with himself. He began his career in country music with guitarist Hank Garland, played jazz with George Shearing and Stan Getz, and then helped to instigate the jazz-rock fusion movement through his group with guitarist Larry Coryell and drummer Roy Haynes. Burton has made marvellous duet albums with Chick Corea and Paul Bley.

Popular Melody

Orenette Coleman – 'Lonely Woman' (1959)

Ron Carter (Bass, piccolo bass, b. 1937)

Ron Carter possesses a distinctive tone and phenomenal dexterity that place him at the upper level of jazz rhythmists. In the early 1960s Carter joined drummer Chico Hamilton's popular quintet, then worked with Eric Dolphy, Don Ellis, Thelonious Monk, Cannonball Adderley and Art Farmer. From 1963–68 Carter played in Miles Davis's rhythm section with Herbie Hancock and Tony Williams. He has an equally sturdy background in classical music.

Don Cherry (Cornet, 1936–95)

Besides serving as the perfect complement for Ornette Coleman in the saxophonist's early quartet, cornettist Don Cherry was a pioneer of the 'world music' movement. Oklahoma-born Cherry moved to Los Angeles where he played in the Jazz Messiahs before meeting Coleman. After leaving the Coleman group, Cherry co-led the New York Contemporary Five. In 1968 he gathered artists from Europe and America, performing music inspired by the Balinese gamelan and Middle Eastern sounds. He continued to investigate sounds inside and outside jazz, working with Turkish musicians, the trio Codona, more mainstream jazz groups, a quartet called Old and New Dreams, and Coleman on occasion.

Cornettist Don Cherry, here playing an African hunter's harp, helped to introduce music from other cultures into the western world.

A-Z of Artists

Larry Coryell (Guitar, b. 1943)

Guitarist Larry Coryell got his start in New York with Chico Hamilton. He was a trailblazer of both free jazz and jazz-rock fusion in groups such as the Free Spirits – with saxophonist Jim Pepper and drummer Bob Moses – and in vibist Gary Burton's band. A remarkable technician, Coryell also ventured into free-jazz territory with the Jazz Composers Orchestra Association, dug deeper in to pyrotechnic fusion with the Eleventh House and performed crystalline acoustic jazz in the mid-1970s.

Jack DeJohnette (Drums, piano, b. 1942)

Few drummers successfully bridge the gap between free jazz and bebop to the same extent as Jack DeJohnette. An intensely intuitive player, young DeJohnette played early on with Jackie McLean and Charles Lloyd. In 1969 he replaced Tony Williams in Miles Davis's electric ensemble, appearing on the essential *Bitches Brew* (1969). After leaving Davis he led the fusion ensemble Compost and the expansive, compositional groups New Directions and Special Edition. He has also recorded many albums in trio with Keith Jarrett and bassist Gary Peacock.

'I hear overtones and chords in the cymbals as well as the drums. I am hearing orchestrally.... I am hearing colors. I consider myself somebody who colors the music.'

Jack DeJohnette

Eric Dolphy (Alto saxophone, bass clarinet, flute, 1928–64)

In the six years before his untimely death, Eric Dolphy became one of the most beloved and influential musicians in jazz. Brilliant on alto saxophone, he also helped to legitimize the flute and bass clarinet as viable jazz horns. Dolphy worked in relative obscurity until 1958, when he was discovered and hired by popular drummer Chico Hamilton.

He earned positive attention from the jazz press and moved on to work with Charles Mingus in 1960. Dolphy also looked into 'third stream' fusions of jazz and classical music with John Lewis and Gunther Schuller, as well as intense music with Ornette Coleman, John Coltrane and his own groups. Oliver Nelson's 1961 album *Blues And The Abstract Truth* featured the imposing front line of Dolphy and Freddie Hubbard. *Out To Lunch*, recorded in February 1964, is perhaps his most fully realized work. Not long after touring Europe with Mingus, Dolphy died suddenly in Berlin.

In addition to his skilful saxophone playing, Eric Dolphy raised the profile of the flute and bass clarinet in jazz music.

A-Z of Artists

Kenny Dorham (Trumpet, 1924–72)

The star of fame never shone brightly enough upon trumpeter Kenny Dorham, who too often took a back seat to his peers. He played with Dizzy Gillespie, Billy Eckstine and Lionel Hampton before joining Charlie Parker's bebop band in 1948. Dorham was a founding member of Art Blakey's Jazz Messengers in 1954, then replaced Clifford Brown in Max Roach's quartet. He led several fine sessions for Blue Note and Riverside before dying of kidney disease.

Art Farmer (Trumpet, flügelhorn, 1928–99)

Art Farmer was largely responsible for popularizing the mellow-toned flügelhorn as a solo jazz instrument. A wonderfully lyrical player, he came up in Los Angeles' Central Avenue jazz clubs in the 1940s and worked with Lionel Hampton, Horace Silver, Gerry Mulligan and alto saxophonist Gigi Gryce. In 1959–62 he and tenor saxophonist Benny Golson led the Jazztet, which had a hit with 'Killer Joe'. Farmer was based in Europe from 1968 onwards.

Key Tracks

'Osmosis' Kenny Dorham
'Straight Ahead' Kenny Dorham
'I Remember Clifford' Art Farmer
'The Girl From Ipanema' Stan Getz
'Desafinado' Stan Getz

Stan Getz (Tenor saxophone, 1927–91)

Stan Getz was one of many white tenor saxophonists influenced by Lester Young, but as he matured he developed a distinctive sound of his own. After working with Jack Teagarden, Stan Kenton, Jimmy Dorsey and Benny Goodman, Getz became one of the 'Four Brothers' in Woody Herman's Second Herd. From the 1950s onwards Getz led his own sessions, heading the massive bossa nova craze of the early 1960s. He initiated many original projects and was widely admired – by John Coltrane among others – for his lyrical virtuosity.

Art Farmer (right), pictured with fellow leader of the Jazztet Benny Golson, was jazz music's main exponent of the flugelhorn.

A-Z of Artists

Charlie Haden (Bass, b. 1937)

As a child in Iowa Charlie Haden performed on radio with his family's country and western band. At 15 he took up the bass while recovering from polio, acquiring a novel technique that makes his notes resonate deeply. Haden moved to Los Angeles in 1957 to find work. He met pianist Paul Bley and altoist Ornette Coleman. After leaving the Coleman quartet, Haden began looking into folk music and assembled his Liberation Music Orchestra in 1969. Haden has worked in a trio with saxophonist Jan Garbarek and guitarist Egberto Gismonti, and duetted with Pat Metheny; he has also collaborated with pianists Gonzalo Rubalcaba and Hank Jones. In the 1980s he formed the popular Quartet West.

Elvin Jones (Drums, 1927–2004)

Powerhouse drummer Elvin Jones was the engine of John Coltrane's legendary quartet in the 1960s, appearing on most of the saxophonist's most popular recordings. He was the younger brother of pianist Hank and trumpeter Thad Jones and had worked with Bud Powell, Miles Davis, Sonny Rollins and J.J. Johnson prior to joining Coltrane. A masterful innovator of polyrhythms, after a brief stint with the Duke Ellington Orchestra, he formed Elvin Jones Jazz Machine and helmed it until his death. In his last years he also collaborated annually with pianist Cecil Taylor.

Key Tracks

'Song For Ché' Charlie Haden
'Favorite Things' John Coltrane Quartet
'The Inflated Tear' Rahsaan Roland Kirk

Rahsaan Roland Kirk (Saxophones, clarinet, flute, various invented instruments, 1936–77)

Reeds player Rahsaan Roland Kirk developed a method for playing two or three horns simultaneously. Accidentally blinded at the age of two, Kirk taught himself to play several instruments. At 15 he joined an R&B band, and at 20 he made his first record. He modified his unusual pawn-shop horns, the manzello and stritch, with extended keys, developed the skill of circular breathing, enabling him to hold notes indefinitely, and eventually built the discipline to play two separate melodies at once. In 1961 Kirk worked with Charles Mingus, then continued his solo career with exceptional recordings, such as *Rip, Rig And Panic* (1965). He regularly modified his instruments and took on the mysterious name 'Rahsaan' after a dream. Although partially paralyzed by a stroke at 40, Kirk kept playing his horns until his death in 1977.

One of jazz's most colourful characters, Rahsaan Roland Kirk developed a unique method of playing multiple horns, often simultaneously.

A-Z of Artists

Charles Lloyd (Various saxophones, b. 1938)

Charles Lloyd was an inspirational figure in 1960s jazz. He moved from playing blues in Memphis to West Coast jazz. His quartet with pianist Keith Jarrett, bassist Ron McClure and drummer Jack DeJohnette was the first American jazz group to tour the Soviet Union. In 1969 he retired before returning triumphantly at the 1982 Montreux Jazz Festival. Lloyd has since made a series of excellent albums.

Herbie Mann (Tenor saxophone, flute, 1930–2003)

Herbie Mann was a popularizer of the flute in jazz, an investigator of far-flung ethnic music traditions and a pioneer of jazz-rock fusion. Mann began as a tenor saxophonist but eventually became the most commercially successful of the few jazz players to concentrate exclusively on the flute. He fronted an Afro-Latin group in the late 1950s, and popular success with *Memphis Underground* (1968). Mann focused upon Brazilian-tinged jazz later in his career, and at the end of his life explored the music of his Central European Jewish ancestry.

Key Tracks

'East Of The Sun' Charles Lloyd
'Comin' Home Baby' Herbie Mann
'Impressions' Wes Montgomery
'The Sidewinder' Lee Morgan

Wes Montgomery (Guitar, 1925–68)

Wes Montgomery was a premier jazz guitarist; his unique guitar sound came from plucking octave figures with his thumb instead of a pick. Born into a musical family, Wes taught himself to play the guitar and toured with Lionel Hampton in the late 1940s. He performed with his brothers, bassist Monk and vibist Buddy, before beginning a solo career that brought him to the top of the jazz sales charts. He moved successfully into pop-jazz crossovers, under the direction of producer Creed Taylor, before his sudden death from a heart attack.

Lee Morgan (Trumpet, 1938–72)

Born in Philadelphia, trumpeter Lee Morgan led one of the storybook lives in jazz. He joined Art Blakey's Jazz Messengers in 1958, having already worked with Dizzy Gillespie and John Coltrane. A magnificent hard-bop stylist who effectively utilized half-valve techniques and *staccato* blowing, Morgan was a star of the Blue Note Records roster, hitting the R&B top 10 in 1964 with the instrumental 'The Sidewinder'. Tragically, he was murdered by a woman who considered herself his wife outside a jazz club in 1972.

Self-taught guitarist Wes Montgomery created his own unique sound by using his thumb in place of a pick.

A-Z of Artists

Sunny Murray (Drums, b. 1937)

James 'Sunny' Murray's most enduring legacy may be his many recordings with Cecil Taylor and Albert Ayler, which belie his beginnings with stride pianist Willie 'The Lion' Smith and Swing Era trumpeter Henry 'Red' Allen. Murray was as melodic on drums as Taylor was percussive on the piano, resulting in a stellar combination. He moved to France in the 1980s and has since led his own sessions.

Joe Pass (Guitar, 1929–94)

Although drug addiction nearly killed the promising career of Joe Pass, he became one of the most influential guitarists in jazz. As a young man he played with various swing bands, then fell into heroin abuse while in the military. He recorded his first album while in rehabilitation in 1962, showcasing his impressive technique of splitting melodic and accompanying figures. From the mid-1970s until his death, Pass was a true jazz star, particularly as a solo performer and in recordings with Ella Fitzgerald.

Key Tracks

'Too Many Drummers, Not Enough Time'
Sunny Murray
'All the Things You Are' Joe Pass
'Beatrice' Sam Rivers
'Hambone' Archie Shepp

Sam Rivers (Various saxophones, flute, b. 1923)

Sam Rivers boasts a most impressive resumé: bebop with Tadd Dameron and Dizzy Gillespie, hard bop with Miles Davis and free jazz with Cecil Taylor and Anthony Braxton. Born in Oklahoma, Rivers played around Florida and Boston in the 1950s before settling in New York City. His 1960s Blue Note records were edgy and impressive. He hosted free jazz sessions at his loft Studio RivBea through the 1970s and helped to launch the careers of bassist Dave Holland and saxophonist Steve Coleman, among others.

Archie Shepp (Tenor and soprano saxophones, b. 1937)

Saxophonist Archie Shepp was a principal figure in the second wave of free-jazz artists. Also recognized as a playwright and poet, Shepp was an articulate spokesman for Black Power. He emerged in 1960 as a member of Cecil Taylor's group, then collaborated with trumpeter Bill Dixon, Don Cherry and John Coltrane. In the late 1970s Shepp moved decisively away from free jazz into more mainstream projects, such as a programme of ballads and gospel songs in duet with pianist Horace Parlan.

Archie Shepp developed a distinctive sound that drew inspiration from the jazz of his contemporaries as well as the jazz giants of the 1930s.

A-Z of Artists

Wayne Shorter (Tenor and soprano saxophones, b. 1933)

Wayne Shorter's most significant early position was in Maynard Ferguson's orchestra in 1958, where he met pianist Joe Zawinul. In 1959 Shorter joined Art Blakey's Jazz Messengers and soon thereafter made his debut as a leader. He gained prominence as a member of Miles Davis's ambitious groups from 1964–70, in which his unusual, compelling compositions were often featured, and as a Blue Note Records leader and sideman. Shorter teamed with Zawinul and bassist Miroslav Vitous in 1970 to form Weather Report, which became one of the world's most popular fusion bands.

Shorter's album *Native Dancer* (1974) introduced Brazilian singer Milton Nascimento to North America, and he was also in the repertory group VSOP with Herbie Hancock and Freddie Hubbard. Shorter left Weather Report in 1985, then toured with rock guitarist Carlos Santana and recorded with Joni Mitchell and Steely Dan. His own projects were intermittent until 1992, when a dying Miles Davis urged him to step forth. Shorter has led his own ensembles since then, acknowledged as a major, if still elusive, jazz voice.

'Is Cecil Taylor old? ... when he jumps on that piano, what are you hearing? Are you hearing age or are you hearing a vision that is sharper and sharper and more refined?'

Evan Parker

Cecil Taylor (Piano, b. 1929)

Since the late 1950s, pianist Cecil Taylor has maintained a prime position in the pantheon of free jazz. He was one of the first jazzmen to jettison standard chord changes, fixed rhythms and expected ensemble roles in the interest of musical democracy. Taylor developed his unorthodox style while studying at New England Conservatory. Duke Ellington, Thelonious Monk and Lennie Tristano were among his major influences. Taylor debuted in 1956 with *Jazz Advance!*.

He treats the piano as a percussion instrument and has been both condemned and praised for his innovations. Besides leading magnificent ensembles – the best of which featured alto saxophonist Jimmy Lyons – and collaborating with artists ranging from Mary Lou Williams and Max Roach to the dancer Mikhail Baryshnikov, Taylor is also a commanding solo performer. He is tirelessly adept at forming beauty out of seeming chaos, and his performances can last for hours.

Cecil Taylor is a great innovator of free jazz and has a distinctive, percussive piano style.

A-Z of Artists

Stan Tracey (Piano, accordion, vibraphone, composer, arranger, b. 1926)

Stan Tracey is one of the UK's most original and talented jazz musicians, yet he has always remained underrated by critics. Londoner Tracey was playing professionally from the age of 16, before landing the job of house pianist in Ronnie Scott's Soho jazz club. There he accompanied the big names of the day, including Zoot Sims, Stan Getz, Roland Kirk and Sonny Rollins, with whom he recorded the soundtrack for the film *Alfie* (1966). He played solo and in various line-ups, and had a big hit with his 1965 album *Under Milk Wood*, inspired by Dylan Thomas's audio play.

Tracey has released over 45 albums and has received an OBE as well as various music awards. He has continued to compose, tour and record and has also taught for many years at London's Guildhall School of Music. Despite his long career and life in the jazz fast-lane, Tracey has remained refreshingly self-effacing and down-to-earth.

Key Tracks

'Starless And Bible Black' Stan Tracey
'Naima' McCoy Tyner
'Blue Monk' McCoy Tyner
'Sister Cheryl' Tony Williams

McCoy Tyner (Piano, b. 1938)

McCoy Tyner will forever be remembered for his role in John Coltrane's great 1960s quartet. Born in Philadelphia and a member of jazz groups including the Jazztet, Tyner proved to be perfectly compatible with Coltrane until the saxophonist moved into free jazz, at which point the pianist left the band. Tyner worked as a sideman and leader for Blue Note during the rest of the decade, and gained further recognition after signing with Milestone Records. He has continued to lead his own sessions, ranging from solos, trios and larger combos to big bands.

Tony Williams (Drums, 1945–97)

Aged 14, Boston-born drum prodigy Tony Williams worked professionally with tenor saxophonist Sam Rivers. In 1962 he went to New York, played with Jackie McLean, then became part of one of Miles Davis's greatest bands. A dazzling colourist and dynamic rhythm-maker, Williams recorded two albums for Blue Note and played with many of the label's stars before establishing the breakthrough fusion band Lifetime. After a hiatus, Williams re-emerged in the late 1980s, leading a post-bop quintet of promising young players. He died of a heart attack in 1997 aged 51.

Stan Getz, instigator of the early 1960s bossa nova trend, was often accompanied on stage by the talented pianist Stan Tracey.

The Seventies

Following on from the radical social and cultural developments of the previous decade, the 1970s was unavoidably an era of change, albeit more gradual. The Vietnam War continued until 1973 and America remained divided even after the conflict had ended. President Nixon was forced to resign in 1974 in the aftermath of the notorious Watergate scandal, in which members of the Nixon administration had staged a break-in at the headquarters of the National Democratic Committee.

But while the 1970s was a time of political unrest, high inflation, poor economy and high unemployment levels, there were also many positive changes taking place, such as advances in civil rights and the consequent social empowerment of African-Americans, homosexuals and women. Space travel continued to explore new horizons, there were major advances in computer technology and environmental awareness was on the increase.

Key Artists

Art Ensemble of Chicago
John McLaughlin

Jazz music continued to redevelop itself and began to fuse with other musical styles. Jazz rock, usually thought to have begun with Miles Davis' 1969 album *Bitches Brew*, became very popular, while other US jazz artists looked to Europe, Japan and other musical traditions for inspiration. More synthetic music forms, particularly funk and disco, dominated the airwaves for most of the 1970s, but there were certain jazz influences to be heard in these genres – and so jazz was able to keep its place in the public consciousness while also retaining its dignity.

One of the most versatile jazz musicians of his time, Herbie Hancock was at the forefront of electric jazz in the 1970s.

What Miles Hath Wrought

In many ways, the 1970s can be seen as a transition point in the evolution of jazz. The generational divide became evident with the ascendancy of young artists such as Jaco Pastorius (1951–87), George Benson and Chick Corea, and the deaths of Louis Armstrong (1901–71) and Duke Ellington (1899–74).

Jazz musicians were in the pop-music charts for the first time since the 1950s, but this was a new breed of improvisers who were influenced as much by the Beatles or Motown/soul music as by Armstrong or Charlie Parker (1920–55), and used electric instruments to express themselves. The free-jazz movement of the 1960s grew even more politicized and spread its branches to Chicago, St Louis, Los Angeles and beyond. Artists who trod the middle ground between electricity and the avant-garde found it difficult to get live jobs, yet some still had a productive decade, recording some of their best work.

Trumpeter Miles Davis (1926–91) ushered in the new decade at New York City's Village Gate. The live shows bisected an intensive period of studio work that produced a stunning pair of albums, whose influence would continue to resonate three decades later: *Bitches Brew* (1969) and *Jack Johnson* (1970). While not the first jazz artist to use electric guitar, piano and bass, Davis was the highest-profile leader to adapt the popular approaches of Jimi Hendrix (1942–70), Sly Stone, James Brown and Stevie Wonder to his own ends. His imprimatur cannot be overrated.

'Jazz is not dead, it just smells funny.'

Frank Zappa

Davis had been brewing up his new direction since 1968, and several of his collaborators from the period had ideas of their own about how to fuse elements of rock with jazz. Drummer Tony Williams (1945–97) formed Lifetime, which emulated the guitar-driven power trio sound of Cream and the Jimi Hendrix Experience; saxophonist Wayne Shorter (b. 1933) and keyboardist Joe Zawinul (b. 1932) started Weather Report to explore colour with amplified instruments; pianists Chick Corea and Herbie Hancock (b. 1940) put together their own distinctive electric bands. Marketing played a more important role, too. Gone was the underplayed artwork of Blue Note Records and Impulse!; in its place were rock-inspired themes and, in the case of Corea's *Return To Forever*, a series of grandiose sci-fi fantasies. Instead of nightclubs, the bands played university campuses and outdoor festivals. On FM radio, Weather Report was featured next to rockers like Pink Floyd and the Allman Brothers Band.

Keyboardist Joe Zawinul, a co-founder of Weather Report – one of the most important electric-jazz combos of the decade.

Electric Shock

Miles's musical progeny were making improvised instrumental music attractive and commercially viable. Bitches Brew and Hancock's Head Hunters (1973) set sales records for jazz.

Rock artists, including guitarists Carlos Santana and Jeff Beck, blurred the lines between the genres from the opposite direction, while well-established jazz musicians such as Freddie Hubbard (b. 1938) and Donald Byrd, whether because of commercial pressures or artistic curiosity, began to add electric instruments and broaden their repertoire beyond jazz standards. Even musical iconoclast Ornette Coleman (b. 1930) went electric in the 1970s with his radical septet Prime Time.

However, as with all trends, the fascination wore off for many audiences as the second and third wave of participants arrived, and by the end of the 1970s jazz-rock fusion had become an artistic dead end of overlong solos and overblown imagery. As his former sidemen and acolytes delved into electric jazz rock, Davis moved deeper into dense, pan-cultural music that combined African rhythms, Indian instruments and distorted guitar. All but crippled by leg injuries, sickle-cell anaemia and drug abuse, Davis retreated from music completely in 1975.

Coltrane's Children

If Davis's followers found commercial fortune in tracking his lead, the influence of John Coltrane (1926–67) was no less powerful. The concept of making music on your own terms and seeking freedom through your instrument was Coltrane's legacy, and there were many younger musicians ready to take up where he had left off. By the 1970s, Chicago had already launched the careers of several distinctive artists, including saxophonist Roscoe Mitchell and trumpeter Lester Bowie. With the Association for the Advancement of Creative Musicians (AACM), a musicians' collective that was formed by pianist Muhal Richard Abrams (b. 1930) and others in 1965, Chicago began to develop younger players such as saxophonists Henry Threadgill (b. 1944) and Chico Freeman, trombonist George Lewis and bassist Fred Hopkins, and to attract creative musicians from other Midwest cities, such as St Louis saxophonists Oliver Lake and Julius Hemphill.

Popular Melody

Herbie Hancock – 'Chameleon' (1973)

Trumpeter Miles Davis revolutionized jazz yet again in the 1970s with his jazz-rock fusion.

The Loft Scene

In California, Coltrane's influence touched two young saxophonists who would make important contributions in the 1970s. Alto saxophonist Arthur Blythe cut his musical teeth with influential pianist Horace Tapscott in Los Angeles. Further north, in Berkeley, David Murray was translating the harmonic freedom of Jimi Hendrix to the saxophone.

By the mid-1970s, many of these players had made the time-honoured trek to New York City, where they found a common musical outlet in venues that collectively became known as 'the loft scene'. Cross-fertilization became commonplace, with musicians such as Murray, Freeman, drummer Philip Wilson, trumpeter Olu Dara and organist Amina Claudine Myers playing together frequently. In 1976, four of the most prolific reed players – Murray, Hemphill, Lake and Hamiet Bluiett – formed the World Saxophone Quartet. Along with Threadgill's trio Air, Murray's thorny octet, the quartets led by multi-reed player Anthony Braxton and the Art Ensemble of Chicago, the World Saxophone Quartet pointed to a renewed period of creativity for avant-garde jazz.

Popular Melody

Keith Jarrett – 'In Front' (1971)

Mainstream Struggles

While electric jazz-rock dominated live venues, acoustic jazz was having a rough ride, with the exception of a few well-established names. Pianist McCoy Tyner (b. 1938) released several superb albums while saxophone colossus Sonny Rollins (b. 1930) explored a range of approaches, from solo improvisation to all-star touring units. Alto player Phil Woods returned from France and formed an outstanding quartet. Tenor giant Dexter Gordon's (1923–90) December 1976 stand in Greenwich Village resulted in one of his best recordings – *Homecoming: Live At The Village Vanguard* (1976) – and a renewed belief in some quarters that acoustic jazz was back on solid ground.

In West Germany, meanwhile, former bassist Manfred Eicher was establishing a hybrid of electric and acoustic music, using a signature crystalline studio sound that would be widely influential. The Canadian trumpeter Kenny Wheeler released two luminous LPs on ECM – *Gnu High* (1975) and *Deer Wan* (1977) – while Norwegian tenor player Jan Garbarek helped define the 'ECM sound' with his evocative *Witchi-Tai-To* (1974).

The commercially successful avant-garde innovators, the World Saxophone Quartet.

Key Artists: Art Ensemble of Chicago

With its tribal masks, arcane percussion instruments and grand sense of theatre, the Art Ensemble of Chicago always seemed to be more than just a jazz band. Indeed, the group grew from the communal activities of the Chicago-based AACM, which quickly became a magnet and laboratory for freedom-seeking African-American musicians in the city.

Those included were saxophonists Roscoe Mitchell (b. 1940) and Joseph Jarman (b. 1937), trumpeter Lester Bowie (1941–99) and bassist Malachi Favors (1927–2004). AACM founder Muhal Richard Abrams' Experimental Band (est. 1961) and Mitchell's quartet, which formed two years later, were early models in the sprawling musical vision of the former and the latter's use of unusual timbres created by small percussion instruments.

French Sojourn

In June 1969, as the Roscoe Mitchell Art Ensemble, Mitchell, Bowie, Favors and Jarman travelled to Paris, where they re-christened themselves the Art Ensemble of Chicago. The band's impact was as much visual as musical; Favors and Jarman painted their faces and wore African robes and hats, while Bowie donned a white lab coat. Onstage, multiple saxophones and percussion devices surrounded the quartet. The effect was further heightened when drummer Don Moye (b. 1946) joined in September 1969. Moye called his array of drums, cymbals and hand-crafted instruments 'sun percussion' and liked to climax percussion movements by igniting magician's flash-paper between his fingers.

'Jazz is so difficult. A lot of people think once they've learned these licks they can get up and play them for the rest of their life. But that's not being truthful to the music 'cause it's not developing.... I've built a whole career out of making mistakes!'

Lester Bowie

During its two years in Europe, the band recorded 11 albums and three film scores, and toured widely, frequently accompanied by soul singer Fontella Bass, Bowie's wife. The band's music escaped classification. The first three tracks on the 1969 album *A Jackson In Your House* capture part of the range: anthemic horn statements offset by a bicycle horn; antic vocal effects; melodies reminiscent of the Jazz Age; free-blown horn choruses that defy

Right: Trumpeter Lester Bowie was a co-founder of the Art Ensemble of Chicago and also led several of his own groups.

the shouted order to 'Get in line'; and a waltz performed at half-tempo with the horns stretching the melody line like taffy. The band also integrated Bowie's R&B background, with Moye laying down a backbeat and Favors switching to electric bass.

A Pragmatic Agenda

Returning to the US in 1971, the band's members determined that they would focus on building an audience through performances at jazz festivals, universities and large concert venues. Throughout the 1970s, the Art Ensemble steadily spread its name and its motto: 'Great Black Music, Ancient to the Future'. Two recordings for Atlantic Records exposed them to a broader audience, and a breakthrough commercial contract with ECM initiated the band's most financially successful period. With *Nice Guys* (1978) and *Full Force* (1980) the band achieved a much higher profile and reached new levels of accessibility. During this period, several members – most notably Bowie and Mitchell – re-established recording and performing careers independent from the band.

Surviving Deaths

The Art Ensemble maintained a relatively high level of creativity and productivity through the 1980s, switching labels to the Japanese DIW company and touring only every other year in order to permit individual projects. In 1993, Jarman left the band to establish a martial arts and Buddhist spiritual centre in New York City, and the others carried on as a quartet. After Bowie's death from cancer in 1999, they re-formed again as a trio. Jarman returned to the fold in 2003, and the group recorded *The Meeting* (2003), as well as announcing an extended concert tour just prior to Favors's death. The remaining members kept the scheduled dates and have plans to continue as a trio or with younger AACM players.

Next Page: Art Ensemble of Chicago at AACM's twentieth anniversary festival in 1995.
(l–r) Roscoe Mitchell, Famodon Don Moye, Lester Bowie, Malachi Favors and Joseph Jarman.

Key Artist: John McLaughlin

By turns avant-garde adventurer, high-voltage rocker and Third World explorer, Yorkshire-born guitarist John McLaughlin has seldom repeated himself.

Born in 1942, McLaughlin studied piano from the age of nine and taught himself guitar after becoming interested in country blues, flamenco and Django Reinhardt. A gig with Pete Deuchar's Professors of Ragtime in 1958 was his ticket to London, where the storm that would become the British Invasion of the US was brewing. He played with Georgie Fame, Graham Bond and Brian Auger, and picked up studio session jobs – ranging from Petula Clark to David Bowie.

Choosing Jazz

By 1967, McLaughlin had tired of session work and moved to Germany to play with vibraphonist Gunter Hampel. Occasionally, he returned to London to jam with musicians such as bassist Dave Holland and drummer Tony Oxley and, eventually, to record the album *Extrapolation* (1969), one of the most exciting debuts in contemporary jazz. Already in place were the remarkably fluid technical facility, diamond-hard tone and harmonic imagination that would set him apart from most jazz guitarists.

Concurrent with this recording, McLaughlin was invited by drummer Tony Williams to join his new band, Lifetime. Within hours of landing in the US, McLaughlin was jamming at Count Basie's club in front of an audience that included Miles Davis. Davis, several months into a two-year period of intensive recording activity, did not waste time; he invited McLaughlin to the studio on 18 February 1969 for what would form part of the seminal *In A Silent Way* (1969). While working with Lifetime, McLaughlin helped shape four other key Davis recordings: *Bitches Brew* (1969), *Jack Johnson* (1971), *Live-Evil* (1971) and *Big Fun* (1974).

Above: Guitarist John McLaughlin, who worked as a session musician before playing with key jazz artists, including Miles Davis.

Following a New Leader

McLaughlin was extraordinarily prolific during his first 18 months in the US. In addition to the work with Davis and the Tony Williams Lifetime albums *Emergency!* (1969) and *Turn It Over* (1970), he recorded the rock-influenced *Devotion* (1970), the adventurous *Where Fortune Smiles* (1970) and the acoustic *My Goal's Beyond* (1970). The title and meditative mood of the latter album pointed to a major turning-point in his life, a spiritual awakening that would find him pledging allegiance to a mystic, re-christening himself Mahavishnu John McLaughlin and launching a band that would set the bar much higher for instrumental prowess in the burgeoning jazz-rock movement.

'McLaughlin to me is the most important, certainly the most influential voice in the last decade on the guitar, without a doubt.'

Pat Metheny

The Mahavishnu Orchestra debuted in July 1971 and stunned listeners with rapid-fire unison melody lines played between McLaughlin, violinist Jerry Goodman and keyboardist Jan Hammer, unusual time signatures and advanced dynamics. The band's first recording, *The Inner Mounting Flame* (1971), remains a landmark work of the era. McLaughlin continued to use the Mahavishnu Orchestra name for subsequent bands, but none matched the original for power and invention. The second group is notable for McLaughlin's collaboration with an ensemble conducted by Michael Tilson Thomas, documented on the album *Apocalypse* (1974).

Discovering Other Worlds

In 1976, McLaughlin surprised devotees by releasing *Shakti*, a recording of his acoustic encounter with four traditional Indian musicians. While McLaughlin's trademark lightning arpeggios were still there, the volume was reduced significantly. Never again could fans pin him down to a single style. His subsequent works included renewed interest in jazz rock, *Electric Dreams* (1978) and *Electric Guitarist* (1979); collaborations with classical pianist Katia Labéque, his then-partner; and spirited meetings with guitarists Paco de Lucía and Al DiMeola.

In the 1990s and the early years of the twenty-first century, McLaughlin continued his pattern of going wherever his imagination took him. He recorded and toured with organist Joey DeFrancesco in a trio, continued his occasional forays with De Lucía and DiMeola, and delved back into ragas with Shakti Remembered.

Next Page: McLaughlin (second from left) in Shakti, a group with its roots in traditional Indian music.

A-Z of Artists

Gato Barbieri (Tenor saxophone, b. 1934)

An acerbic-toned saxophonist heavily influenced by John Coltrane, Barbieri is an enigmatic figure, best known for his trademark black borsalino and his successful excursions into commercial music. Argentinean by birth, he first surfaced in Paris as a member of trumpeter Don Cherry's group. After two years with Cherry, Barbieri began to actively seek ways to fuse Latin-American music and jazz. His soundtrack for *Last Tango In Paris* (1972) received widespread acclaim.

Anthony Braxton (Various saxophones and clarinets, flute, piano, b. 1945)

'I've been isolated and kicked out of jazz as a black man who is not "black" enough, a jazz guy who is not "jazz" enough,' said Chicago native Braxton, looking back on a highly iconoclastic career that has been documented on more than 130 recordings. After military service, Braxton emerged in 1966 with a musical conception that, while influenced by older saxophonists like Roscoe Mitchell, Warne Marsh and John Coltrane, was wholly original.

Key Tracks

'Latino America' Gato Barbieri
'Composition 6 C' Anthony Braxton
'Lovely Lady' Brecker Brothers

His debut recordings as a leader in 1968 – *Three Compositions Of New Jazz* and *For Alto* (both on Delmark) – were stunning in their conceptual maturity. In the 1970s, Braxton's music began to reflect his interest in composers Karlheinz Stockhausen and John Cage, as well as his love of marches by John Philip Sousa. His musical output includes solo works and compositions for massed orchestras of 160 players, but he is best known for his quartets, including the group Circle.

Brecker Brothers (Randy Brecker, trumpet, flugelhorn, b. 1945; Michael Brecker, tenor and soprano saxophone, EWI, b. 1949)

Philadelphia-born brothers Randy and Michael Brecker were already experienced players when they collaborated with drummer Billy Cobham in 1970 to form Dreams, one of the first groups to attempt combining elements of jazz and rock. In 1975 the siblings formed the Brecker Brothers. Over six years, the band was one of the most popular in jazz, featuring musicians such as David Sanborn, George Duke and Don Grolnick. The brothers reformed briefly in 1992, by which time Michael had established himself as one of jazz's pre-eminent soloists.

The Brecker Brothers, who led one of the most popular jazz-rock groups of the 1970s.

A-Z of Artists

Herbie Hancock (Piano, electronic keyboards, b. 1940)

A classical prodigy in Chicago, Hancock became one of the most versatile jazz pianists of the post-war era. At the age of 20, he moved to New York City to play with trumpeter Donald Byrd. After his debut as a leader, *Takin' Off* (1962), he joined Miles Davis for five years. In the 1970s, his Mwandishi sextet and jazz-funk unit Head Hunters were at the forefront of electric jazz, and he subsequently alternated between electric and acoustic music, becoming an articulate and much-quoted spokesperson for jazz.

Dave Holland (Bass, b. 1946)

A professional musician since the age of 13 in his native Wolverhampton, England, Holland became one of jazz's most in-demand bassists after Miles Davis persuaded him to emigrate to the US in 1968. Holland performed on two of Davis's seminal studio recordings, *In A Silent Way* (1969) and *Bitches Brew* (1969), before leaving to co-found the quartet Circle. His debut recording as a leader, *Conference Of The Birds* (1972), is one of the era's masterpieces. Having led two quintets and participated selectively in others' projects, he started a distinctive big band in 1999.

'... [Dave Holland]'s so consistent a group player. He just makes it all possible for you to take it easy. He allowed everyone else to stretch.'

John Scofield

Abdullah Ibrahim (Piano, b. 1934)

Born Adolphe Johannes 'Dollar' Brand in Capetown, South Africa, Abdullah Ibrahim successfully fused African rhythms and lilting melodic lines with the piano styles of Duke Ellington and Thelonious Monk. In 1960, with trumpeter Hugh Masekela and others as the Jazz Epistles, he released the first contemporary South African jazz album. The racial climate in his country forced him and his wife, singer Sathima Bea Benjamin, to seek exile in Switzerland, where he met and recorded for Ellington.

Exposed to a wider audience through extensive jazz-festival work, the pianist played with Elvin Jones after the drummer left John Coltrane, and toured Europe with Don Cherry and others. Assuming his Muslim name in the 1970s, he worked frequently as a solo artist, but in 1976 he settled in New York City and established the sextet Ekaya; subsequently, he wrote soundtracks for French film director Claire Denis.

Dave Holland was the pre-eminent bass player of the era, following a stint with Miles Davis.

A-Z of Artists

Keith Jarrett (Piano, keyboards, flute, soprano saxophone, percussion, b. 1945)

Few artists are as demanding of themselves and their audiences as Allentown, Pennsylvania native Keith Jarrett. A child prodigy, Jarrett first caused a stir while playing in saxophonist Charles Lloyd's quartet. In 1970, he joined Miles Davis on electric piano and organ. Jarrett soon eschewed electronic keyboards and entered into a long relationship with the German-based label ECM.

In the 1970s he pursued three streams of jazz: improvised solo concerts; knotty, blues- and gospel-inflected works in a quartet with saxophonist Dewey Redman, bassist Charlie Haden and drummer Paul Motian; and more cerebral performances with saxophonist Jan Garbarek, bassist Palle Danielsson and drummer Jon Christensen. In 1983, Jarrett formed a trio with bassist Gary Peacock and drummer Jack DeJohnette to focus on the harmonic and melodic possibilities of the Great American Songbook. Work with this so-called Standards Trio dominated the following two decades, although he continued to pursue other projects, including some recordings of classical works.

Thad Jones (Flugelhorn, cornet, valve trombone, 1923–86)

The middle brother in Detroit's musical Jones family, Thad Jones joined older sibling Hank at age 16 and, after wartime service, played with younger brother Elvin in Billy Mitchell's band. He rose to prominence with Count Basie during a nine-year tenure (1954–63), but he became best known for the 13-year period in which he co-led a big band with drummer Mel Lewis every Monday night at New York's Village Vanguard. In 1979 Jones moved to Denmark, where he formed the Thad Jones Eclipse.

Key Tracks

'Bop-Be' Keith Jarrett
'My Song' Keith Jarrett
'Tiptoe' Thad Jones
'Little Pixie' Thad Jones
'Zoom' Volker Kriegel

Volker Kriegel (Electric guitar, 1943–2003)

As a sociology student in Frankfurt, Germany, Kriegel's playing caught the ears of older musicians, who convinced him to pursue music. After working with visiting US players he joined the nascent Dave Pike Set in 1968. Kriegel's *Spectrum* (1971) was an important step in the development of European jazz rock. In 1973, he formed Spectrum with bassist Eberhard Weber, and in 1976 co-founded the long-running United Jazz and Rock Ensemble.

Thad Jones (left) jams with Mel Lewis, 1976.

A-Z of Artists

Steve Lacy (Soprano saxophone, 1934–2004)

Born Steven Lackritz in New York City, Lacy began his career playing Dixieland music with veterans Henry 'Red' Allen and Rex Stewart, but became best known as a highly lyrical and adventurous champion of the soprano saxophone. His adoption of the straight horn, neglected since the heyday of Sidney Bechet, inspired John Coltrane to double on the instrument. Lacy moved to Paris in 1970 and recorded extensively, often taking inspiration from poets and painters.

Albert Mangelsdorff (Trombone, 1928–2005)

Although he played violin and guitar, Frankfurt native Albert Mangelsdorff did not take up the trombone until the age of 20. However, despite this relatively late start, he became a pioneer of multiphonics on the horn and a leader of the European avant-garde. Recordings with pianist John Lewis and sitarist Ravi Shankar in the 1960s helped to make his name, but it is as a member of the Globe Unity Orchestra, beginning in 1967, that he was perhaps best known. He died on 25 July 2005.

Key Tracks

'Blinks' Steve Lacy
'The Owl' Steve Lacy
'Zores Mores' Albert Mangelsdorff
'Aurora' Oregon

Oregon (Instrumental group, 1971–present)

The antithesis of the fusion music of the 1970s, Oregon comprised Paul McCandless (oboe, English horn, tenor saxophone, bass clarinet), Glen Moore (bass, violin, piano, flute), Ralph Towner (guitar, piano, French horn, trumpet, flugelhorn) and Colin Walcott (tabla, sitar, clarinet, percussion). In some ways, Oregon resembled a chamber-music quartet more closely than a jazz combo, introducing diverse musical elements from far-flung cultures long before 'world music' came into vogue. After Colin Walcott was killed in a car accident in 1984, the group disbanded, but re-emerged in 1986 with Indian percussionist Trilok Gurtu and an even broader range of influences.

Steve Lacy brought the straight soprano saxophone back to prominence and inspired John Coltrane to experiment with the instrument.

A-Z of Artists

Jaco Pastorius (Electric bass, piano, 1951–87)

The Pennsylvania native burst on to the music scene in 1974 with a debut recording, *Jaco*, which redefined electric playing. A veteran of R&B and pop bands in Fort Lauderdale by the age of 24, Pastorius collaborated with his good friend, guitarist Pat Metheny, before being hired to join the band Weather Report. In 1980 he formed his own group, Word of Mouth. Increasingly troubled by mental illness, Pastorius died homeless after being beaten by a bouncer outside a Florida nightclub.

Woody Shaw (Trumpet, flugelhorn, composer 1944–89)

A lyrical soloist, composer and bandleader, Shaw's career was cut tragically short by deteriorating vision and an accident that cost him an arm. After early work with Willie Bobo and Eric Dolphy, Shaw played extensively in Europe with Bud Powell, Kenny Clarke and Johnny Griffin. Returning to America, he worked with Horace Silver, Art Blakey and others. In 1976, he co-led a series of high-profile New York City gigs with Dexter Gordon and thereafter led his own combos.

Key Tracks

'Donna Lee' Jaco Pastorius
'Rahsaan's Run' Woody Shaw
'Hotel Hello' Steve Swallow
'In A Silent Way' Joe Zawinul

Steve Swallow (Electric bass, b. 1940)

Swallow is one of a handful of electric-jazz bassists who have shaped the sound of the instrument. An apprenticeship with pianist Paul Bley grew into a long-term association and the two recorded frequently. Vibist Gary Burton provided another ongoing musical relationship. After a number of years teaching and playing in California, Swallow became involved with pianist-composer Carla Bley, and the pair co-lead numerous projects.

Joe Zawinul (Piano, electronic keyboards, b. 1932)

Born in Vienna, Josef Zawinul was 27 when he arrived in the US on a music scholarship, but this did not prevent him from becoming an enormously influential composer and bandleader. Following brief stints with Dinah Washington and Maynard Ferguson, Zawinul joined Cannonball Adderley's band and attracted the attention of Miles Davis, to whom he contributed compositions during the transition to electric jazz. In 1970, Zawinul and Wayne Shorter co-founded Weather Report. After 1985 he led a series of bands under the name Zawinul Syndicate.

Jaco Pastorius, who redefined the role of the electric bass in jazz, played with Pat Metheny and Weather Report, among others.

The Eighties

In the 1980s, as the baby boomers began to develop their own careers and families, the world saw a huge population growth. The burgeoning middle class helped to create a consumer culture that cultivated high-flying career men and women in search of ever greater success and power, and obsessed with wealth and luxury material possessions. Major advances in science and technology brought computers and other electronic equipment into people's everyday lives, and the 1980s came to be seen as a decade of flamboyant wealth and greed.

Ronald Reagan, elected President in 1981, set about restoring America's economy and morale after the disquieting events of the 1960s and 1970s, as well as negotiating with the USSR to implement an eventual end to the long-running Cold War. The subsequent destruction of the Berlin Wall, in 1989, became the ultimate symbol of the fall of Communism.

While advanced digital sound and recording technology led to the compact disc becoming the medium of choice, many old jazz recordings were reissued, often being restored digitally and becoming available for the first time in stereo. This sudden influx of traditional jazz music, sounding so much clearer and brighter than the previously available recordings, may have contributed to the influence of jazz music from the past on the leading artists of the era, which included Pat Metheny, Miles Davis and Wynton Marsalis.

Key Artists

Wynton Marsalis
Pat Metheny

Pat Metheny (left) was one of the most original jazz guitarists of the 1980s and is seen here with the rest of 1986's Song X line-up, Jack DeJohnette (centre) and Ornette Coleman (right).

Traditional vs Modern

By the late 1970s, the jazz-rock fusion movement had become codified and diluted. Groups and individual artists such as the Crusaders, George Benson, Ramsey Lewis, Spyro Gyra and Jeff Lorber began producing a more palatable strain of pop-influenced jazz that sought to cross over to a mainstream audience. This tamer brand of fusion from the late 1970s paved the way for New Adult Contemporary (NAC) in the 1980s and the smooth-jazz movement of the 1990s.

Meanwhile, with the rise to prominence in the early 1980s of Wynton Marsalis – a gifted young trumpeter from New Orleans who took an earnest stand to play strictly acoustic jazz – a major schism had been set in place in jazz. Marsalis quickly became leader of the so-called 'Young Lions' movement, which sought a return to jazz's acoustic roots. Meanwhile, Australian broadcaster and sound engineer Robert Parker developed a technique of digitally remastering the classic jazz recordings of the 1920s and 1930s, resulting in his *Jazz Classics In Digital Stereo* series and a further surge of interest in the early days of jazz music. This swinging, neo-conservative (neo-con) trend developed in parallel with a trend towards smooth jazz, marked by simpler, more melodious and accessible radio-friendly sounds, and represented by the movement's leader Kenny G (b. 1959).

'Whatever you have to say to the world, it comes down to that basic thing. It's your own voice ... that's what music is – somebody's point of view about the world.'

David Sanborn

But a few fusion renegades persisted during the 1980s, notably drummer and Ornette Coleman disciple Ronald Shannon Jackson, whose Decoding Society accounted for some of the most fiercely uncompromising music of the decade. Alongside him were harmolodic guitarist James 'Blood' Ulmer (b. 1941), alto saxophonist Steve Coleman (b. 1956) and former Weather Report bassist Jaco Pastorius (1951–87). Fusion pioneers Chick Corea and John McLaughlin (b. 1942) both returned to the electronic arena with a vengeance in the mid-1980s – Corea with his Elektric Band, and McLaughlin with a new edition of his Mahavishnu Orchestra. Another fusion pioneer, Herbie Hancock (b. 1940), scored a massive radioplay hit in 1983 with 'Rock It', a streetwise melding of techno and funk that updated his own early 1970s jazz-funk hit 'Chameleon' while presaging the hip hop–jazz movement of the 1990s.

Pianist Chick Corea (foreground), shown here with tenor saxophonist Bob Berg, was a major force in electronic jazz in the 1980s with his Elektric Band.

The Stalwarts of Jazz

Another influential and widely imitated musician of the decade was guitarist-composer Pat Metheny (b. 1954), whose refreshingly original sound affected a generation of listeners and players alike. The 1980s also marked the return of Miles Davis (1926–91), who had been in self-imposed retirement since 1975. Davis's comeback band of 1980 included bassist Marcus Miller, guitarist Mike Stern and saxophonist Bill Evans (1929–80), each of whom became a bandleader in his own right later in the decade.

Other jazz giants still active on the scene in the 1980s included trumpeter and bebop pioneer Dizzy Gillespie (1917–93), tenor saxophonist and Gillespie protégé James Moody (b. 1925), alto sax burner Jackie McLean (1931–2006), tenor saxophonist Johnny Griffin, drummer Mel Lewis and tenor sax titan Dexter Gordon (1923–90), who appeared in the 1986 film *Round Midnight*. Also significant in this period were vocalist/talent scout Betty Carter – whose band served as a training ground during the 1980s for promising young talent including pianists Benny Green, Marc Cary and Stephen Scott, saxophonists Don Braden and Craig Handy, drummers Winard Harper and Gregory Hutchinson, and bassists Curtis Lundy and Taurus Mateen – and the great drummer Art Blakey (1919–90), who continued to tour with his Jazz Messengers. The group's ranks during this period included future bandleaders Wynton and Branford Marsalis, trumpeters Terence Blanchard, Philip Harper and Brian Lynch, saxophonists Bobby Watson, Billy Pierce, Donald Harrison and Javon Jackson, pianists James Williams, Donald Brown, Mulgrew Miller and Geoff Keezer, and bassists Charles Fambrough and Lonnie Plaxico.

Popular Melody

Miles Davis – 'Jean Pierre' (1981)

It was also possible to see legendary jazzmen, such as trumpeters Clark Terry and Doc Cheatham (1905–97), saxophonists Stan Getz (1927–91), Sonny Rollins (b. 1930), Benny Carter (1907–2003) and Jimmy Heath (b. 1926), guitarists Barney Kessel (1923–2004) and Joe Pass (1929–94), trombonist J.J. Johnson (1924–2001), violinist Stephane Grappelli (1905–97), pianists Oscar Peterson (b. 1925), Dave Brubeck (b. 1920) and Eubie Blake (1883–1983), drummers Kenny Clarke (1914–85), Buddy Rich (1917–84) and Max Roach (b. 1924), and bandleaders Count Basie (1904–84), Benny Goodman (1909–86), Cab Calloway (1907–94) and Woody Herman (1913–87).

Tenor saxophone legend Dexter Gordon portrays lonely musician Dale Turner in the 1986 film Round Midnight.

Key Artist: Wynton Marsalis

In the 1980s, trumpeter Wynton Marsalis leapt from jazz-steeped New Orleans to international artistic prominence. In 1979 he was enrolled in New York City's Juilliard School and was jamming with Art Blakey's Jazz Messengers, and 10 years later he had seeded what has become an unrivalled international jazz performance centre. In between, Marsalis established himself as a hot soloist, bandleader, composer and recording artist, as well as an eager educator, media charmer and ad-hoc ambassador of American values.

Born in New Orleans on 18 October 1961, Marsalis is the second of six sons of jazz pianist and educator Ellis Marsalis. His elder brother Branford is a saxophonist while younger siblings Delfaeyo and Jason play the trombone and drums respectively. At the age of eight Wynton was in the Fairview Baptist Church band, organized by veteran jazz banjoist and guitarist Danny Barker. He also played in marching bands and classical youth orchestras, performing the Haydn Trumpet Concerto with the New Orleans Philharmonic at the age of 14. He left his studies in 1980 for the front line of Blakey's Messengers with Branford. In July 1981, Wynton toured Japan with Miles Davis's famed 1960s rhythm section – pianist Herbie Hancock, drummer Tony Williams and bassist Ron Carter. Their recording *Quartet* (1982) was released as Marsalis's debut on Columbia Records.

The Neo-Conservative Style

Marsalis's youth, energy, technical facility, directness of expression, breadth of repertoire and articulation of a neo-conservative aesthetic were in strong contrast with Davis's flagging health and fading iconoclasm. He was promoted as king of the Young Lions – a fresh crop of skilled, musically educated instrumentalists who abjured free jazz and commercial fusion to stand for the achievements and ambitions of an African-American middle class. Marsalis proclaimed the primacy of blues, swing, bebop, Louis Armstrong, Duke Ellington, Blakey, mid-period Davis and Thelonious Monk, but he scorned jazz rock, funk and fusion (music Miles was playing at the time).

Above: Wynton Marsalis (right) and brother Branford (left) were important figures in the neo-conservative revival of traditional jazz values.

After leaving Blakey, Marsalis formed a quintet (with Branford, Kenny Kirkland on piano, and Jeff 'Tain' Watts on drums) that expanded on post-bop conventions. Marsalis's *Think Of One* (1983) and his first album of classical trumpet fare both won Grammy Awards, an unprecedented feat he repeated with *Hot House Flowers* and *Baroque Music* in 1984. His *Black Codes (From The Underground)* from 1985 is another early peak. Subsequently, Marsalis recorded two three-volume sets of jazz standards and of original, intertwined material entitled *Soul Gestures In Southern Blues* (1988). As Branford launched his own career (the brothers still appear together, and occasionally *en famille*), Wynton discovered other collaborators, including pianist Marcus Roberts, drummer Herlin Riley and trombonist Wycliffe Gordon.

Marsalis at Lincoln Center

In summer 1987 Marsalis presented a concert series, Classical Jazz, under the auspices of Lincoln Center, New York's premier performing-arts institution. So began a unique collaboration between artist and establishment that has developed far-reaching jazz education programmes, jazz collaborations with chamber-music ensembles, orchestras and ballet troupes, countless radio and television productions, the globe-trotting Lincoln Center Jazz Orchestra, and Wynton himself.

'I try to play whatever I'm hearing. And that's part of jazz music. That's what it is.'

Wynton Marsalis

Marsalis is a celebrity, but he has never sold out. He has consistently applied serious efforts to his ensembles, film scores, chamber works and art songs. His oratorio *Blood On The Fields* (1995), featuring vocalists Cassandra Wilson, Miles Griffith and Jon Hendricks, was the first jazz piece awarded the Pulitzer Prize, and he wrote *All Rise* for big band, 100-voice choir and the New York Philharmonic Orchestra to celebrate the turn of the twenty-first century.

In October 2004, Marsalis realized a fondly nurtured dream – the opening of Jazz@Lincoln Center's state-of-the-art Rose Hall, a multi-venue, multi-use facility billed as the first ever specifically designed for jazz. By 1990, Wynton Marsalis was already as he remains today: a tireless advocate for jazz (particularly its African-American strains), a communicator of jazz principles and a virtuoso instrumentalist, credibly interpreting diverse genres and styles, and able to improvise deeply affecting personal statements.

Next Page: Marsalis's Lincoln Center Jazz Orchestra, which is based in New York but tours festivals and concert halls worldwide.

Key Artist: Pat Metheny

Guitarist Pat Metheny emerged in the mid-1970s with a fully realized approach to his instrument that was wholly unique for its time, offering a refreshing alternative to both bop and fusion styles.

His sweeping, warm-toned, reverb-soaked lines and liquid phrasing, once described by *Down Beat* magazine as 'the sound of wind through the trees', had a huge impact on a generation of guitarists and forged a new direction in jazz in the late 1970s. Metheny also made a significant impact as a composer, with original, genre-stretching music that artfully blended his own folk influences with elements of rock, Brazilian music, bebop, new age and free jazz.

A Precocious Student

Born on 12 August 1954 in the small midwestern town of Lee's Summit, Missouri, Metheny started on trumpet aged eight before switching to guitar at the age of 12. By 15, he was already a local legend in Kansas City, where he gained invaluable bandstand experience working with veteran players on the jazz scene. In 1972 he moved to Florida and at 18 became the youngest teacher ever at the University of Miami. In 1973 he joined the faculty at the Berklee College of Music in Boston and became the youngest musician ever to be on the staff there (he received an honorary doctorate at Berklee in 1996).

'To me if it's anything, jazz is a verb – it's more like a process than it is a thing.'

Pat Metheny

Metheny established his reputation through his work as a sideman with Gary Burton's group – he is featured on Burton's ECM albums *Dreams So Real* (1975) and *Passengers* (1976) – and as a leader of such acclaimed recordings as his 1976 ECM debut, *Bright Size Life* (a trio date with bassist Jaco Pastorius and drummer Bob Moses) and two powerful follow-up recordings for the label: 1977's *Watercolors* (which established his long-running partnership with keyboardist Lyle Mays) and 1978's *Pat Metheny Group* (which introduced the band featuring Mays on keyboards, Mark Egan on electric bass and Danny Gottlieb on drums).

Pat Metheny took jazz guitar in a new direction and was refreshingly open to the influence of other musical styles.

Metheny Meets the Mainstream

Metheny broke into mass-market acceptance with 1979's *American Garage*, a far more rock-oriented recording than the typically introspective and searching ECM fare. He achieved mainstream popularity and attained gold-record status (sales of 500,000 copies) during the 1980s with a string of melodic, Brazilian-tinged albums, including 1983's *Travels*, 1984's *First Circle*, 1987's *Still Life (Talking)* and 1989's *Letter From Home*. And yet he never stopped taking risks and expanding his musical boundaries throughout the decade, as evidenced by such uncompromising side projects as 1980's free-boppish *80/81* with bassist Charlie Haden, drummer Jack DeJohnette and the twin tenors of Michael Brecker and Dewey Redman; 1981's ethereal duet with keyboardist Mays on *As Falls Witchita, So Falls Wichita Falls*; 1982's abstract *Off Ramp* (which introduces his use of guitar synthesizer); 1983's *Rejoicing*, a subdued guitar-trio setting with bassist Haden and drummer Billy Higgins; 1984's film soundtrack *The Falcon And The Snowman*, which included a collaboration with pop star David Bowie on 'This Is Not America'; and 1986's provocative *Song X*, an historic collaboration with one of his boyhood idols – free-jazz icon Ornette Coleman.

An Experimental Superstar

By the end of the 1980s, Metheny was a bona-fide jazz superstar whose name was on a par with Miles Davis, Keith Jarrett, Herbie Hancock, Joe Zawinul and Wayne Shorter. Through the 1990s, he continued to release recordings of consistently high quality that appealed to his massive fan base (particularly 1992's *Secret Story*, 1994's *We Live Here* and 1997's *Imaginary Day*) while also indulging in purely experimental projects such as 1992's solo guitar synth noise onslaught *Zero Tolerance For Silence* and 1997's *The Sign Of 4*, an edgy free-jazz collaboration with British avant-garde guitar pioneer Derek Bailey, recorded live at New York's Knitting Factory with drummers Paul Wertico and Gregg Bendian.

Over the years, Metheny has won countless polls as 'Best Jazz Guitarist', as well as earning three gold records and 15 Grammy Awards. His Pat Metheny Group, now in its twenty-fifth year, remains one of the longest-standing acts in jazz.

Vibist Gary Burton, in whose group Metheny established his original playing style.

A–Z of Artists

George Adams (Tenor saxophone, flute, 1940–92)

A passionate voice on tenor sax in Charles Mingus's last band (1973–76), Adams co-led one of the most dynamic quartets of the 1980s with pianist Don Pullen; it also featured drummer Dannie Richmond and bassist Cameron Brown. Through the 1980s, the Adams-Pullen band brilliantly straddled the inside-outside aesthetic, perhaps most successfully on 1983's two-volume *Live At The Village Vanguard*.

Steve Coleman (Alto saxophone, b. 1956)

Chicago native Coleman worked in funk and R&B bands before switching to jazz and learning under tenor sax great Von Freeman. He moved to New York in 1978 and worked with the Thad Jones–Mel Lewis Orchestra and Sam Rivers. He had a tenure in the early to mid-1980s with Dave Holland before forming his own group, Five Elements, which blended solid funk rhythms with angular lines.

Coleman was also a co-founder of the Brooklyn-based M-Base Collective (short for 'Macro-Basic Array Of Structured Extemporization'), whose ranks included such forward-thinking players as trumpeter Graham Haynes, bassist Lonnie Plaxico, tenor saxophonist Gary Thomas, trombonist Robin Eubanks, keyboardist Geri Allen and vocalist Cassandra Wilson. While enjoying high-profile sideman work with artists such as Sting and Abbey Lincoln, he went on to spearhead adventurous hybrid collaborations with rappers, Cuban percussionists and singers, with his bands Mystic Rhythm Society, Council of Balance and Five Elements.

Key Tracks

'Big Alice' George Adams
'The Twelve Powers' Steve Coleman
'Tropicana Nights' Paquito D'Rivera

Paquito D'Rivera (Saxophone, clarinet, b. 1948)

Growing up in Havana, D'Rivera saw many legendary Cuban musicians, but it was a Benny Goodman recording that inspired him to play jazz. He performed with the National Theater Orchestra of Havana at the age of 10, and in 1973 joined Irakere, which fused jazz, rock and Cuban music in an exhilarating hybrid. In 1981, D'Rivera defected to the US and made his recording debut as a leader with *Paquito Blowin'*. He released a string of recordings during the decade and in 1988 joined Dizzy Gillespie's 15-piece United Nations Orchestra. Since then he has led small group recordings that highlight his virtuosity.

After moving to New York, Steve Coleman worked with Sam Rivers (pictured) in his All-Star Orchestra, a move that helped launch his career.

A-Z of Artists

Dirty Dozen Brass Band (Instrumental group, 1975–present)

Drawing from the parade-band tradition of New Orleans, the Dirty Dozen Brass Band revolutionized the form by drawing on the bebop repertoire and incorporating elements of contemporary R&B into the mix. The innovative group revitalized the brass-band tradition in the 1980s, inspiring a new generation of brass bands to incorporate popular themes of the day into those infectious grooves. During the 1980s the DDBB recorded for Concord, Rounder and Columbia.

Digby Fairweather (Cornet, trumpet, b. 1946)

The Essex-born trumpeter worked as both a sideman and a leader in a variety of settings before branching out as a jazz educator, author and broadcaster. A key figure in establishing the jazz section of Britain's Musician Union, he also founded the National Jazz Foundation Archive. He led his own groups in the 1980s, including the Jazz Superkings, and has worked with the Great British Jazz Band.

'If I ever DO see [Kenny G] anywhere ... he WILL get a piece of my mind, and maybe a guitar wrapped around his head.'

Pat Metheny

Kenny G (Soprano and alto saxophones, b. 1959)

Kenny Gorelick came up as a sideman in Jeff Lorber's fusion band of the 1970s, before releasing his first R&B-flavoured recordings as a leader in the early 1980s. He hit pay dirt in 1986 with his phenomenally successful *Duotones*, which sold millions. His lyrical, emotive soprano sax playing has come to define smooth jazz, earning him a huge following (as well as hordes of detractors).

Stanley Jordan (Guitar, b. 1959)

In the early 1980s, Chicago native Jordan developed a revolutionary approach to the guitar, in which he sounded notes by tapping on the fretboard with the fingers of both hands. This technique allowed Jordan to play completely independent lines on the guitar simultaneously. His dazzling polyphony soon captured the attention of Blue Note Records, which released his debut, *Magic Touch*, in 1985. He recorded six more albums for Blue Note before switching to Arista Records in 1994. He continues to perform in solo and trio settings and in 2003 collaborated with the Italian pop group Novecento.

Stanley Jordan's innovations on the guitar allow him to play two lines simultaneously.

A-Z of Artists

Bobby McFerrin (Vocals, b. 1950)

A vocal gymnast and daring improviser, McFerrin is one of the most distinctive and uncategorizable singers in contemporary music. His remarkable range (he makes uncanny leaps from deep bass tones to the highest falsetto zone), elastic delivery and incredibly open-minded nature allow him to convincingly cover everything from pop, R&B, jazz and rock to demanding classical pieces. His 1982 self-titled debut on Elektra introduced an extraordinary talent, while his 1984 follow-up, *The Voice*, was a milestone in jazz – the first time a singer had recorded an entire album without any accompaniment.

His Blue Note debut, *Spontaneous Inventions* (1986), earned him respect from the jazz community and 1988's *Simple Pleasures* made him a household name on the strength of his surprise hit 'Don't Worry, Be Happy'. McFerrin continued to challenge himself through the 1990s with his vocal group Voicestra and his duet collaborations with classical cellist Yo-Yo Ma and pianist Chick Corea, and has also been a conductor and performer at the BBC Proms in London's Royal Albert Hall.

Key Tracks

'Don't Worry Be Happy' Bobby McFerrin
'Good Lovin' Bobby McFerrin
'Children Of The Ghetto' Courtney Pine
'Giant Steps' Courtney Pine

Courtney Pine (Tenor and soprano saxophones, bass clarinet, b. 1964)

Starting out in reggae and funk bands in high school, the British saxophonist became interested in jazz in the early 1980s and eventually gravitated towards the music of his biggest influences, Sonny Rollins and John Coltrane. He began playing with John Stevens's Freebop band and by the mid-1980s had formed the Jazz Warriors, an adventurous big band that combined elements of reggae, calypso and ska with jazz.

Pine later formed a sax quartet called the Saxophone Posse and made his recording debut as a leader with 1986's *Journey To The Urge Within* on Island Records. Through his work as a composer-bandleader and virtuosic player – along with his high-profile guest appearances in the UK with the George Russell Orchestra, Art Blakey's Jazz Messengers and the Elvin Jones Jazz Machine – Pine became a role model for a generation of young black jazz musicians in London in the mid-1980s.

With his vocal range and eclectic musical tastes, Bobby McFerrin carved a unique role for himself in the 1980s jazz scene.

A-Z of Artists

David Sanborn (Alto saxophone, b. 1945)

One of the most instantly recognizable and widely imitated voices in jazz during the 1980s, Sanborn emerged from the New York studio session scene – and a seat in Gil Evans's orchestra – to gain crossover success worldwide on the strength of seven R&B-infused outings for Warner Bros., beginning with 1980's breakthrough album *Hideaway*. His intensely expressive phrasing, marked by leaps into the *altissimo* register, remains a Sanborn signature, while his pungent tone and urgent attack are indebted to Hank Crawford's bluesy alto playing.

John Scofield (Guitar, b. 1951)

A masterful improviser who is equally adept at funk, fusion, bebop and ballads, Scofield came up in the mid-1970s with the Billy Cobham/George Duke fusion band before recording as a sideman with Charles Mingus, Gary Burton and Dave Liebman. In 1982–85 he worked with Miles Davis, and through the 1980s made six powerhouse recordings as a leader for Gramavision. His 1990s Blue Note recordings established him as one of the premier guitarists in jazz. His sixth recording for Verve, 2005's *That's What I Say*, is a tribute to the late Ray Charles.

Key Tracks

'It's You' David Sanborn
'Blue Matter' John Scofield
'I'll Take Les' John Scofield
'Soul Eyes' Steps Ahead

Steps Ahead (Instrumental group, 1979–present)

Originally an acoustic jazz quintet led by vibist Mike Mainieri and featuring tenor saxophonist Michael Brecker, pianist Don Grolnick, bassist Eddie Gomez and drummer Steve Gadd, Steps changed personnel through the early 1980s, changed its name to Steps Ahead in 1983 and by 1985 had become a high-tech fusion outfit, with Mike Stern on electric guitar and both Brecker and Mainieri playing MIDI controllers. Mainieri continued to lead the band with new personnel through the 1990s.

David Sanborn is an influential alto saxophonist with a distinctive tone and unusual phrasing.

A-Z of Artists

Henry Threadgill (Alto saxophone, flute, composer, b. 1944)

One of the most prolific and original composers of his generation, Chicago native Threadgill was a charter member of the Association for the Advancement of Creative Musicians (AACM) in the mid-1960s. During the 1970s he collaborated with several AACM colleagues and also worked with Air, his trio with drummer Steve McCall and bassist Fred Hopkins. After moving to New York, he began composing through the 1980s for his acclaimed Sextet and Very Very Circus. He has also written ambitious works for symphonic forces and uncategorizable ensembles such as his Make A Move quintet.

James 'Blood' Ulmer (Guitar, b. 1941)

Drawing on systems that are both ancient and modern, this experimental guitarist forged an original vocabulary on his instrument that has rarely been imitated and remains one of the most individual approaches in jazz. Ulmer began his career working in organ bands around the Midwest in the 1960s, before moving to New York in 1973. Hooking up with Ornette Coleman that same year introduced him to the harmolodic theory of musical composition and improvisation, altering his approach for all time.

Key Tracks

'Subject To Change' Henry Threadgill
'Theme From Captain Black' James 'Blood' Ulmer
'Rush Hour' Yellowjackets

Through the 1980s Ulmer led three record dates for Columbia, which helped to expose his music to a wider audience. He also worked with tenor saxophonist David Murray and drummer Ronald Shannon Jackson in the Music Revelation Ensemble, and then in 1987 formed the edgy group Phalanx with tenor saxophonist George Adams, bassist Sirone and drummer Rashied Ali.

Yellowjackets (Instrumental group, 1981–present)

Bassist Jimmy Haslip and keyboardist Russell Ferrante joined drummer Will Kennedy as the backing band for a 1979 recording by guitarist Robben Ford. By 1981, that same quartet recorded its fusion debut for Warner Bros. under the band name Yellowjackets. When Ford left the band the following year, he was replaced by alto saxophonist Marc Russo. Through the 1980s they pursued a Zawinul-influenced sound; saxophonist Bob Mintzer brought more jazz credibility to the group in the 1990s.

James 'Blood' Ulmer has a highly original approach to jazz music and plays a blend of blues and free jazz.

The Contemporary Era

The 1990s and 2000s saw major advances in technology and communication, in particular with the development of the World Wide Web, email and mobile telephones. Suddenly, instant contact and an almost limitless amount of information were available at all times to people everywhere, and new aspects of language and social interaction began to form as a result.

Following the Gulf War of the 1990s, the US has undergone some turbulent times, with events such as the terrorist attacks on the World Trade Center in 2001, the subsequent war in Iraq and the dubious political treatment surrounding Hurricane Katrina resulting in a certain amount of political unease and conflicting opinions. The UK has found itself in a similar position while, on the other side of the world, China has emerged as the new centre of mass-production and is beginning to rival the West as a global superpower. The threats of global warming and environmental destruction are ever-present, casting a shadow over the many exciting developments in science and technology.

Meanwhile, jazz in the current climate continues its relentless journey. There are strains that look back to former styles and others that constantly follow new directions. Jazz music has also entered the mainstream in a more accessible, generic form, via a new generation of talented singers and musicians who use their interests and influences from this field to give a jazz flavour to their music. The Internet has provided a forum for jazz websites, communities and chat rooms, as well as a resource for tracking down what were once obscure jazz records. Even at 100 years old, the flame of jazz music still burns strong – long may it continue to do so.

Key Artists

Joey DeFrancesco
Diana Krall
Abbey Lincoln
Arturo O'Farrill
Cassandra Wilson

Charlie Hunter is a flexible guitarist and was a key figure in the acid-jazz movement which rose to prominence in the 1990s.

A Dwindling Audience

In the first decade of the twenty-first century, musical culture is blown every which way and some feel that jazz bears the brunt of the storm. The increased corporate consolidation of the media means that celebrity vocalists mouthing formulaic pop songs rule the airwaves, while vapid, mid-tempo fantasies dominate commercial, 'lite' jazz, also known as instrumental pop.

At its inception, commercial radio was highly diversified and characterized by local programming. It has since become centrally owned and operated, promulgating a limited playlist. Jazz seldom, if ever, makes that list. Only non-commercial, government-supported 'public radio' in the US and Britain, and the newly burgeoning satellite radio systems, seek to serve niche markets, of which the audience for jazz is one. A couple of generations ago, adults on a given night might have danced to a swing band in a ballroom or relaxed at a nightclub; today, their grandchildren are transfixed by home entertainments. So far, jazz has not proved very telegenic, nor has the downloading of jazz music via the Internet proved particularly popular or profitable.

With each death of a jazz veteran – from the demise of the still-provocative Miles Davis (1926–91) through the close of the Swing Era with the passings of Lionel Hampton (1908–2004) and the scornful, long-retired Artie Shaw (1910–2004) – direct links of jazz to its prior golden ages are lost. At every turn, economic factors and new trends threaten not only the maintenance, but the very growth and development of jazz.

'I feel musicians can ... accomplish certain things that maybe even governments and industries can't accomplish.'

Jack DeJohnette

A Global Phenomenon

And yet simultaneously, jazz education at high school and college levels has never enjoyed higher enrolment. Jazz has been embraced by musicians and audiences around the globe, with the European Union, West and South Africa, the Caribbean, South America, Russia and the Far East advancing gifted musicians, as well as stalwart support networks (Jazz Institute of Chicago, San Francisco Jazz, New Orleans Jazz & Heritage Foundation, Monterey Jazz Festival, Earshot Jazz, Northsea Jazz Festival, Umbria Jazz Festival, etc.), which comprise entrepreneurs and semi-professionals alike.

The New Orleans Jazz & Heritage Festival – proof that the jazz spirit lives on in the city where the music was born.

Jazz Raises its Profile

In autumn 2004 Wynton Marsalis (b. 1961) presided over the opening of the first major performance facility ever designed specifically for jazz. Rose Hall, home of Jazz@Lincoln Center, the world's leading multi-purpose jazz institution, offers three venues (Manhattan nightclub, Greek theatre, Italian opera house), classrooms, rehearsal space, an art gallery and production facilities in a glamorous site in New York City, with an ambitious calendar of staged shows, big band concerts and combo bookings.

Jazz – and Wynton himself – was celebrated in a 19-hour series by video documentarian Ken Burns; biographers are publishing volumes on figures as disparate as Django Reinhardt (1910–53) and Wayne Shorter (b. 1933), and jazz's rich, associative legacy has been tapped for literary purposes by the likes of Toni Morrison and Edgardo Vega Yunqué, and in films by Robert Altman, Clint Eastwood and Spike Lee.

The Meaning of 'Jazz' Today

Is jazz a thriving art or a fading pastime? Is jazz, in 2007, still fundamentally the realm of black Americans? Or does jazz belong to a worldwide elite whose members add their own accents to jazz's trademark themes, rhythms, strategies and variations? The jazz industries can accurately be described as threatened, but jazz itself, the art of a functional culture, may be securing itself through consolidation. Virtuosic saxophonists such as Bobby Watson and Kenny Garrett, steeped in hard swing and deep blues, and sophisticated pianists such as Mulgrew Miller and Bill Charlap (b. 1966) define the young to middle-aged mainstream. Neo-conservatives such as the Marsalis brothers canonize the very greatest names of the jazz past, although with selectivity: Duke Ellington (1899–1974) and Count Basie (1904–84), yes; Glenn Miller (1904–44) and Stan Kenton (1912–79), no. Many working musicians pay homage to jazz repertoire by launching outright tribute projects (such as pianist Michael Wolff's Children on the Corner) or by stylistically emulating their heroes, such as alto saxophonist Vincent Herring taking off from Cannonball Adderley (1928–75), and trumpeter Nicholas Payton from Louis Armstrong (1901–71). Direct 'quotes' of historic jazz also proliferate, due to hip hop's rage for digital samples. Turntable artists recycle licks of soul jazz artists of the 1950s and 1960s to make new hits from scraps of the old.

> **Popular Melody**
>
> Wayne Shorter – 'Aung San Suu Kyi' (1997)

Wynton Marsalis at the opening procession for the Rose Hall jazz venue at New York's Lincoln Center.

A Brighter Future?

The bland noodlings of soprano saxophonist Kenny G (b. 1959) remain the bestselling recordings by an instrumentalist of all time. The quasi 'chamber jazz' of pianist Bob James's Fourplay, the California glitz of studio ensembles such as the Rippingtons, the innocuous effusions of Canadian singer-pianist Diana Krall (b. 1964) and the youthful moxie of British pianist-singer Jamie Cullum all top jazz CD sales lists.

However, with purer forms of jazz struggling in the US but thriving abroad, audiences have been more willing to lend an ear to far-flung ensembles. The Ganelin Trio, darlings of the 1980s Russian avant-garde, have reconvened sporadically since the fall of the Soviet Union, despite the pianist-leader's emigration to Israel. Pierre Dorge's New Jungle Orchestra of Denmark has gained renown, as Denmark has become famous for bestowing the world's most prestigious jazz honour, the annual JazzPar Award.

Individuality, originality and iconoclasm still exist, launched from platforms in jazz. Experimentalists such as British guitarist Derek Bailey (b. 1932) and saxophonist Evan Parker (b. 1944), American reedsmen Charles Gayle and Roscoe Mitchell and saxophonist-composer John Zorn (b. 1953) continue to test the bounds of their instruments. Vocalists including Siberian throat singer Sainkho Namchylak, Brooklyn-born Shelly Hirsch and New Jersey's Lisa Sokolow explore the flexiblities of language, while

Popular Melody

Cassandra Wilson – 'Last Train To Clarksville' (1996)

Lawrence Douglas 'Butch' Morris, William Parker (b. 1952) and Walter Thompson conduct large ensembles through instant, scoreless compositions. Folkloric elements from Spain and Latin American settlements in the Western Hemisphere have been embraced as basic to jazz – in the words of Jelly Roll Morton (1890–1941), 'the Spanish tinge' –

so Panamanian-born pianist Danilo Perez, Dominican pianist Michel Camilo and Nuyorican trumpeter-conguero Jerry Gonzalez with his *piratas del flamenco* attain full measures of respect and influence.

Jazz continues to mirror contemporary society. Culture is fragmented; so is jazz. Communications are global, and jazz is a worldwide phenomenon. Values everywhere are in dispute; jazz has its internal debates, feuds and competitions. The best news is that the music hasn't been frozen for museum display. Fertile, free of untoward constraints and fighting as always for self-definition, jazz lives!

Musicians such as saxophonist and composer John Zorn continue to question the limits of jazz.

A-Z of Artists

Geri Allen (Piano, b. 1957)

Raised in Detroit, pianist-composer Allen emerged in New York City with older midwestern avant-gardists such as Lester Bowie and Oliver Lake, and hometown colleagues including saxophonist Kenny Garrett. Her albums feature elusive but lyrical compositions for small ensembles. She toured briefly and recorded *Feel The Fire* (1993) with singer Betty Carter, and has worked with her husband, trumpeter Wallace Roney. Allen performed as Mary Lou Williams in Robert Altman's film *Kansas City* (1996).

Fred Anderson Jr (Tenor saxophone, b. 1929)

Admired by post-1960s Chicago improvisers as a founding member of the Association for the Advancement of Creative Musicians, tenor saxophonist Fred Anderson's reputation spread after his first trip to Europe in 1977, but he was very sparsely recorded until the 1990s. Since then his huge tone and gutsy statements have been captured on numerous albums, and his music club, the Velvet Lounge, has become an internationally renowned venue.

Key Tracks

'Lullaby Of The Leaves' Geri Allen
'Straight, But Not Straight' Fred Anderson Jr
'What It Is' Derek Bailey
'Ani Mamin' Steven Bernstein

Derek Bailey (Guitar, b. 1932)

The British guitarist is uncompromisingly cerebral, exploring atonal, anti-melodic yet associative 'sound', abjuring musical conventions. Yet his solos and collaborations with master improvisers of jazz and beyond are compelling. The author of *Improvisation: Its Nature And Practice In Music* (1993), Bailey considers traditions from Africa and India as well as the West. In the early 1990s he produced the television series *On The Edge* for Britain's Channel 4.

Steven Bernstein (Trumpet, composer, arranger, b. 1961)

A member of several populist-experimental-fun jazz bands since the late 1980s (including Hieroglyphics Ensemble, Kamakazi Ground Crew, Lounge Lizards, Spanish Fly, Sex Mob and the Millennial Territory Orchestra), Bernstein continues to perform on slide trumpet (or soprano trombone), cornet and other standard brass instruments, and to compose and arrange film soundtracks. His projects include adaptations of Jewish folk and liturgical themes with Cuban mambo and New Orleans R&B rhythms.

Trumpeter Steven Bernstein has played in various experimental jazz ensembles.

A-Z of Artists

Dee Dee Bridgewater (Vocals, b. 1950)

First heard in the 1970s with the Thad Jones-Mel Lewis Orchestra, then in the Broadway musicals *The Wiz* and *Sophisticated Ladies* and later in pop/jazz contexts, Bridgewater relocated to Paris in 1983. Leading a trio, she regained career momentum in the 1990s with tribute projects commemorating Billie Holiday, Horace Silver and Ella Fitzgerald, and has also performed jazz-related standards.

Uri Caine (Piano, b. 1956)

Born in Philadelphia, Caine pursued classical studies and performances with locally based jazz stars (Philly Joe Jones, Grover Washington Jr) prior to moving to New York in the late 1980s. He has productive associations with clarinettist Don Byron and trumpeter Dave Douglas, among others, and his output ranges from mainstream and electric piano trios to neo-klezmer, to post-modern revisions of works by Mahler, Wagner and Bach, and a concept album depicting early-twentieth-century Tin Pan Alley.

James Carter (Various saxophones, b. 1969)

A musical prodigy, saxophonist James Carter toured Europe at the age of 16, worked with Wynton Marsalis and starred in Julius Hemphill's saxophone opera *Long Tongues*. Since 1990, his New York ensemble has recorded a variety of romantic jazz, Django Reinhardt-style gypsy jazz, hard-core fusion and jazz standards. At the fiftieth anniversary Newport Jazz Festival he upped the stakes by improvising 33 choruses of Duke Ellington's 'Diminuendo And Crescendo In Blue'.

Key Tracks

'Dear Ella' Dee Dee Bridgewater
'Now Will The Sun Rise As Brightly' Uri Caine
'Take The 'A' Train' James Carter
'Don't Mess With Mister T.' Regina Carter

Regina Carter (Violin, b. 1966)

Violinist Regina Carter has stabilized her instrument's precarious role in jazz after advanced work in classical, jazz-pop and experimental formats. From childhood Suzuki lessons (a method of teaching music that stresses listening over reading skills), she joined the Detroit-based band Straight Ahead, then the String Trio of New York. She was a featured soloist in Wynton Marsalis's Pulitzer Prize-winning *Blood On The Fields* oratorio (1995) and was the first jazz musician, person of colour or woman to play and record on Paganini's Stradivarius, 'the Cannon'.

The violin has made a comeback on to the jazz scene in the hands of Regina Carter.

A-Z of Artists

Bill Charlap (Piano, b. 1966)

The son of composer Moose Charlap and singer Sandy Stewart, Bill Charlap was inducted into professional jazz by Gerry Mulligan and has been acclaimed for his deft playing, superb taste and unfailing swing feel. In 2004 he succeeded pianist Dick Hyman as director of the prestigious jazz series at New York's 92nd Street Y (Young Men's and Young Women's Hebrew Association).

Ravi Coltrane (Tenor and soprano saxophones, b. 1965)

Ravi Coltrane, the son of John and Alice Coltrane, faces problematic expectations to which he has responded with modesty and genuine accomplishment. Raised by his spiritually devout mother, Ravi joined Coltrane drummer Elvin Jones's band in his early 20s. The loosely organized Brooklyn M-Base Collective supported his individuality and, while touched by the influence of his parents, he mines a progressive rather than radical musical style.

Joey DeFrancesco (Organ, b. 1971)

The son of jazz organist Papa John DeFrancesco, Joey's keyboard skill and enthusiasm were well-recognized even before 1987, when he was a finalist in the annual Thelonious Monk Competition. Indebted in style to Jimmy Smith, DeFrancesco played with Miles Davis and recorded on Columbia Records prior to his graduation from high school. His prodigious youthful energy has attracted audiences and revitalized an interest in jazz organ.

Key Tracks

'Slow Boat To China' Bill Charlap
'Monk's Mood' Ravi Coltrane
'Blues A La Carte' Ravi Coltrane
'The Champ' Joey DeFrancesco
'Moon Of The West' Dave Douglas

Dave Douglas (Trumpet, b. 1963)

Dave Douglas spans musical abstraction and gutsiness in acclaimed albums and a busy, international touring schedule. After attending Berklee School of Music, New England Conservatory and New York University, he studied with classical trumpeter Carmine Caruso and toured with Horace Silver. He has recorded for a variety of small labels, as well as BMG-RCA Victor, and is known for his Tin Hat Trio (jazzing Balkan music) and John Zorn's Sephardic-tinged jazz quartet Masada. In 2005 Douglas introduced his own record label with *Mountain Passages*.

Pianist Bill Charlap, who has played with Benny Carter, Clark Terry and Gerry Mulligan, among others.

A-Z of Artists

Bill Frisell (Guitar, b. 1951)

A distinctive electric guitar stylist, Frisell evokes longing and wonder through melodic selectivity, *legato* attack and strategic outbursts. Originally a clarinettist, then inspired by Wes Montgomery, he studied at Boston's Berklee School of Music and with Jim Hall. He recorded for ECM and won fame in the New York noise/improv scene, exploring pastoral Americana imagery in his own projects. Besides playing in Paul Motian's trio with Joe Lovano, Frisell has recorded colouristic accompaniments for rock and pop singers.

Roy Hargrove (Trumpet, b. 1969)

Encouraged by Wynton Marsalis, Hargrove has a jauntier approach to trumpet than his mentor. He principally employs hard-bop vocabulary, but has also led the Latin jazz band Crîsol with Cuban pianist Chucho Valdés, recorded with hip hop/soul singer D'Angelo, and co-starred in Herbie Hancock's New Standards quintet with saxophonist Michael Brecker. In his own programmes, Hargrove plays both tender ballads and R&B/funk hits.

Shirley Horn (Vocals, piano, 1934–2005)

Shirley Horn was successful from 1954 in her hometown of Washington, DC. She was promoted by Miles Davis and Quincy Jones and owned a club called the Place Where Louie Dwells, but gradually turned full attention to her family. She returned with records, club dates and concert tours in the mid-1980s, and was admired for her unadorned, expressive ballad singing and self-accompaniment. Horn suffered a diabetic foot amputation in 2004 and sadly later died in 2005.

Key Tracks

'Strange Meeting' Bill Frisell
'Greens At The Chicken Shack' Roy Hargrove
'You Won't Forget Me' Shirley Horn
'Lulu's Crawl' Charlie Hunter

Charlie Hunter (Guitar, b. 1967)

The leading exponent of briefly trendy 'acid jazz', guitarist Charlie Hunter has learned to emulate the organ-bass runs of his inspiration, Larry Young. Raised in Berkeley, California, the son of a guitar repairer, he was a street musician in Europe prior to founding Disposable Heroes of Hiphoprisy in the early 1990s – the first of his series of popular combos, which draw on the R&B, soul, alternative rock and reggae repertoires.

Roy Hargrove plays both ballads and funk tracks in a clean, hard-bop-influenced trumpet style.

A-Z of Artists

Vijay Iyer (Piano, composer, b. 1971)

Raised in Rochester, New York, Vijay Iyer started Suzuki violin lessons at the age of three and taught himself to play piano. He performed professionally while pursuing advanced studies at Yale and the University of California, Berkeley and moved to New York in 1998, having released two albums and toured with saxophonist Steve Coleman. Iyer incorporates socio-political concerns and South Asian musical elements into his cross-genre projects, frequently in collaboration with saxophonist Rudresh Mahanthappa.

Norah Jones (Vocals, piano, b. 1979)

An overnight sensation, Norah Jones's debut album *Come Away With Me* (2002) won numerous Grammy Awards and its sales revitalized Blue Note Records. Introduced by her mother to Billie Holiday's music, Jones won *Down Beat* Student Music Awards in 1996 and 1997 and studied jazz piano at North Texas State University prior to arriving in New York City in 1999. Her warm voice and intimate delivery lend compelling inflections to pop, folk and country songs in basic arrangements with 'jazz' content from sidemen.

Diana Krall (Vocals, piano, b. 1964)

From western Canada, Diana Krall attended Berklee School of Music, was encouraged to sing by Los Angeles-based pianist-singer Jimmy Rowles and was mentored by bassist Ray Brown. Her first trios, co-led by guitarist Russell Malone, emulated Nat 'King' Cole's; her accessible stylings led to international festival tours, bestselling recordings and increasingly nuanced vocal shadings. In 2004 Krall married British singer-songwriter Elvis Costello and released her first album of all-original material.

Birelli Lagrene (Guitar, b. 1966)

A French gypsy, Lagrene was hailed as Django Reinhardt's heir upon the release of his first album at the age of 13. He has performed gypsy jazz in the company of swing veterans Benny Carter, Benny Goodman and Stephane Grappelli, but has also developed a personal, fusion-oriented style and mixes both approaches in collaborations with guitarists John McLaughlin, Al Di Meola, Paco de Lucia, Christian Escoudé and Stanley Jordan, among others.

Key Tracks

'Memorophilia' Vijay Iyer
'Come Away With Me' Norah Jones
'Don't Know Why' Norah Jones
'The Look Of Love' Diana Krall
'Coquette' Birelli Lagrene

French gypsy guitarist Birelli Lagrene is one of the many bringing new flavours to jazz music.

A-Z of Artists

Abbey Lincoln (Vocals, composer, b. 1930)

Lincoln caps her long, diversified singing and acting career as an iconic songwriter and performer. Her first record, in the 1950s, was with Benny Carter's orchestra; in the 1960s she recorded politicized material with then-husband Max Roach. In the mid-1980s she re-emerged, paying tribute to Billie Holiday and embodying an African-American feminism. Employing top younger instrumentalists in her bands, she has also become a model for younger vocalists such as Cassandra Wilson, Erika Badhu and Lizz Wright.

Joe Lovano (Various saxophones, clarinet, drums, b. 1952)

The son of Cleveland saxophonist Tony 'Big T' Lovano, Joe Lovano attended Berklee School of Music before working in organ groups. He was in Woody Herman's 1970s Thundering Herd and Mel Lewis's Vanguard Jazz Orchestra, freelanced extensively and joined drummer Paul Motian's trio with Bill Frisell in 1990. He has become a leading voice of mainstream modernism, applying himself to diverse contexts. He has collaborated with his vocalist wife, Judi Silvano, various saxophonists and rhythm sections, and composer Gunther Schuller.

Key Tracks

'Left Alone' Abbey Lincoln
'When Malindy Sings' Abbey Lincoln
'Fort Worth' Joe Lavano
'Uprising' Joe Lavano
'Note Bleu' Medeski, Martin & Wood

Medeski, Martin & Wood (Instrumental group, 1991–present)

In the 1990s John Medeski (keyboards, b. 1965), Billy Martin (drums, b. 1963) and Chris Wood (bass, b. c. 1969) established an energized form of lengthy improvisations over powerful grooves, playing student venues and festivals. All three members have impressive resumés, including conservatory training and experience with experimental jazz leaders. Their recordings have taken increasing liberties with the basic jam band formula, adding DJs, vocalists, compositional complexity and collage effects.

Abbey Lincoln has become a mentor for younger musicians and vocalists.

A-Z of Artists

Arturo O'Farrill (Piano, orchestra leader, b. 1960)

Arturo O'Farrill is the pianist and music director of the Latin jazz orchestra his father, Cuban-born Chico O'Farrill, organized upon his comeback in the mid-1990s; he has also worked with keyboardist-composer-bandleader Carla Bley, trumpeter Lester Bowie and the Fort Apache Band. Upon Chico's death in 2000, Arturo inherited his bandbook and legacy. In 2003 he was named leader of Jazz@Lincoln Center's Afro-Latin Jazz Orchestra.

Greg Osby (Alto and soprano saxophones, b. 1960)

After playing in R&B bands in St Louis, Greg Osby studied at Washington, DC's Howard University. He quit Berklee School of Music to tour with Dizzy Gillespie, then moved to New York City and joined Steve Coleman's M-Base Collective. At first their styles were mirror images, but Osby gradually found a unique voice based on phrase displacements. He has recorded with Cassandra Wilson, older iconoclasts and acoustic groups with new talents such as pianist Jason Moran.

Evan Parker (Tenor and soprano saxophones, b. 1944)

Bristol-born Evan Parker has been an important experimentalist in the UK and Europe for 40 years with the Spontaneous Music Ensemble, Music Improvisation Company, London Jazz Composer's Orchestra, Brotherhood of Breath, Dutch-based ICP and Globe Unity Orchestra. His mastery of circular breathing and alternate fingerings have resulted in inimitable, atonal improvisations. Live shows by his Electro-Acoustic Ensemble feature interactive electronics.

Key Tracks

'Moment's Notice' Arturo O'Farrill
'Pent-Up House' Greg Osby
'Chicago Solo' Evan Parker
'Harlem' William Parker

William Parker (Bass, b. 1952)

William Parker apprenticed with major bassists in New York City's Jazzmobile programme, studied privately with Jimmy Garrison and Wilber Ware, and performed with Cecil Taylor's group at the age of 21. He has anchored many ensembles, including the David S. Ware Quartet. His prodigious work ethic, instrumental steadiness, dependability and selflessness have made Parker central to activities that culminate annually in a week-long interdisciplinary Vision Festival, produced by his wife, dancer-choreographer Patricia Parker.

Melow vocalist Cassandra Wilson perfomed with Greg Osby in Steve Coleman's M-Base Collective in the 1980s.

A-Z of Artists

Chris Potter (Various saxophones, b. 1971)

A Chicago native, Chris Potter emerged professionally in bebop trumpeter Red Rodney's combo, before moving on to roles in the Mingus Big Band and bassist Dave Holland's quintet and big band. He became the youngest musician to win Denmark's prestigious Jazzpar Prize in 2000. Personally self-effacing, Potter is a virtuosic instrumentalist with an adventurous frame of melodic mind, equal to any musical challenge.

Enrico Rava (Trumpet, b. 1939)

Raised in Turin, Italy and taught piano by his conservatory-graduate mother, Rava began playing traditional jazz on trombone as a teenager but, inspired by Miles Davis, switched to trumpet. He worked with expatriate American jazzmen in Rome and travelled throughout Europe and around South America and New York. Through broad perspective and international experience he has arrived at a distinctive sound, with a melodic style that embraces both conventional and radical gestures.

Joshua Redman (Tenor and soprano saxophones, b. 1969)

Joshua Redman neé Shedroff grew up in Berkley, California and played reeds throughout high school. He was accepted by Yale Law School, but his victory at the 1991 Thelonious Monk competition persuaded him to take up music professionally. He was quickly accepted by jazz elders, peers and audiences due to his strong, blunt tone, populist taste, articulate manner and voracious style. In 2000 he was appointed artistic director and artist-in-residence of the San Francisco Jazz Festival, and continues to record and tour widely.

Key Tracks

'Stella By Starlight' Chris Potter
'Tea For Two' Enrico Rava
'Blues For Pat' Joshua Redman
'Better Days' Dianne Reeves

Dianne Reeves (Vocals, b. 1956)

Dianne Reeves's parents were musicians and her cousin, pianist George Duke, encouraged her. She sang in Los Angeles studio sessions in the late 1970s and 1980s, and with Caldera, Night Flight and Sergio Mendes's troupe. Her albums blend jazz, gospel, African and Brazilian accents with pop-music production. She has recorded a tribute to Sarah Vaughan and in 2002 was appointed Creative Chair for Jazz by the Los Angeles Philharmonic, to curate jazz bookings and educational workshops at the Hollywood Bowl and the Walt Disney Concert Hall.

Like his father Dewey, Joshua Redman is a versatile and successful jazz reedsman.

A-Z of Artists

Gonzalo Rubalcaba (Piano, keyboards, b. 1963)

A pianist with Romantic sensibilities, Rubalcaba is from a revered musical family. He led an electric Grupo Proyecto on tours of Europe and Asia in the 1980s, representing triumphs of Castro-era Cuba, but the US denied him entry until 1993. Bassist Charlie Haden sponsored his first Blue Note Records albums and remains an important collaborator, while Rubalcaba has continued to compose lush yet abstract works for trio, quartet and quintet, occasionally employing electronics.

Maria Schneider (Composer, arranger, bandleader, b. 1960)

Schneider studied several instruments and composition prior to an internship with arranger Gil Evans in New York City in 1985. After further work with Bob Brookmeyer and Mel Lewis, she established a jazz orchestra that performed weekly in Greenwich Village from 1993–98 and recorded three albums. In 2004 she self-produced *Concert In The Garden* and distributed it over the Internet. She has written for orchestras in Paris, Denmark and Stockholm, and for the Pilobolus Dance Theater company.

Matthew Shipp (Piano, b. 1960)

Shipp considers himself to be a follower of bassist William Parker, with whom he has worked on many projects including the David S. Ware's Quartet. His style is rhythmically propulsive; he lays dense harmonic accompaniments for single-note instruments. In 1999 he contracted with Thirsty Ear Records to produce his own imprint, Series Bleu, featuring himself with associates including hip hop DJs and punk-rock bands.

Key Tracks

'Contagio' Gonzalo Rubalcaba
'Concert In The Garden' Maria Schneider
'Cohesion' Matthew Shipp
'Mr Bruce' Chuco Valdés

Chucho Valdés (Piano, b. 1941)

Chucho remained in Cuba after his father, pianist Bebo Valdés, defected in the late 1950s. In his mid-20s Chucho established Orquesta Cubana de Musica Moderna, which became the internationally touring jazz showband Irakere; he turned it over to his son in 1998. A large man with huge hands, Valdés is capable of sweeping ballads as well as dazzling fast display. He teaches at Havana's Beny Moré School of Improvised Music and at the Banff Center for the Arts in Canada, and directs the annual Cuban Jazz festival.

Versatile pianist Gonzalo Rubalcaba is one of the most important artists to emerge from Afro-Cuban jazz in the 1990s.

A-Z of Artists

Ken Vandermark (Tenor saxophone, clarinet, b. 1961)

Ken Vandermark studied film before turning to music with a trio in Boston in the mid-1980s. He moved to Chicago in 1989, playing reeds with a flinty, aggressive sound. His investigations of free improvisation won him a five-year MacArthur Foundation 'genius' grant in 1999 and he has used the funding to invest in further recordings and his international career, including membership in saxophonist Peter Brotzmann's high-energy Tentet.

Jeff 'Tain' Watts (Drums, b. 1960)

Watts played timpani in the Pittsburgh Youth Symphony Orchestra during his teens and vibraphone at Berklee School of Music, where he met the Marsalis brothers. He recorded with Wynton Marsalis from 1981 and then with Branford. An explosive polyrhythmist who can also provide restrained accompaniment, 'Tain' is much in demand for sessions by many jazz modernists.

Cassandra Wilson (Vocals, composer, b. 1955)

Raised in Mississippi, smoky contralto Wilson sang R&B and folk music, but emerged in New York City in the early 1980s as a member of the M-Base Collective and with Henry Threadgill's band. Her breakout album *Blue Skies* (1988) reprised jazz standards and she starred in Wynton Marsalis' oratorio *Blood on the Fields*, but the cornerstone of her mature tyle is *Blue Light 'Til Dawn* (1993), in which she performs original songs, famous blues and unusual rock/pop choices with interesting arrangements.

Popular Melody

Wynton Marsalis – 'Knock-Moe-King' (1983)

John Zorn (Alto saxophone, composer, b. 1953)

New Yorker John Zorn deconstructed bebop themes in the late 1970s and created musical games that dictated improvisational structures. He plays in bands such as Masada, purveying electric funk, Japanese pop and punk rock. Zorn has encouraged other renegade musicians by establishing music policies at venues and curating international festivals. As principal of Tzadik Records, he jump-started the avant-garde klezmer and 'Radical Jewish Culture' movements. He remains a prolific composer and has also branched into film soundtracks and chamber music.

Jeff 'Tain' Watts started out playing with the Marsalis brothers and has become one of the foremost drummers of his generation.

STYLES OF JAZZ

The diversity and flexibility of jazz music is due in part to the high calibre of its artists – a long line of hugely talented and inventive players and bandleaders through the decades, such as Louis Armstrong, Jelly Roll Morton, Count Basie, Coleman Hawkins, Lester Young, Dizzy Gillespie, Charlie Parker, Miles Davis, Bill Evans and John Coltrane, have ensured that jazz has continued to move along and develop at an extraordinary rate and in unprecedented directions, never remaining in one place long enough to become stale or uninteresting.

From the syncopated rhythms of ragtime to the unrestricted outpourings of free jazz; from the stripped-back, simple musical structures of the Dixieland revival to the outlandish sounds of jazz rock and from the often minimalist recordings of cool jazz to the passionate invocations of Latin jazz, this multi-faceted genre embraces an incredibly wide range of different styles, reflecting the changing times and the many cultural, social and geographical influences that informed its creators. The fact that conflicting factions exist within the jazz scene (e.g. the Modernists v Moldy Figs debate of the 1950s) is surely testament to the enormous musical variety that it encompasses.

This section of the book examines in detail each of the main styles of jazz, describing the circumstances, people and events that helped to develop the music, as well as discussing the most important artists, composers and recordings and looking at the defining features of the style's sound.

Saxophonist Sonny Stitt (left of standing group) with Thelonious Monk (seated far left) and (l–r) Clark Terry, Roy Eldridge and Al McGibbon, some of the greatest names in jazz history, performing at Monterey, 1971.

Ragtime

A forerunner of jazz, ragtime was derived from brass-band music and European folk melodies, African-American banjo music and spirituals, minstrel songs, military marches and European light classics.

The 'raggy' style, or ragged-time feeling, of this jaunty, propulsive, toe-tapping piano music refers to its inherent syncopation, where loud right-hand accents fall between the strong beats of the left-hand rather than on top of them. One noted practitioner, the pianist Eubie Blake (composer of the 1920s hit song 'I'm Just Wild About Harry'), summed it up simply: 'Ragtime is syncopation and improvising and accents'.

'Scorned by the Establishment as ephemeral at best, trashy at worst, ragtime was the fountainhead of every rhythmic and stylistic upheaval that has followed in a century of ever-evolving American popular music.'

Max Morath

While this highly syncopated style involved only limited improvisation and lacked a jazz-swing feel, it directly informed the work of the early jazz giant Jelly Roll Morton and served as a precursor to the Harlem stride piano movement of the 1920s, pioneered by James P. Johnson, Willie 'The Lion' Smith and Fats Waller. Ragtime could be heard as early as the 1880s in camps of workers building the great railroads across the American continent, as well as in travelling minstrel shows and vaudeville shows. By 1892, the composer Charles Ives had come across it in his hometown of Danbury, Connecticut. At the Chicago World's Fair that same year, many people heard ragtime for the first time. By 1896, the first pieces labelled 'ragtime' were published. The following year, some 20 rags were published. By 1899, 120 rags were issued in New Orleans.

As piano rolls and sheet music appeared at the turn of the century, a ragtime fad swept the nation. Hordes of young people shocked their parents by kicking up their heels to this infectious new music, which was described alternately by critics and newspaper columnists as 'syncopation gone mad' and 'the product of our decadent art culture'.

Eubie Blake and Noble Sissle began writing songs together in 1915 and went on to have a successful writing and performing partnership, calling themselves 'The Dixie Duo'.

The Ragtime King

Although Scott Joplin became the figurehead for this burgeoning new American music movement, there were several ragtime piano players who preceded him, including Walter Gould (known as One Leg Shadow), Tom Turpin, James Scott and One-Leg Willie Joseph, along with other ivory-tinkling 'professors' who plied their trade in brothels, gambling joints, saloons and private clubs.

Following the phenomenal success of Joplin's 'Maple Leaf Rag', which sold 75,000 copies of sheet music in 1899 for the publisher John Stark and 500,000 copies within 10 years, Joplin was dubbed 'King of Ragtime Writers' and presided over ragtime's reign as the main popular musical style of the US for nearly 20 years.

Key Artists

Eubie Blake
Scott Joplin
Joseph Lamb
James Scott
Tom Turpin

The son of a former slave, born in Texarkana, a town in the northeast corner of Texas, on 24 November 1868, Joplin was a piano prodigy with a musical education financed by his mother's work as a domestic servant. With aspirations to become a classical concert pianist, he played at the Chicago World's Fair in 1892 and later enrolled at the George R. Smith College for Negroes in Sedalia, Missouri (where he would write 'Maple Leaf Rag'). In 1901, Joplin moved to St Louis to begin working with Stark, where he began to expand his writing from ragtime tunes to full-length pieces such as ballets and operas. The first of these, *A Guest Of Honor*, emerged in 1903.

Rather than being improvised, Joplin's music was as formally composed and carefully worked out. And while he easily enchanted the masses with catchy numbers such as 'Maple Leaf Rag' and 'The Entertainer', Joplin longed to be taken seriously as a composer. He saw himself as a black American counterpart to Chopin or Strauss, a composer of new music for a new century.

Thomas 'Fats' Waller, who pioneered the stride piano style that grew out of ragtime.

Ragtime Revival

Joplin's death in 1917, just before the end of the First World War, effectively marked the beginning of the end of ragtime's supremacy in America, and although Zez Confrey had some success in the early 1920s with tunes such as 'Kitten On The Keys' and 'Dizzy Fingers', by the second decade of the twentieth century, attention had shifted dramatically to the new phenomenon of 'hot music' or 'jazz'.

By 1930, ragtime was largely extinct. The legacy of the early ragtime pioneers lived on only through sheet music and piano rolls of their compositions: there were no recordings of any of the music. In fact, the year Joplin died was the same year in which the Original Dixieland Jazz Band made the first jazz recording.

More than half a century after Joplin's death, this rollicking, syncopated music enjoyed a revival in the early 1970s, sparked by three significant events. In 1971, the musicologist and pianist Joshua Rifkin recorded an album of Joplin's pieces for Nonesuch, which caught on with critics and the public alike. The following year, Joplin's 1915 ragtime opera, *Treemonisha*, was resurrected and staged at Atlanta's Memorial Arts Center. Then, in 1973, the pianist-composer Marvin Hamlisch used Joplin's 'The Entertainer' as the main theme for the Hollywood blockbuster *The Sting*, starring Paul Newman and Robert Redford. That Academy Award-winning film made Joplin a household name, helping to trigger renewed interest in his jaunty and sophisticated music.

Ragtime Style

Ragtime is a composed piano style which consists of pieces of simple, cheerful-sounding melodies with simple syncopation in which the right hand is rhythmically supported by the left.

Treemonisha was again staged by the Houston Grand Opera in May 1975 and brought to Broadway that October, contributing to Joplin being posthumously awarded a special Pulitzer Prize in 1976 for his contribution to American music. Joplin's legacy has been kept alive through the 1980s and 1990s by ragtime piano interpreters such as Terry Waldo, Butch Thompson, Dick Hyman and Marcus Roberts, as well as by prominent jazz instrumentalists such as Anthony Braxton, Archie Shepp, Ran Blake, Ron Miles, Bill Frisell and Wynton and Branford Marsalis. Original composers in the ragtime style, such as Mississippi's David Thomas Roberts and Chicago's Reginald Robinson, have helped to keep this nearly extinct music alive on the concert and recording scene over the past 10 years.

Scott Joplin wisely secured a royalty contract on 'Maple Leaf Rag', one of his most successful compositions. He received one cent for each copy sold.

New Orleans Jazz

Conditions were ripe for jazz to evolve in New Orleans at the turn of the twentieth century. A thriving port of immigration, where Africans and Creoles lived side by side with Italians, Germans, Irish, French, Mexicans and Cubans, New Orleans' unprecedented ethnic diversity allowed for a free and easy mingling of musical ideas between cultures.

Other factors contributed to the coalescing of jazz as a cultural expression unique to New Orleans. The call-and-response tradition of West African music was retained in many Baptist churches of the South, particularly in New Orleans, while concepts of polyrhythm and improvisation within group participation (qualities inherent in African drumming ensembles) were kept alive in the Crescent City at Congo Square, an authorized venue where slaves would gather to recreate their drumming and dancing traditions. These African drumming concepts, and indeed the very notion of percussiveness as musical expression, would seep into the cultural consciousness of New Orleans.

'Arguably the happiest of all music is New Orleans jazz. The sound of several horns all improvising together on fairly simple chord changes with definite roles for each instrument but a large amount of freedom cannot help but sound consistently joyful.'

Scott Yanow

Let the Good Times Roll

The foundation for a new hybrid music was set by a combination of the African notion of rhythm that swings, or has a propulsive motion, with the European classical influences brought into the mix by ragtime and sophisticated Creole musicians. Add a thriving brass band tradition, which developed in the late-nineteenth century from the plentiful supply of cheap brass band instruments left behind after the Civil War, blend in rhythmic and melodic elements from Cuba, the West Indies and the Caribbean, and factor in the slightly decadent and pervasive 'party time' atmosphere of the City That Care Forgot (typified by the pageantry of Mardi Gras, as well as the city's unofficial motto, 'Laissez les bons temps rouler' or 'Let the good times roll'), and you have a potent recipe for jazz.

Canal Street, New Orleans, c. 1900, as jazz music was developing.

The Cornet Kings

Out of a rich cultural gumbo came Charles 'Buddy' Bolden, the first bona fide jazz star of the twentieth century. A cornetist of unparalleled power, Bolden's innovative approach took the essence of ragtime and put a looser, hotter, bluesier spin on it, grabbing dancers in the process.

By 1895, Bolden was leading his own group in residence at New Orleans' Globe Theater, where he held court as 'King' Bolden. By 1901, his popularity spread from playing dance halls scattered throughout the city and in outlying communities, including Preservation Hall, the Tin Roof Café and Funky Butt Hall. In 1903, he began to fade from the scene, plagued by spells of dementia and drunkenness, until he was committed to the East Louisiana State Mental Hospital on 5 June 1907: the first jazz casualty.

Succeeding Bolden as the cornet king of New Orleans was Freddie Keppard, who, in 1906, led the Olympia Orchestra. Legend has it that Keppard, leery of having other cornet players 'steal his stuff', turned down an offer from the Victor Talking Machine Company to become the first New Orleans musician to record. Another prominent cornetist was Joe Oliver, who began playing in local dance bands and with the Onward Brass Band in 1907. By 1917, he became the star cornetist in a popular band led by the trombonist Edward 'Kid' Ory, who billed him as 'King' Oliver. An early master of mutes, Oliver pioneered the 'wah-wah' and other vocal effects on his horn, which would later become a signature of the Ellington trumpeter Bubber Miley. When Oliver went north to Chicago in February 1919, Ory hired the 18-year-old Louis Armstrong as his replacement on cornet.

Key Artists

Sidney Bechet
Buddy Bolden
Freddie Keppard
Jelly Roll Morton
King Oliver

Oliver's contemporary on the New Orleans scene was the Creole clarinettist Sidney Bechet. A child prodigy, Bechet held his own with Freddie Keppard's band at the age of 10. He left school at 16 and began working with various bands, thrilling audiences and players alike with his forceful attack, soaring passion and unusually fast vibrato. Bechet relocated to Chicago in 1918 and, a year later, became one of the first Americans to spread jazz to Europe as a member of the travelling Southern Syncopated Orchestra. It was while he was in London that he ran across the instrument with which he would eventually make jazz history: the soprano saxophone.

Kid Ory's 'tailgate' playing style – in which the trombone plays a rhythmic line beneath the band's trumpets and cornets – may have been influenced by his earlier experiences as a banjo player.

The Jazz Age

A key figure in New Orleans jazz was the pianist, composer, entertainer and raconteur Jelly Roll Morton. A natural extrovert who bragged that he had invented jazz, Morton began embellishing on ragtime, blues and light classics while performing at the 'sporting houses' of the Storyville red-light district as early as 1902.

By 1907, he began touring in vaudeville shows throughout the Gulf Coast and the Midwest. He settled in Chicago in 1914, then relocated to the West Coast from 1917 to 1922. He had composed numerous works by that time, including his classic 'King Porter Stomp' and 'Winin' Boy Blues', but remained unrecorded until 1923.

A plethora of jazz musicians were active in New Orleans during the first decade of the twentieth century, but the first jazz recording was not made until 1917. That honour went not to pioneers such as Keppard, Ory, Oliver, Bechet or Morton (all of whom went unrecorded until after they had left New Orleans), but to a group of five young, white New Orleans musicians calling themselves the Original Dixieland Jazz Band. Led by Sicilian-American cornetist Nick LaRocca, the ODJB assembled in the Victor studio in New York City on 26 February 1917 to record 'Livery Stable Blues'. A lively novelty number that featured passages where the instruments imitated barnyard animals, it immediately caught on with the public. Following the extraordinary success of their recording debut (it would eventually sell 1.5 million copies), the ODJB toured British variety theatres, where they audaciously billed themselves as 'The Creators of Jazz'. The ODJB later introduced such Dixieland standards as 'Margie', 'Indiana' and 'Tiger Rag', spawning a number of copy bands and sparking a craze that quickly swept America, as well as setting the stage for what the writer F. Scott Fitzgerald characterized as 'The Jazz Age' of the 1920s.

New Orleans Style

New Orleans is an ensemble style in which each instrument has a specific role. The piano and banjo provide rhythm and harmony, the trumpet plays the main melody and the clarinet is used for melodic embellishment.

Pianist, composer and bandleader Jelly Roll Morton advocated the 'Spanish tinge' element in jazz music.

Chicago Jazz

Jazz was the by-product of cultures coming together in New Orleans at the turn of the twentieth century. The music, along with some of its greatest practitioners, moved north by 1917. That year Storyville, the red-light district, was forced to close and jazz musicians headed north to Chicago, where jazz matured into a fine art form.

Chicago held the promise of a new life for the Southern black population, which migrated from the fields of the cotton industry to the blast furnaces and factories of big Northern cities. A centrally located, active transportation hub that provided easy access to Los Angeles and New York, Chicago was an attractive destination for working jazz musicians, many of whom worked in the gangster-owned speakeasies created by the Volstead Act of 1919 (outlawing the manufacture and sale of alcohol in the United States).

Blow the Way You Feel

While the North Side of Chicago had its famous clubs – the Green Mill, College Inn, Blackhawk, Kelly's Stables and Friar's Inn – the hottest jazz bands of the early 1920s could, primarily, be found on a nine-block stretch of State Street on the city's predominantly black South Side, known as 'The Stroll'. There, jazz lovers could choose between the Pekin Inn, Dreamland Café, Plantation Café, Elite Café and Sunset Café. Among the patrons who frequented The Stroll was a group of jazz-hungry, white teenage students who attended Chicago's Austin High School – cornetist Jimmy McPartland, tenor saxophonist Bud Freeman, drummer Dave Tough and reedman Frank Teschemacher. Along with developing young players, such as guitarist Eddie Condon, pianist Joe Sullivan, cornetists Muggsy Spanier and Leon 'Bix' Beiderbecke, clarinetist Benny Goodman and drummer Gene Krupa, this next generation of jazz musicians originated the 'Chicago style', building on the rhythmic innovations of the New Orleans pioneers while injecting a frenetic intensity and reckless spirit that reflected the city itself.

> *'Armstrong plays with such bravura and rhythmic intensity that when you listen to it you hear the future. At that moment you know that something is in the works and it's never going to be contained.'*
>
> **Gary Giddins, critic, 2000**

Eddie Condon (seated) played an important part in the desegregation of jazz, as well as in moving jazz performances from underground clubs to concert halls.

Hypnosis at First Hearing

The Austin Gang and other architects of the extrovert Chicago style were fans of the Original Dixieland Jazz Band, but they quickly fell under the spell of another white group from New Orleans, playing in Chicago in 1920 under the name of the New Orleans Rhythm Kings.

They made their recording debut in 1922, and a year later teamed up in the studio with Jelly Roll Morton for one of the first-ever integrated sessions. Another focal point for the Austin Gang's adulation was the dazzling cornet virtuoso Louis Armstrong, who came to town in 1922 to join his mentor King Oliver in the ranks of the Creole Jazz Band. With its two-cornet frontline, underscored by an intuitive call-and-response chemistry between its leader and 22-year-old star, the impact of King Oliver's Creole Jazz Band on young audiences was devastating. As guitarist Eddie Condon recalled in his memoirs, *We Called It Music: A Generation of Jazz* (Henry Holt): 'It was hypnosis at first hearing. Armstrong seemed able to hear what Oliver was improvising and reproduce it himself at the same time. Then the two wove around each other like suspicious women talking about the same man'. In the early part of 1923, Oliver's pace-setting group went into a rickety studio in Richmond, Indiana, and cut its first historic recording ('Chimes Blues') for the small but influential Gennett label.

Key Artists

Louis Armstrong
Bix Beiderbecke
New Orleans Rhythm Kings
Joe Sullivan
Frank Teschemacher

Armstrong left Chicago in 1924 to join Fletcher Henderson's band in New York. The following year, he returned to Chicago to lead a band organized by his new wife, Lil (Hardin) Armstrong, at the Dreamland Café. Soon afterward, he began doubling with Erskine Tate's Vendome Theater Orchestra, where he was the featured hot soloist. Then, on 12 November 1925, he went into the Okeh studios in Chicago to make the first of a series of five dozen tracks recorded between 1925 and 1928, which have come to be known as the Hot Fives and Hot Sevens sessions. With these revolutionary recordings, Armstrong single-handedly shifted the focus from jazz as an ensemble music to a soloist's art form. As noted critic Gary Giddins put it, 'It's the moment when jazz becomes an art form. With these pivotal recordings, he virtually codifies what jazz is going to be for the next half century'. By 1929, Armstrong shifted his home base from Chicago to New York, where jazz was poised for its next evolution.

Louis Armstrong's Hot Five recordings may represent the greatest jazz of all time. Pictured (l–r) are Armstrong, Johnny St Cyr, Johnny Dodds, Kid Ory and Lil Hardin-Armstrong.

Swing

The popularity of jazz hit a peak after the Depression years of 1929–1933. By the end of 1934, huge numbers were tuning in to the NBC radio series Let's Dance, which broadcast performances by the Xavier Cugat, Kel Murray and Benny Goodman orchestras. Goodman's orchestra in particular caught on with the public and created a demand for live performances.

When Goodman went on tour in the US, scoring his first big success before a packed house of ecstatic teenagers at the Palomar Ballroom in Los Angeles on 21 August 1935, it signalled the beginning of a new national youth craze to rival the turn-of-the-century ragtime fad. Symbolically, it was the birth of the swing era, the predominance of big bands in jazz.

Reaching Fever Pitch

Following Goodman's triumph at the Palomar Ballroom, the floodgates opened wide and several bands followed in his wake. By 1937, Kansas City pianist and bandleader William 'Count' Basie had recorded his first swinging sides, including the anthemic 'Jumpin' at the Woodside' and 'One O'Clock Jump', both featuring the tenor saxophonist Lester Young and the all-American rhythm section of bassist Walter Page, drummer Papa Jo Jones and guitarist Freddie Green. That same year, Jimmy Dorsey scored hits with 'Marie' and 'Song of India', featuring classic trumpet solos by Bunny Berigan. Shortly after, Berigan formed his own big band and had a hit in August 1937 with 'I Can't Get Started', still part of the standard jazz repertoire to this day. Swing-era momentum reached fever pitch with Benny Goodman's historic Carnegie Hall concert in New York in January 1938, which was recorded for posterity and included the classic instrumental version of Louis Prima's 'Sing, Sing Sing', the frantic number that made drummer Gene Krupa such a star that he left the BG Orchestra to form his own big band.

'There was a time, from 1935–1946, when teenagers and young adults danced to jazz-oriented bands, when jazz orchestras dominated pop charts and when influential clarinettists were household names. This was the Swing era.'

Scott Yanow

Django Reinhardt was a key player in European jazz during the swing era. After losing two fingers on his fretting hand, Reinhardt developed his own unique style of playing which became hugely influential.

DJANGOLOGY

DJANGO REINHARDT

DJANGOLOGY
BLUE DRAG
DINAH
CLOUDS
SOME OF THESE DAYS
LENTEMENT MADEMOISELLE
NUAGES
JUST ONE OF THOSE THINGS
MELODIE AU CREPUSCULE
PORTO CABELLO
SWEET CHORUS
SWING 39

jazz doubles

vogue

Swing is the Thing

The year 1939 saw a flurry of activity in swing: Harry James, an outstanding trumpeter in the Goodman organization, formed his own orchestra. The clarinettist Woody Herman scored his first big band hit with 'At the Woodchopper's Ball' and the saxophonist Charlie Barnet became a household name that same year on the strength of his big- band hit 'Cherokee'.

Meanwhile, singer Ella Fitzgerald took over the Chick Webb Orchestra following the drummer-bandleader's death that summer. Glenn Miller's Orchestra rose to prominence by blending pop elements with the highly polished big band formula, scoring several Top Ten hits in 1939 and 1940 with popular recordings such as 'Little Brown Jug', 'In The Mood' and 'Pennsylvania 6-5000'. In that same year, trumpeter Dizzy Gillespie joined the Cab Calloway Orchestra; tenor-sax great Coleman Hawkins recorded his immortal 'Body And Soul'; and bassist Jimmy Blanton and tenor saxophonist Ben Webster joined the great orchestra led by Duke Ellington. Ellington's orchestra had been a monumental force in jazz since the early 1920s and he remained a major name during the swing era on the strength of anthemic hits such as 'It Don't Mean A Thing If It Ain't Got That Swing', 'Rockin' in Rhythm' and 'Drop Me Off In Harlem'.

Key Artists

Count Basie
Cab Calloway
Duke Ellington
Benny Goodman
Woody Herman

As the 1930s came to a close, one thing was eminently clear: swing had become as commercially viable and lucrative as rap music is today. While the swing-era dance bands enjoyed unprecedented popularity, there was never any attempt at playing to the lowest common denominator. The general level of musicianship had risen incrementally in the early 1930s due to the towering influence of Louis Armstrong, whose pyrotechnic playing on the Hot Five sessions of 1925 and collaboration with Earl Hines in 1928 (particularly on anthemic showpieces like 'Weather Bird' and 'West End Blues') had raised the bar for instrumental virtuosity in jazz. The combination of Armstrong-influenced hot soloing, well-honed ensemble playing and an infectious 4/4 beat proved irresistible for listeners and dancers through the 1930s and into the early 1940s.

Virtuoso clarinettist Benny Goodman messes around with Gene Krupa, a drummer so innovative that he was able to upstage Goodman.

From a Flurry to a Fall

With the size of the ensembles ranging from 10 to 20 pieces or more, big band music flowed smoothly on a steady 4/4 pulse, propelled by a foundation of string bass 'walking' in synch with the drums, which kept time on the high-hat cymbal and bass drum while providing syncopated accents on snare and tom-toms.

The distinctive big band quality came from the use of separate trumpet, trombone and saxophone (alto, tenor, baritone) sections to provide chordal or contrapuntal blocks of sound or add rhythmic punch to an arrangement. Over the top of these intricately voiced, highly polished arrangements was room designated for individual soloists to tell their story. That juxtaposition of discipline and freedom is a hallmark of big band music.

Swing Style

One feature of swing is the drumming. As drum kits developed, drummers moved away from four-in-a-bar bass drum to more subtle patterns.

By 1942, the first full year of American participation in the Second World War, the swing era had suffered some setbacks. Key players and bandleaders like Glenn Miller and Artie Shaw had enlisted in the Armed Services and a recording strike by the Musicians Union from 1942–1944 effectively halted the documenting of this new music's development. By the end of the Second World War in 1945, the swing era was feeling competition from the Dixieland revival and the advent of bebop, creating a kind of Civil War that split the jazz audience into three factions. By 1946, many of the big bands had broken up. Combos were the wave of the future. Name-orchestras like Duke Ellington's, Count Basie's and Woody Herman's persisted in the face of changing times but the swing era as a cultural force was clearly over.

Count Basie was taught piano in the Harlem stride tradition by Fats Waller. He worked in the vaudeville circuit for a number of years before going on to become one of the world's greatest big band leaders.

Bebop

Though it was often referred to as a musical revolution, bebop was actually a natural evolution of jazz, involving innovative approaches to harmony and rhythm that advanced the music forward to a modern era.

Traces of bebop began to emerge during the early 1940s, in orchestras led by Earl Hines and Billy Eckstine. Those adventurous impulses were further developed in Harlem nightspots such as Minton's Playhouse and Clark Monroe's Uptown House, where the architects of an iconoclastic new movement conducted experiments with time, tempo and extended techniques.

An Iconoclastic New Movement

It was there that drummer Kenny Clarke began to employ new methods on the kit – implying time, accenting in unpredictable ways and generally colouring and embellishing the music spontaneously from measure to measure, rather than keeping strict metronomic time in the manner of swing-era drummers. It was there that pianist Thelonious Monk began to map out sophisticated harmonic modulations and new melodic contours around familiar songs. In the same spirit of discovery, the trumpeter Dizzy Gillespie and alto saxophonist Charlie Parker began to effectively eliminate bar lines by soaring over the chord changes with impunity, injecting their lines with a stream-of-consciousness creativity that cascaded effortlessly through their horns. These young modernists were, largely, reacting to clichés that had begun to saddle big bands towards the end of the swing era. Their ambitious efforts at developing a new lexicon of expression coalesced into a new kind of music that was publicly unveiled on 'Swing Street', the vibrant strip of nightclubs that lined 52nd Street between Fifth and Seventh Avenues in Midtown Manhattan.

'"Bebop" was a label that certain journalists later gave it, but we never labelled the music. It was just modern music, we would call it. We wouldn't call it anything, really, just music.'

Bebop drummer Kenny Clarke

Minton's Playhouse, where the bebop style began to take shape (l–r Thelonius Monk, Howard McGhee, Roy Eldridge, Teddy Hill).

A Divisive Movement

With the emergence of bebop around 1945, the jazz world was suddenly divided into opposing (and at times hostile) camps: those who thrived on the new music and those threatened by its incursion. Some old-guard icons, such as trumpeter Louis Armstrong and bandleader Cab Calloway, readily dismissed bebop, branding its frantic tempos, eccentric rhythms, advanced harmonies and discordant melodies as undanceable and indecipherable. But others, such as tenor saxophonists Coleman Hawkins and Don Byas, successfully made the transition from the old into the new.

John Birks 'Dizzy' Gillespie, with his outrageous stage persona, became a figurehead of the rebellious new movement. Aside from his peerless virtuosity as a trumpeter, Dizzy was also a beloved showman throughout his long and illustrious career. Gillespie, along with his kindred spirit and musical partner Charlie 'Yardbird' Parker, whose blinding speed and dazzling facility placed him a cut above every other improviser of his day, unleashed a torrent of new ideas (some of which were based on pre-existing chord patterns from swing-era standards) that set a new standard for instrumental virtuosity and changed the course of jazz.

Key Artists

Dizzy Gillespie
Thelonious Monk
Fats Navarro
Charlie Parker
Bud Powell

Born in South Carolina in 1917, Gillespie began playing trombone at the age of 14, before switching to trumpet the following year. He played with Philadelphia's Frank Fairfax Band, before he joined Teddy Hill's Orchestra in 1937, filling a spot formerly held by his trumpet-playing idol, Roy Eldridge. In 1939, Gillespie found himself in fast company on a Lionel Hampton all-star date for Victor. He distinguished himself with some singular, muted trumpet work on 'Hot Mallets', which showed a distinct departure from Eldridge's influence and pointed to a new path for jazz trumpet. Following a two-year stint in Cab Calloway's band, Gillespie worked in a succession of bands led by musicians including Ella Fitzgerald, Benny Carter, Duke Ellington and, in 1943, Earl Hines. In January 1944, he put together the Hepsations, the first bebop-oriented jazz group to play on 52nd Street. In June 1944, he joined Billy Eckstine's all-star big band, and by spring 1945 he had teamed up with Parker at The 3 Deuces on Swing Street. Together, they dominated the bop era from 1945 to 1949.

Earl Hines led a big band throughout the 1930s and 1940s that served as a launch pad for the up-and-coming bebop movement.

A Jazz Messiah

With remarkable technical proficiency, coupled with the sheer force of his charismatic personality, Charlie Parker became a jazz messiah in the mid-1940s. His solos were sermons to a faithful flock, hungering for a hipper alternative to Benny Goodman and Glenn Miller.

Parker's virtuosic flights on alto sax, marked by an uncanny fluidity, an inherent bluesy quality and an intuitive harmonic logic that was complex yet crystal clear, earned him a lofty status among critics, fans and contemporaries alike. An early apprenticeship with the Jay McShann Orchestra in 1937 helped him hone his technique, and by the time he first visited New York City in 1939 as an eager 19-year-old, he was prepared to deal with the advanced playing of Art Tatum and take the next step in his musical journey. Parker met and began exchanging ideas with Gillespie as early as 1940. The two later met in Earl Hines' band in 1943 and, for a few months, in Billy Eckstine's Orchestra in 1944. But it was not until late 1944 that they worked together on 52nd Street, startling the world with bop anthems such as 'Groovin' High', 'Hot House' and 'Shaw 'Nuff'.

Bebop Style

In a bebop rhythm section swing drums combine with walking bass and offbeat piano stabs. Melodies and solos typically used counter rhythms.

In the wake of landmark small group recordings by Bird & Diz, documented in May 1945 on the Guild label, other modernists would add to the bebop canon, including pyrotechnic virtuosos such as pianist Bud Powell, trumpeters Howard McGhee and Fats Navarro, saxophonists Dexter Gordon and Edward 'Sonny' Stitt, trombonist J. J. Johnson, and pianists Tadd Dameron and Al Haig, all of whom placed a premium on speed of thought and execution in their music. By 1950, bebop had run its course as a burgeoning new movement. Some of its early practitioners and disciples had evolved, and were already experimenting with two new jazz tributaries – hard bop and cool jazz.

Dizzy Gillespie's incredibly varied and unpredictable playing style created a feeling of excited suspense. Charlie Parker may have developed bebop beyond all expectations, but without Diz it would never have begun.

Dixieland Revival

By the end of the 1930s, the Swing era was in full force, ushered in by big bands led by Benny Goodman, Chick Webb, the Dorsey brothers (Jimmy and Tommy) and Glenn Miller. New Orleans jazz and its stylistic off-shoot, Dixieland, had both largely faded from popularity.

New Orleans pioneers King Oliver and Jelly Roll Morton drifted into obscurity. Original Dixieland Jazz Band leader Nick LaRocca left music altogether and became a building contractor, while New Orleans trombonist-bandleader Edward 'Kid' Ory (once a mentor to the teenage Louis Armstrong in New Orleans and later appearing on Armstrong's revolutionary Hot Five and Hot Seven sessions from 1925–28) had gone into chicken farming.

Goodtime Music From the Past

By 1939, Dixieland was making a solid comeback. A generation of players, including clarinettists Pee Wee Russell and Joe Marsala, saxophonist Bud Freeman, trumpeters Bobby Hackett, Muggsy Spanier, Max Kaminsky and Wild Bill Davison, guitarist Eddie Condon and others, began reinvestigating the extroverted collective improvisational style of early New Orleans music and Chicago-style jazz of the 1920s. Part of the impetus for the revival of Dixieland came in 1938, when New York record store owner Milt Gabler launched his Commodore Records label to document these prominent Dixieland revivalists. Responding to the renewed interest in old-style New Orleans music, Jelly Roll Morton (who had made only one appearance on record between 1931–37 on a little-known Wingy Manone date) led sessions in 1939 with such notable New Orleans sidemen as Sidney Bechet, Red Allen and Albert Nicholas. Ironically, Morton's music became popular again after his death in July 1941, just as the Dixieland revival really started to take off.

'By the mid-1930s the word 'dixieland' was being applied freely to certain circles of white musicians, first by the trade press, then by the public. By the end of the decade it had all but lost any direct 'southern' association.'

Richard Sudhalter

Ken Colyer helped to keep traditional New Orleans-style jazz alive in Britain.

The Moldy Figs

Another figure who spearheaded the Dixieland revival was Bob Crosby. A former singer in the Dorsey Brothers' band from 1934–1935, Crosby led a band through the late 1930s and early 1940s that revived such New Orleans evergreens as 'South Rampart Street Parade', 'Sugarfoot Strut' and 'Muskrat Ramble' while also interpreting popular hits of the day in a Dixieland two-beat style.

Following the example of Tommy Dorsey (who in 1935 formed his Dixieland-flavoured Clambake Seven as a featured smaller group within his big band), Crosby formed the Bobcats from the ranks of his own big band. This smaller Dixieland ensemble featured several New Orleans-born musicians performing faithful renditions of classic fare by Louis Armstrong, King Oliver and the Original Dixieland Jazz Band.

By the early to mid-1940s, New Orleans jazz pioneers like Kid Ory, Bunk Johnson and George Lewis were being persuaded to return to recording studios and concert halls, which touched off renewed interest in the original New Orleans-style jazz and placed more emphasis on interactive ensemble playing and less on extroverted soloing, as was the style of the Dixielanders. Their pure, spirited playing directly inspired the British cornetist and trumpeter Ken Colyer, who would spearhead a wave of traditional New Orleans jazz throughout England in the 1950s.

Key Artists

Buck Johnson
Kid Ory
Ken Coyler
Eddie Condon
Muggsy Spanier

A primary force for a west coast Dixieland revival was Lu Watters' Yerba Buena Jazz Band, which issued its first records in 1942. This revivalist octet emulated the two-cornet approach of King Oliver's Creole Jazz Band with trumpeters Watters and Bob Scobey on the frontline alongside trombonist Turk Murphy and clarinettist Ellis Horne. By the mid to late 1940s, with the advent of the modernist bebop movement, traditional New Orleans jazz and Dixieland players were being dismissed by progressives as 'moldy figs'. Yet the music was carried on in the late 1940s and through the 1950s by its figurehead, Louis Armstrong, who broke up his big band in 1947 and spent the rest of his career leading an all-star sextet which specialized in playing old New Orleans jazz and Dixieland standards like 'Basin Street Blues', 'Royal Garden Blues', 'Sleepy Time Down South', 'Tiger Rag', 'Indiana' and 'Struttin' With Some Barbecue'.

Bunk Johnson ceased playing in 1931 after a fellow trumpeter was stabbed to death on stage. He was rediscovered in the early 1940s.

Spirited Ensemble Music

Guitarist Eddie Condon, a major propagandist for the Dixieland cause, recorded prolifically throughout the 1940s and 1950s with notable Dixieland players such as trumpeters Wild Bill Davison and Max Kaminsky, trombonists Jack Teagarden and Cutty Cutshall, and clarinettists Pee Wee Russell and Peanuts Hucko.

Other Dixieland revivalists during the 1950s included trumpeter Adolphus 'Doc' Cheatham, New Orleans clarinettist George Lewis, trombonist Wilbur de Paris (whose band featured the great New Orleans-born clarinettist Omer Simeon), San Francisco trumpeters Bob Scobey and Turk Murphy and former Bobcats bandmates trumpeter Yank Lawson and bassist Bob Haggart (who would team up in the late 1960s to form their Dixieland-inspired World's Greatest Jazz Band).

In 1961, Preservation Hall opened in New Orleans to keep the tradition alive and provide steady work for old-time New Orleans jazzmen, such as the trumpeters Kid Thomas Valentine and Punch Miller, clarinetist Willie Humphrey and, on trumpet, his older brother Percy. Trumpeter Al Hirt and clarinettist Pete Fountain also brought greater visibility to Dixieland with their popular recordings and frequent television appearances throughout the 1950s and 1960s.

Dixieland Style

Dixieland rejected the more melodically, harmonically and rhythmically complex forms of jazz in favour of simple rhythmic and harmonic structures.

This spirited ensemble music is still being championed today by New Orleans clarinettists Dr Michael White and Pete Fountain, New Orleans-based singer-bandleader Banu Gibson, soprano saxophonist Bob Wilber (whose Bechet Legacy group was active in the early 1980s), cornetists Jim Cullum Jr and Warren Vaché, New Orleans trumpeter Wynton Marsalis and the current edition of the Preservation Hall Jazz Band.

British trumpeter Humphrey Lyttelton blows his horn while guitarist Eddie Condon operates the valves.

Cool Jazz

In the wake of the manifesto that Charlie 'Bird' Parker and Dizzy Gillespie jointly issued on their first recording together in 1945, most musicians on the New York jazz scene began fanning the flames of bebop. Tempos picked up speed, intensity increased and blazing virtuosity became a means to an end.

And yet, the task of topping the two trendsetters who originated and mastered the art of bebop seemed insurmountable to many of their disciples, who, at best, might be considered great imitators but never originators. This frustrating fact caused several forward-thinking musicians to break from the extroverted bebop mould and forge a new, more reflective and deliberate musical path. Like pouring water on the flames of the bebop movement, these thoughtful young player-composers came to epitomize a 'cool school' in jazz.

Key Artists

Miles Davis
Gil Evans
Lee Konitz
Gerry Mulligan
Claude Thornhill

Velvety, Sensuous and Swinging

The roots of this antidote to the hyperactivity of bebop can be heard in the work of Claude Thornhill & His Orchestra, a dreamy-sounding ensemble from the early 1940s that utilized such unusual instrumentation as French horns and tuba as melodic voices. Some of the finest charts in the band's book were contributed by the composer-arranger Gil Evans, who brought his own boppish inclinations to the ensemble's softer quality. By the end of 1947, Evans had become acquainted with Miles Davis, a promising 22-year-old trumpeter from East St Louis who had apprenticed alongside Parker at the height of the bebop craze.

While Davis did not possess the dazzling virtuosity of his idol Dizzy Gillespie, he began developing a sparser approach to trumpet soloing, contrasting with the explosive bravura of the beboppers. This cooler style finally came to fruition on Davis' *Birth Of The Cool*, the 1949 recording that helped usher in a new musical movement in jazz. Davis' landmark nonet sessions of 1949–50 were characterized by a relaxed yet disciplined integration of elements, featuring cool-toned soloists such as alto saxophonist Lee Konitz, trombonist J. J. Johnson and baritone saxophonist Gerry Mulligan. The arrangers – Evans, Mulligan, Johnny Carisi, John Lewis and Davis – incorporated the lush tones of French horns, trombone and tuba in creating a velvety, sensuous yet swinging body of work, that has stood the test of time.

Chet Baker's ethereal, melodic playing style, combined with his androgynous vocals, introduced a fragile element to cool jazz.

Offshoots of the Cool School

Key participants in the seminal *Birth Of The Cool* sessions went on to incorporate various musical precepts of the Davis nonet experience in their own work: Gerry Mulligan with his celebrated, pianoless quartet; John Lewis with the chamber like Modern Jazz Quartet; Lee Konitz in his mid-1950s work with tenor saxophonist Warne Marsh.

So pervasive was the influence of *Birth Of The Cool* among musicians that it spawned a separate movement, known as 'West Coast Jazz'. Some of the leaders of this branch of the cool school included bassist Howard Rumsey and his Lighthouse All-Stars, trumpeter-arranger Milton 'Shorty' Rogers and his Giants, alto saxophonist Bud Shank with his tenor saxophonist partner Bill Perkins, valve trombonist Bob Brookmeyer, trumpeter Conte Candoli, multi-reedman Jimmy Giuffre, vibist Teddy Charles, tenor saxophonist-oboeist Bob Cooper, trombonist Frank Rosolino and drummer-composer Chico Hamilton, who introduced a group in 1955 that featured the unusual instrumentation of cello (Fred Katz), guitar (Jim Hall), flute (Buddy Collette) and bass (Carson Smith).

Cool Jazz Style

The laid back sound of cool jazz is created by using instruments that are traditionally part of the rhythm section, such as the double bass, to provide melody instead.

Another leading light of west coast Jazz was the alto saxophonist Paul Desmond. In 1951 Desmond teamed up with the pianist Dave Brubeck who had led an experimental octet during the late 1940s. Together Desmond and Brubeck found phenomenal success on college campuses, reaching new audiences and turning a younger generation on to jazz. In the wake of 1954's *Jazz Goes To College*, the Dave Brubeck Quartet was so popular that its leader appeared on the cover of *Time* magazine.

While the rich tonal colours, highly wrought arrangements and relaxed, measured solos of west coast or cool jazz emerged in reaction to the urgency and all-out burn of bebop, it in turn triggered another movement that followed in the mid-1950s: hard bop. By 1959 Miles Davis was already on to other groundbreaking work. His landmark album of that year, the influential and bestselling *Kind Of Blue*, would popularize modal jazz – a system of improvising based on modes or scales rather than running chord progressions – and pave the way for the free jazz movement of the 1960s.

The Dave Brubeck Quartet experimented with unusual time signatures on tracks such as the now-classic 'Take Five'. They were advised that such records would not sell, as they were too difficult to dance to.

Hard Bop

Hard bop evolved out of bebop during the early 1950s but its rhythms were more driving. It also tended to have a more full-bodied sound, a bluesy feel with darker textures and shorter improvised lines, and its chord progressions were composed rather than borrowed from popular tunes.

Although Miles Davis made an early foray into hard bop with *Walkin'* (1953), the style did not become established until drummer Art Blakey and pianist Horace Silver joined forces later that year. They played with the trademark hard-driving grooves and gospel-inspired phrasings that would later be associated with the genre.

Many listeners underestimate the impact Horace Silver had on contemporary mainstream jazz: the hard bop style he and Art Blakey developed in the 1950s is still one of the dominant forms of the genre. Silver studied piano at school in Connecticut, where he formed a trio for local gigs. They impressed tenor saxophonist Stan Getz, who immediately brought them over to New York in 1950. Silver worked with Getz for a year there and also began to play with other top jazzers. In 1953 he joined forces with Art Blakey to form a band under their joint leadership. Their first album, *Horace Silver And The Jazz Messengers* (1955), proved to be a milestone in the development of hard bop, with some of the tunes later becoming jazz standards. Silver left the band in 1956 to record a series of albums that showcased his original, funky piano style. His recordings throughout the ensuing five decades have featured many jazz notables, including the trumpeters Donald Byrd, Art Farmer and Randy Brecker, as well as the saxophonists Hank Mobley and Michael Brecker.

Key Artists

Art Blakey
Wes Montgomery
Max Roach
Sonny Rollins
Horace Silver

Art Blakey began as a pianist before he switched to the drums in the 1940s. He drummed with Mary Lou Williams, Fletcher Henderson's Swing Band and Billy Eckstine's band before forming the original Jazz Messengers in 1955. The band varied in size, but they always delivered top-notch jazz, powered by Blakey's driving drums. His accompaniment style was relentless, and even the best players had to be on their toes to keep up with him. He was never really the jazz world's most subtle or versatile drummer, but what he played, he played exceedingly well and with spirit, until his death in 1990.

Art Blakey's style of drumming set a new precedent for jazz percussionists. During the other musicians' solos, Blakey would spur them on with a drum roll when they seemed to be running out of inspiration.

Other Hard Bop Players

Max Roach was another hugely influential bebop and hard bop drummer. He and Kenny Clarke were the first drummers to spell out the pulse of a groove with the ride cymbal to get a lighter texture. This gave them more freedom to explore their drum kits, and to drop random snare 'bombs' while allowing the frontline virtuosos to play with greater freedom at faster speeds. Roach possessed a broader range than Blakey; he was capable of creating a furious drive. He was also very creative with his use of silence, using cymbals as gongs and handling the brushes as deftly as the sticks.

Sonny Rollins, one of jazz's most influential and most-loved saxophonists, also played a key role in the development of hard bop. Rollins started out on the piano before he permanently switched to the tenor sax in the mid-1940s. After a recording debut with Babs Gonzales in 1949, he worked with Miles Davis from 1951, Thelonious Monk from 1953 and the classic Max Roach-Clifford Brown quintet from 1955.

Hard Bop Style

This style typically incorporated a snare 'bomb'. Tempos became ever more frenetic and solos and chords ever more adventurous.

He became a band leader in 1956 and produced a series of brilliant recordings for Blue Note, Prestige, Contemporary and Riverside, including *Saxophone Colossus* (1956), *Tour De Force* (1957), *A Night At The Village Vanguard* (1957) and *Our Man In Jazz* (1962). Rollins was such a good soloist that Miles Davis once called him 'the greatest tenor ever', and a sax player cannot get a better compliment than that! Other notable hard bop saxophonists who helped to expand the style included Julian 'Cannonball' Adderley, John Coltrane and, more recently, Michael Brecker.

The trumpet was also a prominent instrument in hard bop, and some of the trumpeters who played it were exceptional musicians. Freddie Hubbard, one of the all-time great trumpeters, made a number of acclaimed recordings with Sonny Rollins, Philly Joe Jones (drummer) and Slide Hampton (trombonist), while Art Farmer's trumpet gave a lyrical feel to recordings by the Horace Silver Quintet and the Gerry Mulligan Quartet during the mid-to-late 1950s. The electric guitar was not originally a prominent instrument in hard bop, but Wes Montgomery's great soloing on *The Incredible Jazz Guitar Of Wes Montgomery* (1960) and *Smokin' At The Half Note* (1965) influenced a later generation of jazz guitar giants, including Pat Metheny and Mike Stern.

Sonny Rollins (left) and Max Roach (standing, centre) played some incredible music together that was not always popular with the critics, but was admired by peers such as Miles Davis.

Free Jazz

Free jazz is seen by many as an avant-garde art form rather than a type of jazz, with its unpredictable rhythm and chord progressions. Evolving out of bebop in the 1940s and 1950s the exponents of free jazz abandoned traditional forms to expand the music's creative possibilities.

The first documented free jazz recordings were made by the pianist Lennie Tristano and his band for Capitol Records in 1949. He asked the other players to ignore keys, chord structures, time signatures and melodies for the sessions, and just focus on 'reading into each others' minds'. Capitol were not exactly happy about this, but they released the sessions as *Crosscurrents* (1949). Tristano was a pioneer; his unique contrapuntal and improvisational ideas inspired other bebop musicians to try expanding the boundaries of jazz.

'I have always wanted musicians to play on a multiple level with me. I don't want them to follow me. I want them to follow themselves, but to be with me at the same time.'

Ornette Coleman

Radical Thinking

Although Tristano and his fellow musicians had been indulging in free jazz improvisation in the 1940s, the term free jazz was not used in earnest until the saxophonist Ornette Coleman released his first album in 1958. Coleman started out by playing Charlie Parker-style alto sax in Fort Worth, Texas, during the 1940s, before he moved to Los Angeles in 1950. He worked there as a lift operator, studied music theory and developed some radical ideas about jazz composition. Although these ideas were initially rejected by most of Los Angeles' jazz elite, Coleman eventually found enough allies to form a band: Don Cherry (trumpet), Don Payne (bass), Walter Norris (piano) and Billy Higgins (drums). They recorded *Something Else!!!!* (1958), an original collection of atonal jazz compositions, for Contemporary Records, and it took the jazz world by storm. Coleman's next record, *The Shape Of Jazz To Come* (1959), featured himself, Cherry and Higgins with bassist Charlie Haden. This trimmed-down band line-up showed more focus and a better realization of Coleman's vision. The next offering, *Free Jazz* (1960), was the album that gave the style its name, although Coleman denied later that he had any intention of naming the new type of music he had been developing.

Rumour has it that when gigging with Pee Wee Crayton's band in 1953, Ornette Coleman was paid to forfeit his solos, as audiences would stop dancing when he began to play.

Coleman and Taylor

Coleman's music was nothing short of revolutionary. He used traditional instrumentation and his music swung in a relatively conventional way, but the manner in which he dealt with tonality was extremely unusual.

His tunes were based around quirky bebop motifs, and he would use the overall tonality of these to create space for unusually free and expressive solos. Traditional jazz critics initially dismissed this music as 'anti-jazz' because it did not fit in with their conceptions of what jazz should sound like. Nowadays, though, Coleman is seen as a true jazz pioneer, on a par with the likes of Charlie Parker, Louis Armstrong and Miles Davis.

Key Artists

Ornette Coleman
John Coltrane
Eric Dolphy
Cecil Taylor
Lennie Tristano

A seminal figure in the free jazz movement was Cecil Taylor who was inspired by Fats Waller's single-note melodies and Dave Brubeck's chord clusters, and went on to develop what many critics consider to be one of the most extraordinary jazz piano techniques ever heard; recordings such as *Jazz Advance* (1956), *Looking Ahead!* (1958) and *The World Of Cecil Taylor* (1960) featured highly original versions of standards and atonal tunes, the likes of which had never been heard before. Taylor's approach was very different to Coleman's, as Whitney Balliett once observed in *The New Yorker*: 'Coleman's music is accessible, but he is loath to share it; Taylor's music is difficult, and he is delighted to share it'. 'The American aesthetic landscape is littered with idiosyncratic marvels – Walt Whitman, Charles Ives, D. W. Griffith, Duke Ellington, Jackson Pollock – and Taylor belongs with them,' Balliett continued.

Cecil Taylor was a leading figure in free jazz until his success was eclipsed by the advent of Ornette Coleman in 1959.

From Coltrane to Braxton

Possibly the most influential free jazz player to emerge during the late 1950s was John Coltrane. Unlike Coleman, 'Trane was already a well-known figure in the mainstream jazz scene; he had played on seminal recordings by Dizzy Gillespie and Miles Davis.

While Coleman was defining his art by reducing jazz's tonal base to its bare essence, Coltrane increased the complexity of jazz harmony many times over with his *Giant Steps* (1959) recording. He also began to explore modal jazz concepts, and recorded a series of more progressively 'free' jazz albums up until his premature death at the age of 40 in 1967. Other notable free jazz musicians from this period include multiple reed player Eric Dolphy, saxophonist Albert Ayler and the eccentric keyboard playing band leader, Sun Ra, who claimed to have arrived here on Earth from Saturn on a date that cannot be revealed because of its mystical astrological significance!

Free Jazz Style

Free jazz disposes of the inhibitions of diatonic harmony and regular rhythm, relying instead on musicians' interaction. Less standard playing techniques are often used.

Free jazz developed throughout the early 1960s and 1970s as a growing number of new players such as the Art Ensemble of Chicago and David Murray in the US; Keith Tippett, Steve Beresford, Elton Dean, Trevor Watts, Ian Coxhill and Maggie Nichols amongst others in the UK; Peter Brotzmann and Peter Kowald in Germany; and in the Netherlands' Willem Breuker, Misha Mengleberg and Han Bennick decided to follow in the footsteps of Coleman, Coltrane and Taylor, throwing original ideas into the ever-filling free-jazz pot. Derek Bailey, an eccentric guitarist from the UK, pioneered the use of unusual guitar effects and developed a highly idiosyncratic style, completely avoiding conventional melodies, chords or rhythms while Anthony Braxton and Steve Lacy coaxed extraordinary textures out of saxophones and clarinets, on solo and ensemble recordings. These and other free jazz exponents are continuing to produce original and challenging music.

John Coltrane's eagerness to experiment with chords and musical structure led to his being labelled 'eccentric' and even 'unmusical'.

Soul Jazz

Soul jazz stood out from other previous jazz forms. Its melodies were simpler and more rhythmic compared to hard bop, and influences from gospel and R&B were evident. In more traditional jazz forms, soloists would follow walking basslines or metric cymbal rhythms. In soul jazz, they followed a whole groove, which encouraged a different style of phrasing.

Soul jazz, also known as jazz-funk, can be traced back as far as the early 1950s, when Horace Silver was writing groovy jazz numbers for his now famous trio. One of their recordings, *Horace Silver Trio & Art Blakey* (1952), featured one of the earliest recorded jazz-funk tunes, 'Opus de Funk', which even helped to name the emerging style. The much celebrated hard-bop classic, *Horace Silver And The Jazz Messengers* (1954), also boasts a couple of funky little numbers, including 'The Preacher', one of Silver's most well-known tunes.

'Funky means earthy and blues-based. It might not be blues itself, but it does have that 'down-home' feel to it. Soul is basically the same, but there's an added dimension of feeling and spirit.'

Horace Silver

The music developed during the 1960s and 1970s within both the jazz and soul music fraternities, although the more modern sounds of fusion and smooth jazz were to overshadow it by the 1980s.

Horace Silver's relationship with the innovative Blue Note label lasted for 28 years. Blue Note is the most famous and influential jazz label and has remained open-minded about emerging jazz styles since it began in 1939.

King of the Organ

One of the first musicians to be associated with soul jazz was the legendary organist Jimmy Smith. Both of Jimmy's parents played the piano, so it was not long before he did too; he worked with his father in clubs during the 1940s and formed his own trio in 1955.

His brand of 'late night' soul jazz met with almost instant success, and albums such as *Home Cookin'* (1958), *Back At The Chicken Shack* (1960) and *Bashin'* (1962) inspired countless other Hammond B3 maestros, including 'Brother' Jack McDuff, Jimmy McGriff, Richard 'Groove' Holmes and Big John Patten. Smith's influence also extended to many major figures in rock and pop, including Steve Winwood, John Mayall, Georgie Fame, Brian Auger and Jon Lord of Deep Purple. After a string of hits in the 1960s, he went off the boil and recorded a series of unremarkable albums in the 1970s and 1980s. By then, though, his reputation as an influential pioneer of soul-jazz organ was assured.

Key Artists

Horace Silver
Jimmy Smith
Cannonball Adderley
Lou Donaldson
Jack McDuff

Another soul jazz pioneer was the saxophonist Julian 'Cannonball' Adderley. Nicknamed 'Cannibal' at school because of his capacious liking for food, Julian changed this to 'Cannonball' during his early jazz years. He directed a local high school band during the early 1950s, formed his own jazz combo in 1956, and signed to Riverside Records in 1958. They produced a series of albums, often live, that contributed greatly to the soul jazz style. The first of these, *Somethin' Else* (1958), featured the legendary trumpeter Miles Davis as a sideman. In turn, Cannonball played alto sax on Miles's universally acclaimed *Kind Of Blue* (1959). The most influential Adderley soul jazz recordings were made a few years later, with keyboardist Joe Zawinul in the band; *Jazz Workshop Revisited* (1963) spawned a soul jazz classic in 'Mercy, Mercy, Mercy', penned by Zawinul. The keyboard player's electric piano sound became another recognizable texture in jazz-funk and fusion (he later formed Weather Report with the saxophonist Wayne Shorter).

Jimmy Smith has remained faithful to the Hammond organ sound despite advances in keyboard technology. His pioneering, bluesy style was influenced more by saxophonists than fellow keyboard players.

Cool, Velvet Tones

The guitar also began to appear in soul jazz music during the 1960s, and the velvet-toned Wes Montgomery, an exceptional soloist, often appeared with Jimmy Smith. Wes picked out melodies with his right thumb and fingers, a soft style which originally developed out of trying not to upset his neighbours!

His albums were among the first jazz recordings to appeal to a non-jazz public, but in 1968, at the peak of his popularity and aged only 43, he died suddenly of a heart attack. Kenny Burrell was another cool-toned player who graced countless soul jazz recordings during the 1960s and 1970s. His successful career, spanning six decades, has also encompassed hard bop and jazz funk, and his most popular album, *Midnight Blue* (1963), was cited as the main influence for Van Morrison's jazz-pop classic, *Moondance* (1970).

The Next Generations

Many new soul jazz and jazz funk artists began to appear during the 1970s. As the decade progressed, the music became more dance oriented. The guitarist/singer George Benson effortlessly switched between soulful and smooth jazz styles, and the organist Ronnie Foster emerged as a talented mainstream funk keyboardist, whose Blue Note records later became cult items among a younger generation of listeners raised on acid jazz.

Soul Jazz Style

Soul Jazz heralded a return to simple blues-influenced melodies and is characterized by melodic and rhythmic repetition.

A number of soul jazz hits appeared during the 1970s, one of the most famous of which is The Crusaders' 1979 classic 'Street Life'. The guest vocalist on the song was Randy Crawford, who also sang on Cannonball Adderley's *Big Man* (1975), released after the great saxophonist's death. Artists such as the pianist Ramsey Lewis and saxophonist Grover Washington Jr also produced a lot of lighter instrumental soul jazz during the 1970s and 1980s. Although jazz purists dismissed most of this as borderline muzak, it introduced soul jazz – and, indeed, jazz itself – to a wider audience.

Cannonball Adderley's (right) impassioned, open-hearted playing style ensured that he quickly shook off the inevitable, early comparisons to Charlie Parker and established his own role in the jazz scene.

e electronic jazz rock movement that emerged in the late 1960s. S
d the boundaries of both jazz and rock, while others focused on pr
hallow, 'background' music.

s a kind of
because Miles
ss of discovering
d developing it.'

es Brew)

Although fusion records have never sold in h
the style has remained popular within the m
during the past 30 years. The term 'musician
often used to describe the top exponents.

It is widely accepted that Miles Davis's *Bitch*
album was the first influential jazz rock reco
combined modal jazz with rock guitar and d
to a wider rock audience. The album featured an extraordinary se
g Joe Zawinul and Chick Corea (keyboards), Wayne Shorter (saxop
c guitar) and Lenny White (drums). These players went on to form
d influential fusion bands in the early 1970s: Weather Report (Zaw
Corea and White) and the Mahavishnu Orchestra (McLaughlin).

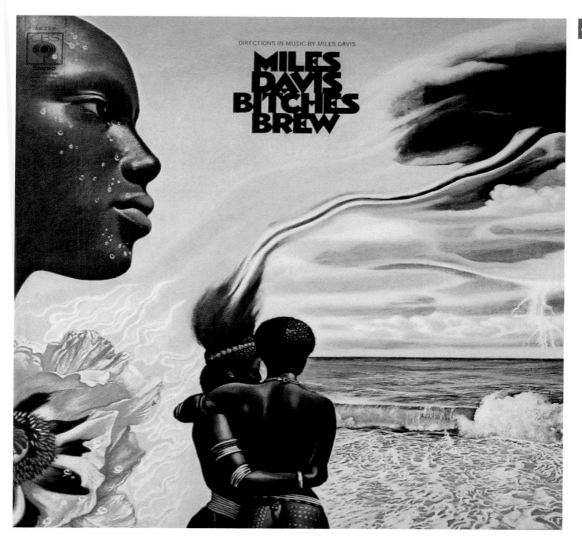

Weather Report and Mahavishnu

Weather Report was one of the most successful fusion bands, with albums reaching the Top 50 charts on both sides of the Atlantic. Their earliest recordings were patchy, but Black Market (1976) featured strong compositions and introduced the legendary Jaco Pastorius on bass guitar.

The combination of strikingly original tunes, Shorter's searing sax lines, Zawinul's colourful synth passages (played on Arp and Oberheim instruments) and Pastorius's jaw-dropping bass work (ranging from 'singing' melodic passages to unusual harmonics and ultra-fast riffs) proved to be an even bigger success with their next album, *Heavy Weather* (1977). Further recordings, such as *Mr Gone* (1978), *Night Passage* (1980) and *Weather Report* (1982), confirmed the band's status as a top-flight jazz act, although Pastorius left in 1982 and the band eventually split in 1986. Sadly, Pastorius died in 1987 after he was beaten up outside a nightclub in Fort Lauderdale, Florida.

The Mahavishnu Orchestra was more rock-oriented than Weather Report. Formed by John McLaughlin during the early 1970s and influenced by Eastern mysticism, the original band featured McLaughlin on electric guitar, along with Jan Hammer (keyboards), Jerry Goodman (violin), Rick Laird (bass) and Billy Cobham (drums). Their explosive creativity broke new boundaries in jazz, both in terms of virtuosity and complexity, and their albums *The Inner Mounting Flame* (1971) and *Birds of Fire* (1972) are widely regarded as fusion classics. Hammer, Goodman and Cobham left to work on their own projects a year later, and McLaughlin reformed the band with various other line-ups for the next two decades. He also formed Shakti, an exploratory 'Eastern' acoustic fusion band, with renowned Indian classical musicians such as L. Shankar (violin) and Zakir Hussain (tablas) during the mid-1970s, as well as a much-celebrated acoustic guitar trio with flamenco virtuoso Paco de Lucía and fusion ace Al Di Meola. The trio's live recording, *Friday Night In San Francisco* (1980), features some breathtakingly fleet guitar work that has to be heard to be believed.

Key Artists

Al Di Meola
Pat Metheny
Mahavishnu Orchestra
Weather Report
John Scofield

John McLaughlin (second from left) with the Mahavishnu Orchestra, whose 1971 album The Inner Mounting Flame *was a jazz landmark.*

Other Influential Bands

The other primary 1970s fusion band to directly emerge out of the *Bitches Brew* scene was Chick Corea's Return To Forever. Their first line-up was a Latin-style band led by Chick on keyboards, but by 1975 the group had developed into an all-out fusion outfit featuring Al Di Meola (guitar), Stanley Clarke (bass) and Lenny White (drums).

Their *Romantic Warrior* (1976) recording was a landmark jazz-rock album, featuring six complex, intricately crafted instrumentals that were to inspire rock and jazz musicians for years to come. It also acted as a launching pad for Di Meola's solo career; he went on to record *Land Of The Midnight Sun* (1976), *Elegant Gypsy* (1976), *Casino* (1977) and *Splendido Hotel* (1979), which resulted in *Guitar Player* magazine readers voting him Best Jazz Player for five consecutive years.

There were a number of other seminal fusion recordings made during the 1970s: *Believe It* (1975) by Tony Williams introduced Allan Holdsworth's unique but influential legato lead-guitar style; Frank Zappa's *Roxy & Elsewhere* (1974) fused jazz and rock with a warped, but much-loved sense of humour; and the Pat Metheny Group with its self-titled album (1978) forged a new, earthy jazz style that eventually earned the group huge audiences, critical acclaim and Grammy awards. Across the Atlantic, Brand X's *Unorthodox Behaviour* (1976) and Soft Machine's *Third* (1970) proved that British bands were also capable of producing world-class fusion, while the French and Belgians also showed their fusion mettle with violinist Jean-Luc Ponty's *Enigmatic Ocean* (1977) and Marc Moulin's *Placebo* (1973).

Jazz Rock Style

Jazz rock utilizes traditional jazz melodies and rhythms and uses rock instrumentation and electrification to create a typical 'fusion' sound.

By contrast, the 1980s were relatively quiet for fusion, although Corea, Holdsworth and the American guitarist John Scofield made some significant recordings during this period. In more recent years, Tribal Tech, led by guitarist Scott Henderson and bass virtuoso Gary Willis, has kept the fusion flag flying. Their recent recordings, *Thick* (1999) and *Rocket Science* (2000), show that jazz rock is still alive and kicking. The latest platform for 'jazz rock' has evolved into the 'jam band scene'.

An incredibly talented and versatile pianist, Chick Corea made forays into fusion jazz that were only a part, albeit an important one, of his musical output. He also peformed Latin and free jazz and music from the classical repertoire.

Acid Jazz

Acid jazz is a lively, groove-oriented music style that combines elements from jazz, funk and hip hop, with an emphasis on jazz dance. The term 'acid jazz' was first used during the late 1980s, both as the name of an American record label and the title of a British jazz funk, 'rare groove' compilation series.

Interest had originally been sparked by a thriving London club scene, where hip DJs were playing rare 1970s jazz funk records. This encouraged British and American underground musicians such as The Brand New Heavies, Jamiroquai, Stereo MC's, Galliano and Groove Collective, who began to popularize the style by the 1990s.

'Acid jazz was the most significant jazz form to emerge out of the British music scene.'

Q magazine, UK

One of the first DJs to be identified with acid jazz was the London-based Gilles Peterson, who began broadcasting jazz funk sets from his garden shed at home and DJing at London clubs in the late 1980s. He teamed up with Eddie Piller, who had previously released a debut album by a young, contemporary Hammond organ virtuoso, James Taylor, to form Acid Jazz Records. The label's first releases were a series of compilations titled *Totally Wired*, which alternated jazz funk obscurities from the 1970s with updated tracks from the new acid jazz movement. Peterson later formed his own acid jazz label, Talkin' Loud Records.

Mainstream Acid Jazz

Acid jazz entered into the mainstream in 1990, after The Brand New Heavies released their self-titled debut album on the Acid Jazz label. Formed in 1985 by drummer Jan Kincaid, guitarist Simon Bartholomew and bassist/keyboardist Andrew Levy – old school friends from London – they were originally an instrumental band inspired by James Brown and The Meters, whose records were getting extensive play around the rare groove scene. The band began recording their own material, added a singer and a brass section, and gained exposure via the club circuit. Their first album was a success and it was followed by a string of hit singles in 1991 in the UK and US. Then came *Heavy Rhyme Experience, Vol. 1* (1992), featuring guest appearances by the rappers Main Source, Gang Starr, Grand Puba and The Pharcyde. The following album, *Brother Sister* (1994), went platinum in Britain, and the band's success has since continued on both sides of the Atlantic with *Original Flava* (1994) and *Delicious* (1997).

N'Dea Davenport, as a member of the Brand New Heavies, was an important figure in the development of acid jazz. After leaving the band in 1994, she embarked on a solo career.

Acid Jazz on the Up

After the emergence of the Heavies, Galliano and a few smaller UK acid jazz bands, a spate of compilations were launched en masse by record labels, leaving many consumers confused over exactly what the style was or who played it.

The confusion increased when even more independent acid jazz communities began to spring up all over the US during the early 1990s. By then, the term could refer to anything from Jamiroquai's commercial soul funk to the James Taylor Quartet's rendering of the 'Starsky And Hutch Theme', or from the ethnic eclecticism of the Japanese producers United Future Organisation to the hip hop poetry of New York's Groove Collective.

Key Artists

The Brand New Heavies
Galliano
Jamiroquai
Courtney Pine
James Taylor Quartet

The creation of the UK singer/songwriter Jason Kay, Jamiroquai has perhaps popularized acid jazz more than any other band. Although some listeners today dismiss them as mere Stevie Wonder imitators, the band has experienced chart success all over the world with an irresistible blend of house rhythms and 1970s-era soul/funk. As he did not originally have a band to back up his songs, Jay came up with his own project and coined its moniker by adding the name of an American Indian tribe, Iroquois, to the music term 'jam'. He assembled a group of musicians and produced some demos, which impressed the Acid Jazz label enough to issue the debut single 'When You Gonna Learn?' in late 1992. A hit, it led to a long-term and lucrative recording contract with Sony, who released *Emergency On Planet Earth* (1992) and *The Return Of The Space Cowboy* (1994), both major hit albums in the UK. This success spread to America with Jamiroquai's third effort, *Travelling Without Moving* (1996), which contained the worldwide hit 'Virtual Insanity'. The band is still going strong, although they now appear to be past their prime.

Jason Kay has been largely responsible for bringing the acid jazz sound into the musical mainstream. The themes explored in his songs include the environment, government incompetence and space travel.

Cutting-Edge Jazz

A number of more 'serious' jazz artists, including the UK's Courtney Pine, the American veteran Pharaoh Sanders (saxophonists) and the American Pat Metheny (guitarist), were also associated with acid jazz forms during the 1990s. Pine and Sanders both contributed to a British compilation series titled Rebirth Of The Cool (named after the classic Miles Davis album Birth Of The Cool), while The Pat Metheny Group used hip hop-style grooves to great effect on their We Live Here (1995) album.

Nu Jazz

Since the 1990s, acid jazz has moved more left-field, evolving into the nu jazz (nu-fusion or future-jazz) movement via the house music-led club dance floor. The cutting edge, springing from the underground, has been exploited commercially by France's St Germain and even the 'establishment's' Herbie Hancock (*Future2Future,* 2002). A serious jazz vibe is being combined with percussion-led, acousto-electric keyboards and programmed beats transfused with the hip hop/drum 'n' bass repetitions of house music, Afro-Brazilian beats and live jazz. Leading the nu jazz field are labels such as Germany's Compost (Jazzanova, Beanfield, Les Gammas, Kyoto Jazz Massive and Minus 8) and UK's 'West London collective' working with producer-DJ IG Culture and artists such as Kaidi Tatham, Modaji and Seiji. In nu jazz, vocalists are coming into their own again, high in both profile and mix – Vikter Duplaix, Robert Owens, Peven Everett and Ursula Rucker in the US, Victor Davies, Joseph Malik, Kate Phillips (Bembé Segué) and Marcus Begg in the UK and Europe.

Acid Jazz Style

Acid jazz artists have effectively cross-fertilized jazz harmonies and melodies with funk basslines and dance orientated drum patterns.

Producers collaborating with live musicians are mixing (today's technological equivalent of scoring/arranging), remixing and sampling to brilliant effect, and new technology is opening up even more possibilities for jazz. Indeed, as Sun Ra predicted as long ago as 1972, 'Space Is The Place', especially for the MP3 generation.

The James Taylor Quartet has kept acid jazz alive through continual gigging and recording. They have also been involved in writing film music, including the theme to Austin Powers: International Man Of Mystery.

Smooth Jazz

Slick, 'radio-friendly' smooth jazz emerged in the 1970s, and it has continued to evolve ever since. The most artful examples can make for rewarding listening, while blander compositions can be recognized by any combination of musical clichés: light funk grooves, cool jazz chords, slapped bass lines, corny horn accompaniments and predictable solos.

The style has drawn fierce criticism from jazz purists, but its unobtrusiveness has often made it popular with restaurants, wine bars and other public places where sophisticated-sounding background music is required to give clients or customers a chill-out vibe.

'Kenny G has long been the musician many jazz listeners love to hate.'

All Music Guide

Many would use the term 'fusion' to describe smooth jazz, even though the same word is more commonly used to describe the more exploratory jazz rock scene that emerged out of Miles Davis's *Bitches Brew* period. This seems rather contradictory, as smooth jazz is normally cool background music while jazz rock is often complex and demanding. But it probably explains why jazz rock fans tend to pour scorn over even the most distinguished smooth jazz acts whenever they are mentioned.

There are many who would dispute the music of Kenny G deserving the name jazz; to his credit he prefers to describe his music as 'instrumental pop'. His records are popular as relaxing background music.

Cool Sounds in the Seventies

The earliest smooth jazz artists were musicians who wanted to make more commercial, accessible music without losing their jazz roots. Born in Pittsburgh, Pennsylvania on 22 March, 1943, George Benson is perhaps the best example.

His stepfather was a musician who taught him to play the ukulele and guitar, and after being enticed by the jazz sounds of saxophonist Charlie Parker and guitarist Grant Green, he decided to become a jazz guitarist. He emerged as a popular soloist in the style of Wes Montgomery, and played alongside top artists such as Herbie Hancock, Jack McDuff and Ron Carter during the 1960s. In the 1970s, he switched over to a more commercial, jazz funk style, and was rewarded with serious album sales. *Breezin'* (1976) sold more than two million units and was the first of several Grammy-winning recordings with Warner Brothers, while *In Flight* (1976) was a polished album that featured Benson – an accomplished vocalist – 'scat' singing in unison with his trademark cool solos. He switched to a more overtly pop vocal sound during the 1980s, to the disgust of some jazz purists, but he later compensated by recording with Count Basie's old band in 1990.

Key Artists

George Benson
Kenny G
Spyro Gyra
Steely Dan
Yellowjackets

Benson's popularity inspired other jazz guitarists to go 'smooth' during the 1970s. Earl Klugh appeared with acoustic guitar albums, including the acclaimed *Earl Klugh* (1976) and *Finger Painting* (1977), while Lee Ritenour produced Latin-influenced recordings such as *Guitar Player* (1976) and *Captain Fingers* (1977), and Larry Carlton delighted listeners with his excellent soloing on *Larry Carlton* (1977). Keyboard players were at it too, with Herbie Hancock using electronically synthesized vocals on *Sunlight* (1977), Ramsey Lewis producing slick recordings such as *Tequila Mockingbird* (1978) and George Duke recording many albums, including his critically acclaimed *Solo Keyboard Album* (1976). On the band side, Spyro Gyra delivered the infectious *Morning Dance* (1979) and even jazz rock heroes Steely Dan fully developed their own unique and sophisticated brand of jazz pop on the albums *Aja* (1977) and *Gaucho* (1980).

The musically open-minded guitarist George Benson infuriated jazz fans with his covers of pop records, but he refuses to be constricted by what is expected of him, explaining that his first duty is as an entertainer.

Further Refinements

Some of the most polished, artistic and commercial examples of smooth jazz emerged during the 1980s and 1990s. Perhaps the most respected band in this period was the Yellowjackets. They formed in 1977, when the guitarist Robben Ford assembled a group of veteran session musicians to work on one of his albums.

Ford and the trio of musicians – keyboardist Russell Ferrante, bassist Jimmy Haslip and drummer Ricky Lawson – enjoyed working together, hence the Yellowjackets. Ford and Lawson left after two well-received albums, but the band continued to refine its sound: by the late 1980s, recordings such as *Politics* (1988) and *The Spin* (1989) demonstrated that they were already a cut above most other smooth jazz bands in terms of artistry. By the mid-1990s, they had developed a definitive smooth jazz sound on the albums *Greenhouse* (1991), *Like A River* (1992) and *Blue Hats* (1997). They are still going strong, and their lively 2002 *Mint Jam* album (Heads Up label) featured among the 2003 Grammy nominations.

Smooth Jazz Style

Smooth Jazz rejects ensemble pieces in favour of unchallenging melodies played by one or two principle instruments.

At the more commercial end of the musical spectrum, Kenny Gorelick (Kenny G) has been introducing larger pop audiences to smooth jazz. He began playing professionally with Barry White in 1976, and, after graduating from the University of Washington, worked with the keyboardist Jeff Lorber before signing to Arista as a solo artist in 1982. His first three albums were moderately successful, but his fourth, *Duotones* (1986), hit the big time with a hugely popular instrumental hit, 'Songbird'. Since then, he has released a succession of popular smooth jazz albums, which have sold more than 30 million copies and annoyed jazz purists who consider them innocuous and one-dimensional. Various other smooth jazz bands, such as the Rippingtons, Fattburger and Acoustic Alchemy, as well as solo artists such as Joyce Cooling, Dave Koz and Boney James, have helped to maintain the popularity of this style.

Donald Fagan, whose distinctive vocals added yet another unusual dimension to the logic-defying band Steely Dan. Their music is an obscure but strangely accessible combination of jazz, rock and pop, with a hint of country.

Latin Jazz

Latin jazz is commonly defined as the fusion of American jazz melodies, improvisation and chords with Latin American rhythms, predominantly those of Afro-Cuban origin. How this marriage of styles occurred is also one of the most significant cultural, musical exchanges in history.

Mention the birth of Latin jazz to any aficionado of the art form and they will invariably reply with two names: Machito and Mario Bauzá. The former was born Francisco Raul Gutiérrez Grillo on 16 February 1912, in Cuba. The young vocalist/maraca man hit New York City in 1937, where he played stints with Xavier Cugat and Noro Morales before forming his own band, Machito's Afro-Cubans. By 1940, Machito asked his brother-in-law, Mario Bauzá (who was married to his sister Estella), a trumpeter, pianist, arranger and composer who had already worked with the likes of Dizzy Gillespie and Chick Webb, to be his band's musical arranger. It was this orchestra that two American musicians – one in Los Angeles, one in New York City – would hear, and the musical world would never be the same again.

'We play jazz with the Latin touch, that's all, you know.'

Tito Puente

The Night that Changed Dizzy's Life

On 31 May 1943, the already legendary Gillespie went to the Park Place Ballroom in New York. There, he heard Machito and his orchestra perform 'Tanga' (meaning marijuana), a dazzling new Afro-Cuban composition written by Bauzá during a rehearsal. The piece is widely recognized to be a breakthrough in the creation of a new style of music, which has been called Afro-Cuban jazz, Cubop and Latin jazz, a term Bauzá reportedly hated. Still, Gillespie would often recall that night as one that changed his life. The trumpet virtuoso was so taken with the conga, bongos, and 'clave' rhythms that he immediately incorporated them into his own group.

Harlem-born Puerto Rican Tito Puente's arrangements of the mambo and cha-cha earned him admiration across a wide cultural sphere. He recorded over a hundred albums and has a star on the Hollywood Walk of Fame.

Wider Audiences

In January 1946, the influential American pianist/bandleader Stan Kenton was awestruck when he heard the same 'Tanga' at a club in Los Angeles. Soon, he too added Latin elements to virtually all of his music.

Gillespie made Latin music history himself with his 30 December 1947 recording of 'Manteca' on RCA Victor, which he co-wrote with a musician introduced to him by Bauzá. It was the master conguero Chano Pozo, another seminal figure in the birth of Latin jazz and the key figure in Gillespie's continued 'latinization' of jazz. 'Manteca' would subsequently become Gillespie's signature tune and one of the most covered standards in the history of the genre.

Following closely behind Machito, Pozo, Gillespie and Kenton is master timbalero, bandleader and composer Tito Puente, also known as El Rey del Timbal and The Mambo King. Born in New York to Puerto Rican parents, Puente was instrumental in taking jazz to a broader audience thanks to his big band orchestrations and his on stage flourish. And, of course, he wrote and recorded 'Oye Cómo Va', later popularized by Carlos Santana, which incorporated a coro section and used other eminently Latin elements, such as a charanga-style flute and, of course, the characteristic syncopated piano cha-cha riff.

Key Artists

Machito
Mario Bauzá
Tito Puente
Eddie Palmieri
Chano Pozo

Another pioneer who took Latin jazz to the mainstream was master conguero Ramón 'Mongo' Santamaría, best known for his hit rendition of Herbie Hancock's 'Watermelon Man' and for authoring jazz standard 'Afro Blue'. It was with Santamaria's band, that a then-young Chick Corea first received major exposure, while present-day conguero Poncho Sánchez cites Santamaría as his mentor and major influence.

Mario Bauzá started out as a professional clarinet and oboe player in the Havana Philharmonic before moving to New York in 1930. It was there, while playing with Noble Sissle, that he took up the trumpet.

A New Generation

Other direct descendants of Machito and Bauzá – Latin jazz's founding fathers – include brothers Charlie and Eddie Palmieri, born in New York to Puerto Rican parents. Both of them pianists, composers, bandleaders and arrangers, they created their separate bands and helped shape the New York salsa sound.

While Eddie is best known for his work with his band La Perfecta, which incorporated trombones and trumpets, Charlie revived the concept of the *descarga* (Latin jam session) originally popularized by veteran Cuban bassist Israel López 'Cachao'. Largely forgotten in the 1980s, Cachao lived a brilliant revival in the mid-1990s when he was rediscovered by Cuban-born Hollywood film star Andy García, who directed a documentary on Cachao's life, *Cachao: como su ritmo no hay dos*. Later on, García would also be involved in a film project based on the life of another Cuban musician, trumpeter Arturo Sandoval. Those two projects, coupled with the 2000 film *Calle 54*, which features a series of Latin jazz performances by the likes of Jerry González and the Fort Apache Band, Cuban percussionist Patato Valdés and fellow countryman and pianist Chucho Valdés, has renewed interest in the genre. Currently, pianist Valdés is the elder statesman of a new generation of highly virtuosic Latin jazz pianists, including Gonzalo Rubalcaba, who freely blend American standards with Cuban rhythms and are also highly experimental in their own compositions.

Latin Jazz Style

A growing Hispanic population in the US brought with them latin percussion rhythms, such as uptempo sambas, which blended with traditional jazz melodies to produce Latin jazz.

Other current leaders of the movement include Sandoval and countryman Paquito D'Rivera, who, like Valdés, were once members of experimental Cuban jazz ensemble Irakere, and are currently living in the US. D'Rivera in particular, expanded beyond his brand of Afro-Cuban jazz to delve extensively in to other styles of Latin jazz, incorporating rhythms from Venezuela, Peru and Puerto Rico into his music.

The openness to rhythms outside of Cuba is congruent with the rise of several Latin jazz musicians from other countries, including pianists Danilo Pérez (Panama) and Michel Camilo (Dominican Republic).

Machito (right) inspired players such as Dizzy Gillespie and Stan Kenton to experiment with Latin sounds. Kenton described him as the 'greatest exponent of Afro-Cuban jazz' and even named a track after him.

Brazilian Jazz

In the mid-1950s, a cultural crossfertilization of Brazilian samba rhythms, American cool jazz and sophisticated harmonies led to the development of bossa nova. In the early 1960s the bossa nova movement swept through the United States and Europe producing a strain of Brazilian-influenced jazz that remains a vital part of the jazz scene.

By the early 1950s, a few pioneering Brazilian composers began listening seriously to American jazz, particularly the limpid-toned west coast variety practised by Chet Baker, Gerry Mulligan and Shorty Rogers. In absorbing that cool influence, composers such as Antonio Carlos Jobim, João Gilberto, Baden Powell and Luiz Bonfá stripped the complex polyrhythms of Afro-Brazilian samba down to their undulating essence and offered a more intimate approach, in which melodies were caressed rather than belted out in the raucous Carnival fashion.

'I just thought it was pretty music. I never thought it would be a hit.'

Stan Getz on his first involvement with Brazilian music, the album *Jazz Samba*

Around the same time, American jazz saxophonist Bud Shank (from the west coast branch of cool jazz) had joined forces with Brazilian guitarist Laurindo Almeida in a quartet that blended Brazilian rhythms and folk melodies with cool jazz improvising. Recorded five years before the term 'bossa nova' was even coined, their 1953 collaboration on the World Pacific label, *Brazilliance*, would have a significant impact on the ultimate architects of the bossa nova movement.

Black Orpheus was an updating of the Orpheus & Eurydice myth, set against the background of a Brazilian Carnival. The intense vitality of the music in the film fascinated viewers and the soundtrack sold in the millions.

Blame it on the Bossa Nova

In 1956, the Bahian guitarist/composer João Gilberto relocated from Salvador to Rio de Janeiro, where the colourful cultural mix was inspiring another brilliant guitarist/composer, Antonio Carlos Jobim. The two began to collaborate, and in July 1958, Gilberto recorded Jobim and Vinícius de Moraes's 'Chega de Saudade' ('No More Blues'), which became the hit single (backed by his own 'Bim Bom') widely considered to be responsible for launching the bossa nova movement in Brazil.

Their follow-up single, Jobim's 'Desafinado' ('Off-Key') was a fully formed masterpiece that floated on Gilberto's distinctive, syncopated guitar rhythm, which would become the basis for this new, hybrid form. Momentum for the movement picked up the following year with the popularity of the Oscar-winning film *Black Orpheus*, a romance set in Rio de Janeiro during Carnival, featuring a beguiling score by Jobim and fellow Brazilian guitarist/composer Luiz Bonfá, and introducing such enduring bossa nova anthems as 'Manhã de Carnaval' and 'Samba de Orfeo'. Then, in 1960, Gilberto and Jobim recorded 12 original bossa nova pieces on the largely overlooked Capitol release, *Samba de Uma Note So*.

Key Artists

João Gilberto
Antonio Carlos Jobim
Charles Byrd
Laurindo Almeida
Luiz Bonfá

Meanwhile, this 'quiet revolution' continued to unfold. In 1961, the US State Department sponsored a good-will jazz tour of Latin America that included American guitarist Charlie Byrd. A swing through Brazil on that tour was a revelation to Byrd, igniting the guitarist's love affair with bossa nova. Back in the States, Byrd played some bossa nova tapes to his friend, the soft-toned tenor saxophonist Stan Getz, who then convinced Creed Taylor at Verve to record an album of the alluring Brazilian music with himself and Byrd. Their historic 1962 collaboration, *Jazz Samba*, introduced the bossa nova sound to mass North American audiences. *Jazz Samba* enjoyed immense popularity on the strength of the hit single, Jobim's 'Desafinado' ('Off-Key'), prompting a rush by American jazz record labels to repeat its success, which produced a flood of copycat releases between 1962 and 1963, including Gene Ammons' *Bad! Bossa Nova*, Dave Brubeck's *Bossa Nova USA*, Herbie Mann's *Do The Bossa Nova With Herbie Mann* and Eddie Harris' *Bossa Nova*.

Versed in rural blues as a boy, Charlie Byrd turned to jazz in 1945 after meeting Django Reinhardt in Paris.

A Universally Appealing Message

In 1963, Jobim and Gilberto came to New York to collaborate with Stan Getz on another bossa nova classic, Getz/Gilberto. The album made Gilberto an international superstar and also introduced his then-wife, the singer Astrud Gilberto, whose seductive vocals graced the mega-hit single, 'The Girl From Ipanema', written by Jobim and Vinícius de Moraes. At this time, de Moraes was also working with the influential guitarist Baden Powell, composing a number of important Afro-sambas, paying tribute to the African tradition in Brazilian music.

Getz's recorded output for Verve during the bossa nova craze also included a collaboration with bandleader/arranger Gary McFarland (1962's Big Band Bossa Nova), guitarist/composer Luiz Bonfá (1963's Jazz Samba Encore!) and guitarist/ bossa nova pioneer Laurindo Almeida (1963's Stan Getz With Guest Artist Laurindo Almeida). All of Getz's important recordings in this genre have been compiled on a five-CD set by Verve, entitled The Bossa Nova Years (Girl From Ipanema).

Brazilian Jazz Style

The standard Bossa Nova drum pattern features an off-beat counter rhythm played by the sidestick over two bars.

While Getz passed away in 1991, Gilberto continues to perform and record. Today, the veteran architect of Brazil's bossa nova movement is known in his native country as simply O Mito (The Legend). His 2000 recording, João Voz E Violão, is stripped down to the bare essentials – João's magnificent voice and his silky-sounding guitar accompaniment.

The alluring sound of bossa nova has continued to thrive over the past four decades. Its universally appealing message has been and is continuing to be spread by prominent Brazilian artists such as singer-composers Milton Nascimento and Ivan Lins; pianist/composer/orchestrator Hermeto Pascoal; pianist/vocalist Eliane Elias; vocalists Joyce and Flora Purim; guitarists Toninho Horta, Carlos Barbosa-Lima, Oscar Castro-Neves and Baden Powell; percussionist Airto Moreira; and the group Trio da Paz (comprised of guitarist Romero Lubambo, bassist Nilson Matta and drummer Duduka da Fonseca), as well as by scores of jazz artists all over the world.

Jobim's prolific songwriting and adaptability to concert hall performances led to comparisons with George Gershwin. His studio albums showcase his gentle strumming technique and haunting vocals.

INFLUENCES OF JAZZ

Over the course of the twentieth century and into the twenty-first, popular music has continued to grow, divide and branch out as a genre, as the influences of diverse sounds, regions and eras have shaped and informed countless new musical styles. Jazz music has always been a forward-thinking and constantly evolving creative force, and so it is perhaps unsurprising that such a wide range of musical styles developed during the last 100 years owe much to its influence.

Jazz and blues share some early influences, and each style has continued to the other, even as they have developed in their own directions. Boogie woogie is a style that straddles both genres, with major exponents falling into both camps. In the 1930s, country music blended with jazz strains to create the hugely popular western swing style performed by the likes of Bob Wills and Milton Brown. Gospel music, in its early days, crossed paths with jazz, while jazz influences were also apparent in the work of the Broadway songsmiths in the first half of the twentieth century, and in musical theatre's bawdier cousin, the cabaret style.

The soulful intonations and sophisticated instrumentation of jazz had a profound influence on the development of soul and R&B music: in particular the northern soul music of late 1960s Britain and, later, the jazzy funk sound that seemed at one stage almost omnipresent during the 1970s. Elements of this jazz influence can still be heard in the contemporary R&B music recorded today.

Jazz has also reached out to inspire more diverse genres such as the relaxed yet inventive strains of lounge and easy listening music, the weird and wonderful compositions of psychedelic rock and the dance-friendly, bouncing beats of ska.

By the 1970s funk dominated Afro-American music and jazz musicians began to incorporate its rhythms. One of the best funk albums was Funkadelic's 1968 One Nation Under A Groove.

Boogie-Woogie

A rollicking, fast piano style characterized by repetitive eighth-note bass figures in the left hand, meshed with sharp, bluesy single-note runs in the right hand, boogie-woogie was an infectious form that had an immediate appeal to dancers.

Although the boogie-woogie fad swept the nation in the late 1930s, its roots go back much further. Jelly Roll Morton and W. C. Handy recalled hearing boogie-woogie-style piano in the American South during the first decade of the twentieth century. By the 1920s, boogie-woogie pianists were making their mark in saloons, juke joints, honky-tonks and at rent parties throughout both the South and North, where their powerfully rhythmic attack could cut through the din of a good time.

One of the pioneers of this raucous piano style was Jimmy Yancey. Born in 1894 in Chicago, he worked in vaudeville as a singer and tap dancer before taking up the piano in 1915. Although he did not make a recording until 1939, his most famous student, Meade 'Lux' Lewis, would become one of the first to document the boogie-woogie piano style on record with his 1927 'Honky Tonk Train Blues', a masterpiece of intricate cross-rhythms that highlights Lewis's remarkable independence between hands.

'They played a rolling rhythm in the left hand so that they could reach for a drink or a sandwich with the right hand.'

Donald Clark, *The Rise and Fall of Popular Music*

That same year, Pine Top Smith garnered attention with his catchy 'Pine Top's Boogie-Woogie', in which the pianist shouts instructions to dancers over the top of his rolling keyboard work. The hit tune also featured the rhythmic 'breaks' that were an essential part of early ragtime.

From Spirituals to Swing

In 1938, a single event helped bring boogie-woogie to wider public exposure. Jazz impresario John Hammond, a producer and talent scout who had a keen interest in boogie-woogie piano, arranged to have Lewis and fellow boogie-woogie pianists Albert Ammons and Pete Johnson appear on the bill of his From Spirituals To Swing concert, held at Carnegie Hall on 23 December 1938. The gala event not only helped launch the boogie-woogie boom but also led directly to the formation of Blue Note Records by the German immigrant Alfred Lion.

Meade 'Lux' Lewis, whose performance at 1938's Spirituals To Swing concert helped kick-start the boogie-woogie craze.

Down-Home Humour

Lion pressed 50 copies each of two 78rpm singles, one by Ammons, the other by Lewis. There followed other sessions with the two boogie-woogie pianists, including an innovative 1941 session with Lewis on celeste, Charlie Christian on guitar, Edmond Hall on clarinet and Israel Crosby on bass.

Ammons recorded in the 1940s with the blues singer Sippie Wallace and in 1949 he cut a session with his son, the great tenor saxophonist Gene Ammons, before passing away later that year. Lewis continued playing after the boogie-woogie craze died down, relocating to Los Angeles and recording until 1962. Pete Johnson, the third member of the Big Three of boogie-woogie (the others being Albert Ammons and Meade Lux Lewis), forged a musical rapport with his Kansas City compatriot, blues shouter Big Joe Turner, releasing popular recordings such as 'Roll 'Em Pete' and 'Cafe Society Rag'. He spent 1947–49 in Los Angeles before moving to Buffalo in 1950 and, subsequently, drifting into obscurity.

Born the year Meade Lux Lewis cut his first tracks, Amos Milburn was a jovial boogie-woogie disciple who picked up the torch and ran with it. The Houston-born pianist pounded out some of the most explosive boogie grooves of the post-war era, beginning in 1946 on the Los Angeles-based Aladdin label. His first hits included the driving, countrified boogie of 'Down The Road Apiece' (covered in 1960 by Chuck Berry and in 1965 by the Rolling Stones). Milburn excelled at good-natured, upbeat romps about booze and partying, imbued with a vibrant sense of humour and double entendre, as well as vivid, down-home imagery in his lyrics. He scored successive Top 10 R&B hits with 1948's 'Chicken Shack Boogie', 1949's 'Roomin' House Boogie', 1950's 'Bad, Bad Whiskey' and 1953's 'One Scotch, One Bourbon, One Beer'.

Key Artists

Albert Ammons
Pete Johnson
Meade 'Lux' Lewis
Amos Milburn
Jimmy Yancey

Milburn's frantic piano-pumping style would have a profound effect on seminal rock'n'rollers such as Floyd Dixon, Fats Domino, Little Richard and Jerry Lee Lewis in the early 1950s. That boogie-woogie piano lineage continues today with explosive players such as Marcia Ball, Billy C. Wirtz and Mitch Woods.

Amos Milburn (piano) & his Chicken Shackers, as the group called themselves after the runaway success of their hit 'Chicken Shack Boogie'.

Western Swing

Western swing is an innovative, free-wheeling yet complex instrumental amalgam drawn from blues, jazz and Dixieland syncopations and harmonies. Central to the style is an emphasis on instrumental solos, often involving the transposition of jazz-style horn parts to fiddle, guitar and steel guitar.

It is indicative of western swing's sophistication that Bob Wills' Texas Playboys, the definitive western swing band, included at various times a Dixieland drummer (Smokey Dacus), a jazz piano player (Al Stricklin) and a jazz-flavoured guitarist (Eldon Shamblin). Wills' innovations with his long-time band the Texas Playboys were crucial to the emergence of this hybrid music that merged horns and the improvisatory spirit of jazz big bands with country fiddle music and elements of honky tonk instrumentation like the electric guitar, steel guitar and twin fiddles.

Rivaling Wills' influence in establishing and propagating early western swing was his fellow Texan Milton Brown. Brown and his band the Musical Brownies were pioneers of a number of the genre's essential ingredients, including New Orleans jazz rhythms, twin fiddles playing in harmony, slap-bass fiddle playing and some of the earliest uses of electrified instruments in country music. Brown, just as importantly, brought a smooth and rhythmic vocal style to western swing that drew more heavily from jazz masters like Jack Teagarden and Cab Calloway than from country sources.

'When dancers spotted the Texas Playboys ... what they saw was a traditional country string band. What they heard, however, was a new kind of jazz band.'

Charles Townsend

Bob Wills' career began modestly in 1929 when a trio he'd formed landed a spot on a Fort Worth, Texas radio station. In the early 1930s Wills added additional players to his band, which was called at various times the Aladdin Laddies, the Light Crust Doughboys and finally, in 1934 the Texas Playboys. Four years later, he had boosted the band to 14 members, but by 1935 Wills assembled what some consider to be the most talented line-up of Playboys. In the next few years, he added an entire six-man horn section. He soon was recording some of the songs that have endured as western swing's universal standards, including 'Time Changes Everything', 'San Antonio Rose', 'Take Me Back To Tulsa' and 'Cherokee Maiden'.

The cover of the first LP reissue of Milton Brown's recordings, released almost two decades after his untimely death.

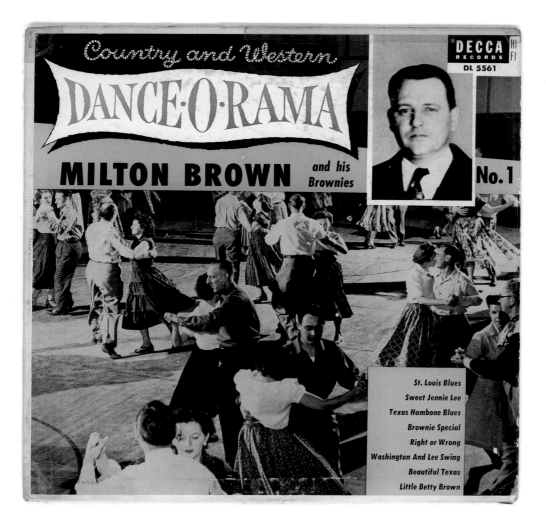

Bob Wills is Still the King

Wills' popularity continued throughout most of the 1940s and the personnel shifts continued. In the late 1940s, he added the brilliant Texas fiddler Johnny Gimble to the Playboys' line-up and employed his brother Billy Jack Wills as his vocalist.

As Wills' popularity had begun to spread in the 1930s, the Texas Playboys became the inspiration for a number of other talented western swing bands. Many of these were led by former Texas Playboys like Leon McAuliffe, Jesse Ashlock and Wills' brothers Lee and Billy Jack. The western swing sound even spread as far afield as Kentucky, where a band called the Prairie Ramblers picked up on it. However, practically all these bands borrowed heavily from Wills' arrangements and repertoire and never quite escaped his long shadow. By the mid-1950s, Wills' star was on the wane and the golden age of western swing had largely run its course. The western swing king was sidelined forever in 1969 by a debilitating stroke and died in 1975 following a series of strokes.

Even decades after its heyday, western swing in general and Wills' repertoire in particular, have been revisited time and again by contemporary country stars like Merle Haggard and George Strait, as well as celebrated honky tonkers like Ray Price, Red Steagall and, most notably, Texan Hank Thompson. A real milestone in western swing revivalism came in 1970 when Merle Haggard reassembled many of the original Texas Playboys and recorded a magnificent salute to Wills called *A Tribute To The Best Damn Fiddle Player In The World*.

Key Artists

Bob Wills & the Texas Playboys
Milton Brown & his Musical Brownies
Hank Thompson
Asleep At The Wheel

Oddly enough, western swing also got a fresh hearing in the 1970s and 1980s through the music of several youthful hippy-era bands like Commander Cody & his Lost Planet Airmen, Dan Hicks & his Hot Licks and Asleep At The Wheel, who became enthralled with the Bob Wills musical tradition. The most enduring of these neo-western swingers is Asleep At The Wheel, who cut their teeth playing clubs in the Washington, DC area in the late 1960s. Through thick and thin the Wheel are still going strong as the most vital contemporary purveyors of this intricate yet robust and eminently danceable music.

Bob Wills (right of drummer) shows jazz and blues influences in his music, which he absorbed from working and playing with the cotton-field slaves. He once travelled 50 miles on horseback to see Bessie Smith perform.

Musicals

From the eclectic musical melting pot of ragtime, Gilbert & Sullivan, early jazz, Viennese operetta, blackface minstrel shows and authentic Deep-South blues emerged the Broadway show tune. 'Show' and 'tune', of course, are the essential indicators of musical style.

The first generation of musical-theatre composers, who included George Gershwin, Irving Berlin, Jerome Kern and Richard Rodgers, were tunesmiths of the highest order. Many were Jewish émigrés. As young men they eagerly embraced the music of a different displaced community of an earlier generation, the African-American. Perhaps it was their distinctly melodic Jewish Cantor tradition, combined with the emerging music of the black ghetto, that was to create the unique, vibrant and soulful sounds of Broadway. Whatever the reason, this generation gave birth to the Golden Age of the musical, dating, roughly, from *Show Boat* in 1927 to *Gypsy* in 1959. The father of them all was Jerome Kern. In Kern's *Show Boat*, part of the purpose of the music was to explore the themes of the show. 'Ol' Man River' has a majestic simplicity, while 'Life Upon The Wicked Stage' has a cheerful mischievousness, brilliantly capturing the 'playful' character of showgirls. And if Kern gave musical theatre its first melodic voice, then it was his lyricist collaborator, Oscar Hammerstein, who gave musical theatre an understanding of its theatrical and dramatic role.

'What's wrong with letting 'em tap their toes a bit? I'll let you know when Stravinsky has a hit – give me some melody!'

Joe, the producer in Stephen Sondheim's musical *Merrily We Roll Along* about a Broadway writing team.

Although he was not a composer, Hammerstein brought theatricality and dramatic intent to the musical form. His songs are often written for a specific time within the show. The '11 o'clock number' will have enough punch and energy to give the show a lift when it might start to sag a little. Equally important is dramatic function. In *The King And I*, when the head wife of the king sings 'Something Wonderful' to Mrs Anna the song not only reveals the wife's feelings for her husband and a side of the king we have not seen; it also dampens Mrs Anna's growing anger towards the king. Such songs may have life as cabaret songs outside the theatre, but to appreciate them fully they must be heard and seen within their theatrical and dramatic context. That is what musical theatre is all about.

Actor and singer Paul Robeson leaving for Hollywood to begin his role in the 1932 revival of Show Boat. *He sang the popular tune 'Ol' Man River' and changed the lyrics to form a protest song.*

Dramatic Integration

Apart from the continuing influence of his own work, Oscar Hammerstein had a second important contribution to make to musical theatre: he was a theatrical and parental mentor to Stephen Sondheim.

A lot is often said about the development of the 'integrated musical', referring to how songs became increasingly integrated into the story so that they naturally arose out of the dialogue, or 'book', of the show. *Oklahoma!* is usually cited as the most important milestone. However, Sondheim rightly points to the 'If I Loved You' section of *Carousel* (Rodgers & Hammerstein) as more seminal. There is no 'number', as such. What you have is a scene in which speaking, underscoring and singing are so interconnected as to appear seamless. This was to become the direction of the musical in the latter half of the last century.

Key Artists

Irving Berlin
George Gershwin
Jerome Kern
Rodgers & Hammerstein
Andrew Lloyd Webber

The score would no longer be integrated into the book of the show; the score would become the show. Sondheim developed a form of the musical in which melodic themes were sometimes fragmented across an entire act or show.

Another devotee of the work of Rodgers & Hammerstein, especially that of Richard Rodgers, is Andrew Lloyd Webber. Early in his career Lloyd Webber, like Kern before him, was embracing an emerging sound. This time, however, it was rock, not blues. And yet the sudden appearance of a waltz, a strong feature of Rodgers's music, in Lloyd Webber's 'sung-through' rock operas – such as *Evita* – shows the continuing influence of an earlier tradition. Even later Lloyd Webber shows continue this mixture of styles, in which elements of a driving rock song (the title song from *Sunset Boulevard*, for example) share the stage with an entrancing, lyrical ballad ('With One Look', again from *Sunset Boulevard*).

This takes us back to where the musical began, with an eclectic variety of influences and sounds. Does the musical have a singular and distinct sound? Perhaps not, but from Kern onwards, the musical has had some of the greatest creators of theatrical melody – or 'show tunes'. The best writers created their own unique style, from the bluesy voice of Kern and the bright, breezily hummable numbers of Irving Berlin, to the sublime waltzes of Rodgers and the rising lyrical ballads of Lloyd Webber. And if there is one influence above all others on musical theatre, it is the theatre itself.

Gershwin completed his folk opera, Porgy and Bess, in 1935. Although this was the composer's favourite and most ambitious composition, it did not receive due acclaim until after his death in 1937.

Jubilee Gospel

In the later years of the nineteenth century, the world of black religion was in ferment. Breakaway sects began to found their own churches and followed the drift of black people from the country to the cities, resulting in the mass migrations from Southern oppression to a newer, but not always easier life in the industrialized cities of North America.

Many of these churches were Pentecostal or 'sanctified' in nature, and they rejected the stiffly formalized rituals of their Baptist or Methodist mother churches in favour of more extreme methods of worship, which could include haranguing sermons, speaking in tongues, dancing (known as 'shouting') and the use of musical instruments. The active involvement of the congregation could induce fits of religious ecstasy during which the worshipper would 'fall out', entering a trance-like state of exaltation. Perhaps the most influential of these new churches was C. H. Mason's Church Of God In Christ (COGIC), which began its life in Mississippi, but found its most fertile ground in the black ghettos of the north. Despite some fierce preaching, these churches projected a tone of joy and a basic message of 'good news'.

'No one but those who have had their slumbers broken by those sacred serenades can realize their sweetness and power.'
Daniel Alexander Payne, *Recollections of Seventy Years* (Nashville, 1888)

The 1920s

In the early years of the new century, black music was very prominent in American life. Minstrelsy had given ground to ragtime, while blues had been noted and, along with jazz, was waiting in the wings. Both Scott Joplin and W. C. Handy had backgrounds in church music. Paralleling these developments was the innovation of sound recordings being made and sold as entertainment. In 1921, soon after Mamie Smith proved that a market existed among blacks, a group from Virginia called the Norfolk Jazz & Jubilee Quartet recorded in New York. Their initial offerings were blues and popular songs, with a sprinkling of religious titles; by 1923, however, jubilee songs had come to dominate their repertoire. By the end of the 1920s, groups such as the Golden Leaf Quartet, the Pace Jubilee Singers and the Birmingham Jubilee Quartet were appearing regularly in record companies' 'race' catalogues. They sang a cappella and introduced more daring and complicated arrangements built on a basic four-part harmony, sometimes utilizing stop-time or bringing forward the bass for novelty effect.

Pioneers of jubilee, the members of the Golden Gate Quartet developed a unique way of performing sacred hymns and enjoyed widespread acceptance outside the church.

Sanctified Recordings

The financial crash of 1929 caused those recording companies that survived to restrict their activities, putting an end to many budding musical careers. However, religion provided solace for people who were hit hard by such desperate times and the popularity of 'sanctified' material with the black audience ensured that it was well represented as the recording industry slowly regained its feet.

The earliest known black composer of religious songs was W. Henry Sherwood, a Baptist who, in 1893, produced a hymnal that found favour in black churches. Another famous collection, by the Methodist C. A. Tindley, followed in 1916. As the black diaspora spread across America, certain cities became famous in black society for their preachers and singers. COGIC was particularly strong in Chicago, and the quartets operating out of Birmingham, Alabama were to become the stuff of legend; even the largely Catholic New Orleans had its own 'sanctified' tradition.

Prior to 1932, Thomas A. Dorsey enjoyed considerable success in the arena of secular music. He employed his instrumental and vocal talents as 'Georgia Tom', first leading a band supporting 'Ma' Rainey and later as half of a hokum duo with Tampa Red, which specialized in lightweight songs of a somewhat salacious nature. Although he had been raised in a religious family, Dorsey never had any problem with 'the Devil's music'. He had been writing religious songs since as early as 1921, and when his wife died he walked away from his secular success and dedicated himself to church music, deliberately marrying elements of jazz and blues to sacred songs. In the process, he became known as the 'father' of gospel and, in association with the entrepreneurial singer Sallie Martin, inaugurated the annual Gospel Singers' Convention and began to charge admission for concerts.

Key Artists

Thomas A. Dorsey
Golden Gate Quartet
Mahalia Jackson
Norfolk Jazz & Jubilee Quartet
Mamie Smith

In 1937 the most influential of all jubilee groups appeared in the form of the Golden Gate Quartet. In this period of secular, jazzy 'rhythm groups' the Gates were as hip as any, with the possible exception of the instrumentally backed Blue Chips. They were to enjoy a career that mixed secular and sacred music, and saw them appearing in churches, nightclubs and even Hollywood movies.

Considered the mother of the blues, Ma Rainey, born Gertrude Pridgett, toured the southern US performing blues, gospel and pop songs on the vaudeville circuit to great public acclaim.

Cabaret

Cabaret thrived on sensuality, wit and an intimacy between performer and audience. Its essence lies in intimate, escapist venues, where charismatic artists perform with ad-hoc backing from piano, brass and bass. Unlike the popularist music hall, cabaret was born from experimentation and a desire to explore the space between mass entertainment and the avant-garde.

A French word that alluded to any business serving alcohol, 'cabaret' acquired its modern definition in 1881, when Le Chat Noir opened its doors to the bohemian denizens of Paris's Montmartre district. At a time when newspapers were controlled by the ruling classes, Le Chat provided a democratic forum where artists could swap ideas and rub shoulders with aristocrats, ne'er-do-wells and inquisitive members of the bourgeoisie. Audiences were treated to a heady mixture of music, dance, poetry, satire and theatre. The biggest cabaret stars were the *diseuses,* multi-talented female performers who were as much actresses as they were singers, and who accompanied their songs with dramatic expressions and expansive gestures. Foremost among these was Yvette Guilbert, who delivered wry, topical chansons and re-worked French folk standards in a voice rich with gruff melancholia.

'Divine decadence, darling!'
Sally Bowles, a principal character in *Cabaret*

Spreading across Europe during the inter-war years, cabaret found a particularly grateful home in Berlin, where a dangerous menu of jazz, satire and pornography flourished. Visual display equalled vocal performance in importance, and the most pungent evocations of this era are on film: Josef von Sternberg's *The Blue Angel* and Bob Fosse's *Cabaret*. The former rocketed Marlene Dietrich to Hollywood stardom, but with her outlandish, half-sung and half-spoken vocals, the German was a relatively minor figure on the live cabaret circuit. More important were such seminal *diseuses* as Rosa Valetti, an oft-overlooked icon of the Roaring Twenties. Valetti was committed to cabaret as a socio-political tool, and roared out provocative political numbers such as 'The Red Melody' in formidable, iron-lunged fashion.

A true cabaret star, Yvette Guilbert started singing at five and began modelling at 16. She performed at the Moulin Rouge and sang at Carnegie Hall, as well as starring in a number of films.

Post-War Accessibility

Despite the intentions of wistful 1960s commentators such as the singer/songwriter Jacques Brel, modern cabaret has been a shadow of its former self in political terms.

In France, it retained a strong sense of sensuality, humour and audience interaction, as the likes of Edith Piaf and the sashaying American Josephine Baker enjoyed considerable popularity. In America, cabaret was reborn in the speakeasies of the Prohibition era and, surviving alongside the gambling halls of Las Vegas, cabaret clubs also enjoyed a glamorous association with vice, as dramatized in films such as *Cabaret* (1972). Performers began to incorporate gutsy torch songs, jazz numbers and Broadway tunes into their routines.

Key Artists

Marlene Dietrich
Yvette Guilbert
Mabel Mercer
Edith Piaf
Sylvia Syms

This period was epitomized by the British-born Mabel Mercer, the piano-playing Barbara Carroll, and Sylvia Syms, a New Yorker and protégée of Billie Holiday who took the night-spots of the Big Apple by storm during the 1960s and 1970s. Syms's husky-voiced renditions of jazz-tinged originals, as well as inspired covers of pop favourites such as 'You Don't Have To Say You Love Me', influenced artists from Tony Bennett to Frank Sinatra, who described her as 'the world's greatest saloon singer'. Combining heartfelt lyrical interpretation with spot-on timing and an acute sense of dramatic irony, Syms was a worthy, accessible successor to *diseuses* like Guilbert and Valetti.

Previously a German cabaret performer, Marlene Dietrich was perfectly suited to her role in the film The Blue Angel. *Her performance as Lola, an aloof and elegant temptress, lifted her from obscurity to sex-symbol status.*

Ska

Ska represents the birth of modern popular Jamaican music, and it does so with the accent on 'Jamaican'. While this raucous, uptempo, good-times music may have had its roots in American big-band jazz and R&B, it was conceived as a celebration of Jamaican independence.

Ska is the link between the virtuoso playing of Kingston's sophisticated nightclub musicians and the vibrancy of the downtown sound systems. It revolutionized Jamaican life and the island's place in the world at the time.

'Ska was our type of music that could lift the youth and make Jamaica known around the world.'

Lloyd Brevett

As an alternative to the very English radio programming in pre-independence Jamaica (light classics, light jazz and light chat), citizens were tuning into the powerful radio stations broadcasting from New Orleans and Miami, which presented a steady diet of R&B, blues and jump jazz. As a result, American music was informing Jamaican popular taste, and while it might have been a great deal of fun, such cultural colonialism in the 1950s, after the island's independence process had been set in motion, no longer fitted the mood. By then, Jamaican-ness was what counted, and so a home-grown soundtrack was obligatory. Ska was that music, and it was taken straight to people's hearts because it was born downtown among those same people at their sound system dances.

Identifiably Jamaican

At its essence, ska is an R&B structure and a jazz attitude, mixed together with enough Jamaican flavouring to give it its own identity. And, like practically every subsequent musical development on the island, it was precipitated by sound men. Coxsone Dodd and Prince Buster, two of Jamaica's biggest sound men, read the mood and wanted to change the beat. By the start of the 1960s, they were running out of new R&B records to play at their dances. They needed a change of music to keep them out in front of their rivals, and they and their crowds were getting swept along by independence fever. As a result, and independently of each other, Buster and Dodd both devised variations on the standard R&B boogie rhythm to create something new that was also identifiably Jamaican.

Prince Buster gave a voice to the people with 'Oh Carolina', which expressed black Jamaican-ness through a commercially viable medium.

Establishing the Sound

Buster and Dodd both retained the shuffle beat from R&B to power ska along as a dance style, and this can be heard when they cut, respectively, tracks like 'Oh Carolina' by the Folkes Brothers or 'They Got To Go' by Buster himself, and 'Easy Snappin'' by Theophilus Beckford or 'Time to Play' by the Mello Larks.

Whereas Dodd, a jazz fan, then looked to add instrumental passages, Buster opted for more intrinsically Jamaican additions such as Rasta drumming. This was the basis of the ska sound and it expanded into music that was virtuosic and largely instrumental, thanks to a pool of superb players on the island. Many of these players had been classically trained and made their livings playing dance music to demanding American hotel crowds. Players as talented as the Skatalites, Don Drummond and Prince Buster's All Stars produced tracks like 'Guns Of Navarone', 'Phoenix City', 'Man In The Street', 'Madness', 'Al Capone' and 'Confucius'.

Key Artists

Prince Buster
Jimmy Cliff
Desmond Dekker
The Wailers
The Skatalites

For much of its lifetime, ska was played more in the dancehalls than in the recording studios, and the classic ska orchestra involved between 10 and 20 players. In true jazz style the soloists worked as hard to impress each other as much as they did the paying customers. Central to ska were the Skatalites, from the rhythm section of Lloyd Knibbs (drums) and Lloyd Brevett (bass) through guitarists Jah Jerry and Ernest Ranglin and pianist Jackie Mittoo, and the brass players: trombonist Don Drummond, saxmen Tommy McCook, Lester Sterling and Roland Alphonso and trumpeter Dizzy Moore. They were the epitome of a ska band and one of the best Jamaican groups ever. The ska era also benefited greatly from a generation of brass players that all came from the Alpha Boys School, an establishment run by nuns for wayward or abandoned boys that mixed strict discipline with the best music department in Jamaica. Horn players Don Drummond, Tommy McCook, Rico Rodriguez, Lester Sterling, Dizzy Moore and Eddie Thornton are all Alpha alumni.

Of course, ska wasn't all about playing, and singers such as Jimmy Cliff, the Wailers, Ken Boothe, Desmond Dekker, Lee Perry, Delroy Wilson, the Maytals and Derrick Morgan were all ska stars. It was as much them as the musicians and producers, including Prince Buster, Duke Reid, Coxsone Dodd and Vincent Chin, that were responsible for ska's laying the foundations of the Jamaican recording industry.

Clement 'Coxsone' Dodd, the sound system man and prolific producer, opened a recording studio and launched his Studio One label in 1963, working with top names of the day, including the Wailers and the Skatalites.

Soul and R&B

In 1949, two apparently small events took place, which in hindsight were to have monumental significance for popular culture. The first of these saw Billboard magazine change the name of its 'Race Records' chart to the more relevant and politically correct 'Rhythm & Blues' chart, reflecting the success of the American dance music of the moment.

Meanwhile, a 19-year-old blind Georgia orphan called Ray Charles Robinson (he dropped the Robinson to avoid confusion with the legendary boxer Sugar Ray Robinson) released his first single 'Confession Blues'. By the mid-1950s, rhythm & blues had mutated into rock'n'roll, the ultimate crossover between black and white popular music, and in the form of R&B would remain the dominant label attached to pop music of Afro-American origin. By 1954, the visionary and eclectic Charles, with his arrangement for bluesman Guitar Slim's 'The Things That I Used To Do' and the irresistible fusion of jazz, blues and gospel on his own 'I Got A Woman' (later covered by Elvis Presley), had invented soul music – rock's spiritual, sensual Afro-American twin.

'It was a slang that would relate to the man on the street, plus it had its own sound: the music on one-and-three, the downbeat, in anticipation.'

James Brown on 'Papa's Got A Brand New Bag'

Soul is an innovative blend of musical styles: the Baptist hymn and the juke joint dance exhortation, the plantation field holler and the sophisticated jazz standard, the romantic vocal flights of doo-wop and the driving rhythms of small-band R&B, the gospel plea for deliverance and the altogether earthier blues lament. It rose to prominence through the innovations of two further black male pioneers from the southern states. Mississippi gospel heart-throb Sam Cooke made a controversial move to secular pop in 1956. By 1957 his 'You Send Me' – a heart-melting mix of teen pop and Cooke's alternately tender and roaring gospel vocals – had gone to number one in the US and truly ignited the soul era. He continued to be one of pop's most loved crossover pioneers until his shocking death in 1964, at the hands of a motel manager who claimed she shot the singer in self-defence after he had allegedly raped another woman.

The Apollo Theatre in Harlem, New York, played a major part in the development of black music. In 1934, the theatre introduced its amateur night, providing performers with a chance to prove themselves. James Brown launched his career at the Apollo.

Unstoppable Energy

Georgia's James Brown released his first single, 'Please Please Please', in 1956, a record so vocally intense and rhythmically tough that it made a romantic plea to a woman sound like a hysterical scream from the very depths of sexual desperation and despair.

Brown's prolific writing and recording schedule was sent into commercial overdrive by the most extreme live performances of the period, a theatrical and almost militarily precise singing and dancing spectacular that had a profound influence on Mick Jagger, Michael Jackson, Prince and every star since who has combined flamboyant sexual display, bravura dance moves and unstoppable physical energy with playful drama and driving rhythm. A recorded document of that show, 1962's *Live At The Apollo*, along with another Ray Charles innovation, *Modern Sounds In Country And Western Music* from the same year, established soul as an album-selling genre. James Brown, of course, was key in turning soul music into funk and disco, and through his ability to make African-derived rhythm into a complex but universally understood musical language, he had the most profound influence upon hip hop and all subsequent genres of dance music.

By late-1963, soul was so dominant in the American singles market that the black chart was abolished, for the first and only time, until early 1965. Over the next 30 years, the original soul impulse was taken in so many different directions that the term is now largely applied only to the 1960s/early 1970s Golden Era. Nevertheless, just as all white rock and pop eventually refers back to the blues, Elvis, the Beatles or Dylan, the black pop we now (rather ironically) call R&B owes its existence to the leaps of artistic faith made by Charles, Cooke and Brown.

Key Tracks

'Papa's Got A Brand New Bag' James Brown
'Georgia On My Mind' Ray Charles
'Let's Stay Together' Al Green
'Jailhouse Rock' Elvis Presley
'Walk On By' Dionne Warwick

Soul superstar James Brown, with his highly charged emotinal vocals and intense showmanship, was to have a profound effect on later generations of dance artists.

Lounge Music

Following on from the lush bombast of the swing era, and established by a colourful group of American artists in the 1950s and 1960s, lounge was easy listening's quirky kid brother. It was more playful than its more populist relative and, when viewed retrospectively, had a high camp factor.

Although ostensibly laid-back and mellow, lounge artists like Les Baxter and Esquivel were not afraid to experiment with tempo and style and helped lounge mutate into new forms. Space-age pop made use of futuristic new instruments and exotica stole influences from Latin America, Africa and beyond. This music was dilettantish rather than authentic, presenting snapshots of far-off countries or future worlds for an audience hungry for escapism. Lounge music was later re-branded as cocktail music, martini music and lounge-core by the trendsetters who rediscovered it in the 1990s. To them, it evoked kitsch 1960s lifestyles. Retro freaks descended in droves on second-hand record shops to unearth vintage LPs like *Equinox* (1967), by Sergio Mendes, and the entire back catalogue of the mighty Burt Bacharach.

'It seems that most of my life I have had inclinations towards ... different, interesting music. I never like to do prosaic.'

Les Baxter

One of the foremost lounge artists was Les Baxter, a pianist from Detroit who is best remembered as the most important pioneer of exotica, which gained considerable popularity in America during the 1950s. His compositions retained the backbone of strings and brass that characterized most popular music of the time. But he also assimilated everything from the striking, four-octave range of the legendary Peruvian vocalist Yma Sumac to the steel guitars of Polynesia and Hawaii. African percussion was another influence: in 1951, Baxter recorded his seminal *Ritual of the Savage* LP, a musical travelogue replete with recorded jungle noises and bird calls. The album remains a classic of exotica.

Back in 1948, Baxter had also experimented with a theremin, one of the world's first electronic instruments, combining its eerie sound with a choir, rhythm section, cello and French horn. The result, an LP titled *Music Out of the Moon*, was the progenitor of space-age pop, a relation of lounge that exploited the possibilities afforded by the stereo format and nascent electronic instrumentation.

Esquivel's bizarre use of instrumentation and innovative arrangements were designed to exploit the new stereo equipment. Futuristic as the music sounded, it dated quickly, but became a kitsch favourite in the 1970s.

A Burst of Latin Lunacy

A prime mover in both space-age pop and exotica was Esquivel, a bona fide lounge eccentric who created some of the strangest music of the late-1950s and 1960s. Much of the Mexican's output was based on the big band format and shot through with exaggerated Latin American rhythms, but he also employed the theremin and an arsenal of other outlandish instruments, including Chinese bells, early electronic keyboards and the ondioline, a vacuum tube instrument that emits a reedy, vibrato sound.

His most infamous recording was 1962's *Latin-Esque*, the first album recorded with full stereo separation: two orchestras performing in separate studios whom he conducted using headphones. He divided opinions during the 1950s and 1960s: some critics were turned off by his wild clashing of styles and tempos. Others became great fans, and Esquivel ended his career as a stalwart of the Las Vegas circuit and a favourite with Frank Sinatra and REM.

Key Artists

Les Baxter
Esquivel
Burt Bacharach
Sergio Mendes
Martin Denny

The popularity of Esquivel and his cohorts declined after the 1970s, but enjoyed a revival in the 1990s, inspiring British electronic artists such as Funki Porcini and receiving a more tongue-in-cheek reworking by Mike Flowers, who achieved UK chart success with a lounge-style cover of Oasis's 'Wonderwall' in 1996. And it was this exposure, along with appearances in the Austin Powers films, that helped to renew interest in another 1960s star – Burt Bacharach – who would come to embody lounge for a new generation of listeners.

Of course, it would be an injustice to one of the twentieth century's greatest musicians to describe the Kansas City-born Bacharach as solely a lounge artist. Since the early 1950s he has written hits for the Carpenters, toured with cabaret star Marlene Dietrich, composed Oscar-winning music for *Butch Cassidy & The Sundance Kid* and released a string of classic collaborations with Dionne Warwick. Bacharach's sophisticated yet light melodies have something in common with those of easy listening titans like Henry Mancini. But his twinkling versatility, which has taken in jazz, bossa nova, soul, Brazilian grooves and pure pop, is even truer to the playful eclecticism of lounge. Today, such tracks as 1965's 'Make It Easy On Yourself', which he wrote for the Walker Brothers, exude a breezy, kitsch panache that makes Bacharach, among many other things, a quintessential lounge hero.

Burt Bacharach, with guest stars (l–r) Mireille Mathieu, Juliet Prowse and Dusty Springfield, on a 1970 television show. Springfield is considered to be one of the best interpreters of Bacharach's songs, along with Dionne Warwick.

Easy Listening

Until it was reclaimed with an ironic wink by 1990s hipsters, easy listening had been hugely popular, but rarely cool. While the teenagers of the 1950s and 1960s were getting off on dangerous rock'n'roll and subversive R&B, their parents were sweetly cocooned in the music of Mantovani and Percy Faith.

Easy listening music never launched any rebellions. It is unobtrusive, pacifying music built around pleasant, easily digestible melodies. Which is not to say it has no artistic value: within its wide borders can be found a rich spectrum of sounds, seasoned with influences from classical to pop to rock to jazz. Though often dismissed as hollow and uninspired, the genre has been distinguished by the work of some lavishly talented musicians, including such immortals as Henry Mancini and Burt Bacharach.

A Birthplace in Business

Beautiful music, mood music, elevator music, background music, adult contemporary, light classical; all fall beneath the umbrella of easy listening, as do the more sugary releases of Frank Sinatra, Dean Martin, Perry Como, Patti Page, Eva Cassidy and the Carpenters. But the genre's origins lie in commerce, and one of its fathers was not a musician but an American soldier. Brigadier General George Owen Squier patented the transmission of background music, which he named 'Muzak', in the 1920s.

'The lighter side of music has always been thrown out and not received its proper dignity.'
Mantovani

Originally designed to soothe the nerves of workers making vertiginous journeys up the first skyscrapers, the supply of watered-down classical, jazz and popular tunes soon became known as 'elevator music'.

Muzak became popular with company bosses, who believed it increased productivity and boosted morale. By the early 1970s, Muzak was played in shopping malls and airport departure lounges, used as telephone hold music, and was even piped into Polaris submarines. Muzak's ability to influence human moods fascinated musicians like Brian Eno, who explored it in his *Discrete Music* LP (1975), generally acknowledged as one of the earliest examples of ambient music. Detractors accused companies of using Muzak as an emotional sedative or a subliminal marketing tool, but the fact remains that it was popular with a large proportion of the millions of workers who were exposed to it.

Mantovani in 1953, leaving London for Amsterdam, where he was to conduct a Dutch orchestra.

The Maestros of Mood

The most notable light classicist, and a name synonymous with easy listening, was Annunzio Paolo Mantovani. Mantovani was a sensation in both America and Britain by the 1950s. He reinvented classical music in a studio-produced style whose hallmarks were 'cathedralized' strings, close harmonies and echo-laden, overlapping sound.

Mantovani topped the charts on both sides of the Atlantic and became the first musician to sell one million records in the US. Many of Mantovani's albums revisited romantic film themes of the day, as did the mood music of Jackie Gleason, but the undisputed master of cinematic easy listening was Henry Mancini. After cutting his teeth on jazz and the big band sound of the 1940s, he developed a knack for creating songs that escaped the confines of the movie or show they were written for and became memorable classics in their own right. It is the elegant simplicity of Mancini's melodies that make his 'Moon River' from *Breakfast At Tiffany's* one of the most perfectly realized pop songs of the past 50 years, and proves that easy listening can be brushed with genius.

Key Artists

Liberace
Henry Mancini
Mantovani
Lawrence Welk
The Carpenters

By the late 1960s, dedicated radio stations were pumping out what had then become known as 'beautiful music' across America. The soft strings of Mantovani, Mancini and Percy Faith dominated the schedules. But, in terms of charismatic showmanship, none of them could hold a candle to Wladziu Valentino Liberace – one of the biggest personalities in popular music. By the 1950s, he was performing a mixture of light classical, lounge jazz and show tunes while exuberantly clad in furs, sequins and gold lamé. Like many easy listening artists, he was never loved by the critics. But his audiences adored him, attending his concerts in droves.

Largely because a lack of vocals was more conducive to its original status as 'background music', the genre had been dominated by instrumentals. But in the 1970s, the beautiful music stations began to play more records by soft-edged pop acts like Barbra Streisand and the Carpenters. The Carpenters' gentle-on-the-ear approach remains one of easy listening's most familiar touchstones. And the genre lives on in the output of both the deeply uncool, like Barry Manilow, and the knowingly trendy, like the Mancini-inspired Stereolab. It seems our appetite for hassle-free melody will never be sated.

Henry Mancini's 'Moon River' appears in various arrangements throughout Breakfast At Tiffany's.

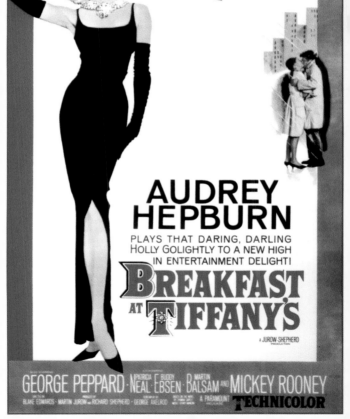

Psychedelic Rock

Several musical movements are associated either directly or indirectly with a specific recreational drug or drugs; psychedelic rock went a step further, and was practically borne out of LSD or acid, as well as other hallucinogens including peyote, mescaline and even marijuana.

Much psychedelic rock attempts to recreate the mind expanding sensations of an acid trip. So, musicians made use of the new studio technology available and used effects and exotic instruments and broke away from traditional song structures. They also looked further afield for inspiration, to jazz or Indian music, for example. George Harrison became interested in the sitar that was used for a scene in the Beatles film *Help!*, which led to the band becoming interested in Eastern culture.

The Yardbirds made a tentative exploration of this area with their 'Heartful Of Soul' single in 1965. In an effort to blend east and west, the band drafted in a sitar player to play the song's instrumental hook. Unfortunately, the hapless sitar player was so used to playing complex eastern rhythms, that he couldn't get the hang of the basic rock beat, so guitarist Jeff Beck imitated the sound of the sitar with a fuzzbox. This anecdote neatly illustrates the problem with some psychedelic rock – mixing disparate musical elements may sound fine on paper, but in practice it might not work. Consequently, when it works psychedelic rock can represent rock music at its most breathtaking, but when it doesn't work it can appear incompetent and foolhardy.

'The psychedelic ethic...runs through the musical mainstream in a still current. Musical ideas are passed from group to group like a joint.'
Richard Goldstein

One of the first psychedelic records, the Byrds' 'Eight Miles High' single (1966), saw the band's guitarist Roger McGuinn attempting to emulate jazz saxophonist John Coltrane and also displaying an Indian influence in his rambling improvisation. John Lennon attempted to recreate the mood of an LSD trip on the Beatles' 'Tomorrow Never Knows' (1966), with multiple tape loops, a processed lead vocal, backwards guitar solo and lyrics inspired by LSD guru Timothy Leary and *The Tibetan Book of the Dead*. The Rolling Stones' 'Paint It Black' single (1966) used a sitar to great effect and their fleeting psychedelic incarnation culminated in *Their Satanic Majesties Request* (1967).

Roger McGuinn, frontman of the Byrds, was deeply influenced by jazzman John Coltrane.

The Summer of Love

1967, the so-called 'Summer of Love', was an important year for psychedelic rock. In the US, the Doors released their self-titled debut album; Jim Morrison's highly poetic lyrics, Ray Manzarek's hypnotic organ and the guitarist Robbie Kreiger's improvizations proved an intoxicating mix. Fellow Americans Jefferson Airplane's Surrealistic Pillow featured 'White Rabbit' with flamenco-influenced, moody introduction. Led by Arthur Lee, Love's Forever Changes included the classic 'Alone Again Or'.

On the other side of the Atlantic, Pink Floyd's debut album, *The Piper At The Gates Of Dawn*, revealed an English sense of whimsy on 'Bike', spacey, sci-fi rock on 'Astronomy Domine' and a taste for almost avant-garde experimentation on 'Interstellar Overdrive'. The Move captured the psychedelia of London's underground scene with 'I Can Hear the Green Grass Grow', conveying the experience of a marijuana high. The Beatles embraced the psychedelic spirit of the times on *Sgt Pepper's Lonely Hearts Club Band*, as exemplified in 'Lucy in the Sky with Diamonds'. One of the longest lasting psychedelic bands was the Grateful Dead, whose free-form live shows earned them an obsessive cult following. Improvization was a big part of the Dead's musical make-up, as can be heard on the *Live/Dead* album (1969) which features 'Dark Star', a song never performed the same way twice. Overall, psychedelic rock was a relatively short-lived phenomenon with bands either splitting up or moving onto new musical territory such as the Byrds, who moved onto country rock with *Sweetheart of the Rodeo* (1968), and Pink Floyd who succeeded in making progressive rock commercially successful with their *Dark Side Of The Moon* (1973).

Key Artists

The Byrds
The Beatles
The Rolling Stones
The Doors
Pink Floyd

Neopsychedelia

Psychedelic rock was largely a 1960s phenomenon, although in Britain Jason Pearce led a valiant one-man crusade for psychedelic rock in the late-1980s and 1990s, first with the ramshackle Spaceman 3, whose chaotic and overwhelming blend of neopsychedelia can be heard on *Playing With Fire* (1989), then as the leader of Spiritualized with the altogether more accomplished and critically acclaimed *Ladies And Gentlemen We Are Floating In Space* (1997). Psychedelic rock's most notable revival, however, occurred with the rise in popularity in the 1990s of trance, a style of dance music of which it is considered to be a forerunner.

Artwork played an important role in psychedelic rock, with record sleeves and concert posters becoming increasingly colourful and ornate. This example is a poster for the Monterey Pop Festival.

Northern Soul

This enduring British cult dance scene takes its name from the post-mod discos in the north-west of England where it developed, rather than the geographical location of the music-makers. Legendary disco venues like Manchester's Twisted Wheel, Blackpool's Mecca and The Wigan Casino, are still spoken about in reverential tones by soul and dance connoisseurs.

The reason northern soul exists is because of the extraordinary amount of quality soul produced in the Motown- and Stax-dominated 1960s. The immediately recognizable northern soul sound derives directly from Motown, and specifically from one key record: the Four Tops' 1965 hit 'I Can't Help Myself (Sugar Pie, Honey Bunch)'. With its circular piano/guitar riff, pounding rhythm, dramatic orchestral arrangement, and masochistic, lovelorn lyric howled like a sermon by lead vocalist Levi Stubbs, this track saw Motown composer/producers Eddie and Brian Holland and Lamont Dozier taking jazz and classical complexity and making it into totally accessible dancefloor R&B. It had an immediate influence on fledgling soul artists and small labels all over America. But, with Motown so commercially dominant, the majority of these more modest soul recordings failed to get radio airplay and slipped into obscurity.

'...until you've been there I don't think any mere written word can fully convey to you that special and unique vibration that generates amongst the brothers and sisters there.'
Dave Godin, soul guru

Meanwhile, England's loyal late-1960s mods, who had made Motown and melodic soul their dance music of choice, were demanding something more from DJs than the familiar big hits. Those DJs began to take more chances on obscure US imports, and the competition to find the most unheard new tunes took off. But by 1968, soul was changing, taking on influences from funk, the blues and roots revival, and psychedelic rock. As they entered the 1970s the serious Twisted Wheel and Mecca dancers wanted their DJs to stick with light, uptempo grooves despite their increasing rarity. DJs began to make trips to the US, often tracking down entire warehouses full of mid- to late-1960s soul singles that no one had bought. Played in the northern clubs, they sent the dancers wild and began a self-contained scene based not around artists or albums, but particular singles.

The Four Tops formed in 1953 after an impromptu performance at a friend's birthday party. Band member Lawrence Payton died in 1997, and the Tops split after an amazing 44 years of performing together.

The Fad that Wouldn't Die

The northern soul cult spread throughout Britain, to Scotland, the Midlands, and eventually London, reaching its peak in 1975 when two novelty groups, Ovation and Chosen Few, both from Wigan, reached the UK singles chart with records designed to exploit the hitherto underground scene.

This caused a split between the 1960s diehards and those – particularly the DJs and patrons of the Wigan Casino – who put crossover pop such as 'A Lover's Concerto' by Toys and 'Love On A Mountain Top' and 'Everlasting Love' by Robert Knight into the mix. By the late-1970s, the Casino, Mecca and Twisted Wheel had closed down, and northern DJs such as Levine and Pete Waterman began mixing light soul with Europop, creating the gay disco of Hi-NRG and having a profound influence over all subsequent forms of British manufactured pop. Nevertheless, northern soul refused (and still refuses) to die, and new generations of DJs and followers continue to emerge, sustaining regular clubs and one-off 'all-nighters', fanzines, a plethora of CD compilations and digital radio shows.

Inevitably, the music associated with northern soul has gone on to encompass an ever-widening range of styles. Scene anthems range from the pure soul stomp of Edwin Starr's 'S.O.S. (Stop Her On Sight)' and the great Jackie Wilson's 'The Sweetest Feeling' to the plaintive orchestral social conscience ballads of Curtis Mayfield and his 1960s vocal group the Impressions; to the girl-group pop of the Velvelettes and the Chiffons; to the R&B of Sugar Pie De Santo and the Capitols; to the soul-jazz instrumentals as 'The In Crowd' by Ramsey Lewis; to records such as Evelyn King's 'Shame' and the O'Jays' 'I Love Music', which typify the northern soul/disco crossover of the scene-splitting late-1970s.

Key Artists

The Four Tops
The Impressions
Edwin Starr
R. Dean Taylor
Jackie Wilson

Apart from the obvious influence on gay disco and manufactured pop, northern soul directly inspired various 1980s British acts. Electro pop duo Soft Cell covered northern classics 'Tainted Love' and 'What'. Dexys Midnight Runners scored their first UK number one with 'Geno', a tribute to club performer Geno Washington. Joboxers had a short shot at fame with northern-inspired hits 'Boxer Beat' and 'Just Got Lucky'. And the 2-Tone bands took a little from the genre too, as is especially obvious on 'Embarrassment' by Madness.

A class northern soul act, Geno Washington achieved chart success with the Ram Jam Band during the 1960s. His album Geno's Back *in 1976 took him back on the road and he continued to tour into the 2000s.*

Funk Soul

Since the dawn of the jazz era, the appeal of pop music had become increasingly intertwined with the demands of the dancefloor. As 1960s rock and soul became more orientated towards youth & hedonism it was only a matter of time before someone would come up with the ultimate dance groove. That someone was soul's greatest innovator, James Brown, who pioneered a music so orientated towards pure, African-derived rhythm that melody would finally be forced to take a back seat .

Funk as a term had been around since the turn of the twentieth century, when it applied specifically to the odours produced by the human body during and after sex. By the 1930s it was used to describe music with a dirty, lowdown feel, and by the 1950s it was an alternative name for hard bop, the post-bebop jazz with a straight-ahead, gospel- and swing-influenced rhythm, as typified by Milt Jackson and Horace Silver. But it was 1964 before funk formally twinned with soul, on James Brown's minor American hit single 'Out Of Sight'. The track had a familiar blues structure, but the hard-but-swinging, hip-grinding rhythm dominated, and was further developed by Brown on 1965's world-changing 'Papa's Got A Brand New Bag' and 1966's 'I Got You (I Feel Good)', by which time the entire JB band – horns, guitar, Brown's screeching staccato vocal – was surrendering melody to beat with a power and vibe as much African as Afro-American. Somewhat surprisingly however, Brown didn't apply the term funk to his new sound until 1967's flop single, the instrumental 'Funky Soul No. 1'.

'He was the true representative of the dream of the crossover between rock and soul and funk and psychedelia.'

Jim Irvin on Sly Stone

As Brown's career progressed, funk began to dominate his oeuvre. As well as making his own genre-defining classics including 'Say It Loud – I'm Black And I'm Proud', 'Sex Machine' (arguably the first disco record) and 'Funky Drummer' (which became the most sampled track of the late-1980s/early-1990s when Clyde Stubblefield's drum break became ubiquitous on hip hop tracks of the period), Brown co-wrote, arranged and produced an enormous catalogue of funk classics for his 'Funk Family'. In some cases, tunes by the likes of Fred Wesley & the JB's, Maceo & the Macks, Bobby Byrd, Vicki Anderson, Lyn Collins and Marva Whitney are more treasured than Brown's own by the funk connoisseur.

Sly & the Family Stone formed in 1967 and, unusually for the time, included male and female and black and white members.

Soul Greats Get Funky

Atlantic Records soul singer Wilson 'The Wicked' Pickett's 1965 anthem 'In The Midnight Hour' is a blueprint for strutting downtempo funk, and arguably the greatest soul singer of all, Memphis's Aretha Franklin, essayed a more subtle, gospel-edged funk sound on 1967 classics 'Respect' and 'Chain Of Fools' and 1971's 'Rock Steady'.

Funk/R&B crossovers like Eddie Floyd's 1966 'Knock On Wood' and Bob & Earl's 1969 'Harlem Shuffle' also added to the burgeoning funk wave. Motown backroom boys Norman Whitfield and Barrett Strong began constructing tracks for the Temptations that blended funky wah-wah guitars, widescreen orchestration, and tough counter-cultural lyrical themes. From 1969's 'Cloud Nine' to 1973's 'Papa Was A Rollin' Stone', the formerly poppy vocal group became an object lesson in funk as artistically ambitious social commentary. Fellow Motown vocal group the Isley Brothers released defiant funk affairs such as 'It's Your Thing' and the same late-1960s/early 1970s period saw Stax writer/producer Isaac Hayes step into the limelight. His 1969 *Hot Buttered Soul* album invented a whole new seduction soul, transforming standards like 'Walk On By' into funk epics.

Key Artists

James Brown
Aretha Franklin
Wilson Pickett
The Temptations
Fred Wesley

Meanwhile, Texan Sylvester Stewart (a.k.a. Sly Stone) was approaching funky soul from a different angle. His inter-racial, multi-gender big band Sly & theFamily Stone grabbed their first US hit with the exuberant 'Dance To The Music' in 1968. Sly & co. mixed funk, soul, big-band jazz, pop and psychedelic rock with brave abandon, making a string of era-defining US hits until 1971's extraordinary *There's A Riot Goin' On* album marked both his peak and his downfall. A powerful funk comment on the disillusion of the times, the album reached number one but also highlighted Stone's increasing emotional decline through drug addiction.

New Orleans, the birthplace of so much jazz and R&B, had its own unique take on the new sound. Dr John was a white piano prodigy already steeped in bayou jazz and blues when he made 1968's *Gris Gris*, a unique mélange of voodoo mysticism, psychedelia and laid-back funk. His friends the Meters responded with their 1969 self-titled instrumental album, which boiled funk down to syncopated beats and infectious 'chicken scratch' guitar, a live-sounding style that reached its height on 1974's vocal *Rejuvenation* album.

By 1976 the Temptations had seen so many line-up changes that only two of the original five members remained. In this year they recorded their final album for Motown – The Temptations Do The Temptations.

Funk

By the 1970s, the new sound of funk dominated Afro-American music. Jazzers such as Miles Davis and Herbie Hancock scored their biggest commercial successes by incorporating its hip-grinding rhythms into what became known as fusion or jazz funk, while soul acts enjoyed a second wave of popularity as funk provided the bridge between the soul and disco eras.

'James has more funk in his little finger than most people have in their life.'
Saxophone player Pee Wee Ellis on James Brown

'The Godfather of Soul', James Brown, continued to develop the funk he'd invented throughout the 1970s and 1980s. Classics such as 1975's 'Funky President' and 1976's 'Get Up Offa That Thing' established him forever as the definitive funk artist. Meanwhile, two other 1960s soul masters blended a mellower form of funk with socially concerned singer/songwriter elements. Former Motown child prodigy Stevie Wonder reached artistic peaks with 1973's 'Superstition' and *Innervisions*, an all-time-great LP mixing tough funk protest, sublime ballads and a jazzy spontaneity. Meanwhile, Chicago's Curtis Mayfield fashioned a unique muse based upon his beautiful falsetto vocals and vivid lyrical pleas for social justice. This produced a funk masterpiece in 1972 with his soundtrack for the movie *Superfly*. All this Sly Stone-influenced funk politics was defined by a classic 1972 single by Ohio's O'Jays. This Philadelphia Sound vocal group produced, in the extraordinary 'Backstabbers', an expression of desperate pop paranoia that matched Marvin Gaye's legendary 'I Heard It Through The Grapevine' in intensity and dread.

The debut album by George Clinton's Funkadelic project took Sly Stone's psychedelic funk on an even weirder trip, mixing hard black rhythm with hallucinogenic guitar freak-outs and sci-fi lyrics. By 1973, former James Brown cohorts Bootsy Collins (bass), Maceo Parker (sax) and Fred Wesley (trombone) had joined Clinton in his two parallel groups, Funkadelic and Parliament, mixed and matched up to 35 members and played the greatest freak-out live shows of their day. They swapped between pounding low-tempo big band grooves and maverick acid funk excursions and became one of America's biggest bands. 1971's *Maggot Brain* (Funkadelic), 1976's *Mothership Connection* (Parliament) and 1978's *One Nation Under A Groove* (Funkadelic) represent the high points of Clinton & co.'s catalogue, which took in equally influential sets by Bootsy Collins's Rubber Band and, in the 1980s, by Clinton as a solo artist.

An all-round musical talent, Curtis Mayfield is a guitarist, singer, producer and songwriter. His movie soundtrack to Superfly proved his greatest solo success, with the tracks 'Freddie's Dead' and 'Superfly' both selling millions in the US.

Low Riders and High Rollers

Four remaining classic funk bands symbolize black American music's swift 1970s journey from rock and jazz-influenced bohemian innovation, through the much-parodied period of sartorial flamboyance represented by Afro dos and outrageous flared jump-suits, to funk's eventual defeat and dilution at the hands of late-1970s disco crossover.

LA's War began as a back-up band for former Animal Eric Burdon before forging their own path with a heavily jazz- and rock-influenced form of funk complexity. Their finest moments veer from the dramatic protest of 1972's 'The World Is A Ghetto' to the irresistible street scene grooves of 1973's 'Me And Baby Brother' and 1976's gravel-voiced 'Low Rider'. But by 1978 their attempts to ride the disco wave floundered and obscurity beckoned. Faring rather better were hardy perennials the Isley Brothers, who, after having adapted to 1950s R&B, Motown pop, early funk, and even superb versions of folk rock protest song covers, encouraged brother Ernie to unleash his coruscating post-Hendrix electric guitar licks. The result was the benchmark 3 + 3 album in 1973, and a prolific stream of small-band funk rock and ballad singles and albums. Again, the Isleys faltered over disco, but bounced back in 1983 with the 'Sexual Healing'-inspired boudoir soul of 'Between The Sheets'.

Key Artists

The Isley Brothers
Kool & the Gang
Curtis Mayfield
Prince
Stevie Wonder

In the wake of P-Funk, horn-driven big bands from all over America mixed infectious chants with grooving jams. Two of those bands gradually changed tack and were two of disco's big winners. Maurice White's Earth, Wind & Fire blended Clinton's cosmic vision with White's own jazz arrangement virtuosity and increasingly sophisticated pop songcraft. Between 1973's *Head To The Sky* and 1981's *Raise!* they were black America's most globally successful act, mixing pop, big-band jazz, funk, soul, disco, hilarious cosmic peace and love pretension, and an incredible theatrical live show. The 1980s advance of machine-driven dance music finally ended their triumphant run. The less flamboyant but similarly adaptable Ohio big band Kool & the Gang hit with a more modest form of funk-to-disco transition. After a string of jam'n'chant successes culminating in 1976's 'Open Sesame', they hired crooner James 'J.T.' Taylor and became disco pop hitmakers from 1979's 'Ladies Night' onwards, before those pesky machines rendered them unKool in the mid-1980s.

Kool & the Gang began life as a jazz quartet during the 1960s, but developed into an internationally successful funk band. Their enigmatic frontman, 'J.T.' Taylor stayed with the band until 1988, when he left to pursue a solo career.

Urban Soul

Although the 1960s golden age established soul as the foundation of Afro-American pop, the 1970s and 1980s saw soul's supremacy challenged and ultimately ended by funk, disco, electro, dance-rock, hip hop and house. Nevertheless, soul, like rock'n'roll, will never die, and a few true soul voices continued to survive and adapt to the new market.

Producer Thom Bell and songwriters Kenny Gamble and Leon Huff set up the Philadelphia International label in the late 1960s. By the mid-1970s, they had established the 'Philly sound', a massively successful blend of gospel- or doo-wop-influenced vocals and heavily orchestrated black pop that informed disco through the music of the O' Jays, Harold Melvin & the Blue Notes, the Three Degrees and the cast-of-thousands house band MFSB. Bell also co-wrote and produced for the three vocal groups who defined the mellifluous sound of sweet soul: the Delfonics, the Stylistics and the Spinners, who all produced a string of much-loved hits in the early 1970s. Bell had no hand in Chicago's Chi-Lites, who mined an identical seam, reaching a peak of tear-stained male masochism on 1972's gorgeous 'Have You Seen Her?' An altogether more defiant gospel-derived take on sweet soul came from Atlanta's Gladys Knight & the Pips, a 1950s Motown vocal group who fronted the first version of 'I Heard It Through The Grapevine' in 1967, and scored their biggest hit in 1972 with 'Help Me Make It Through The Night'. The group became part of the Motown talent drain the following year, when they signed for Buddah and made the extraordinary 'Midnight Train To Georgia', which showcased one of the toughest and most expressive voices in soul history.

'If you got the feeling, you can sing soul. You just sing from the heart.'

Otis Redding

The first solo sweet soul superstar arrived when Teddy Pendergrass, gravel-voiced lead singer of Melvin's Blue Notes, went solo in 1976. His definitive take on boudoir soul seduction produced a string of US hit albums before a car crash in 1982 paralyzed him from the neck down. Undaunted, Pendergrass continued to record throughout the 1980s. An even more tragic story concerns critically acclaimed Chicago vocalist Donny Hathaway. His virtuoso blends of soul balladry, subtle jazz and Latin grooves brought admiration but little commercial impact, aside from hit duets with former classmate Roberta Flack. In 1979 he fell to his death: a suicide brought about by depression over his faltering career.

Roberta Flack and Donny Hathaway studied music together at Howard University. In 1973 she recorded his track 'Killing Me Softly'. It was a huge success and spent five weeks at the top of the charts.

Soul Stars

In the early 1970s, Marvin Gaye made his break from Motown's formula-pop and made music that stands among the greatest in any genre, defining soul's conscience on 1971's *What's Going On* and soul's sensuality on 1973's *Let's Get It On*. After a bitter break from Motown, Gaye returned in 1982 with the extraordinary *Midnight Love*, featuring a single, 'Sexual Healing', that proved that deep soul and new technology could co-exist perfectly.

As disco and its beat-led offshoots dominated, it became obvious that the soul alternative lay in producing a new kind of sweet soul for an adult audience. Cue chubby New Yorker Luther Vandross, who began his career as a session singer before taking centre stage by blending a voice like melting chocolate shot with synthetic backdrops constructed by jazz bassist Marcus Miller. It was masochistic romantic yearning all the way for Luther, hitting heights on 1986's *Give Me The Reason*. The same year saw jazzy soul siren Anita Baker seduce the world with the smoky sensuality of her *Rapture* album, which took adult soul into a level of sophistication.

Key Artists

Anita Baker
Marvin Gaye
Donny Hathaway
Teddy Pendergrass
Luther Vandross

Flip back to the turn of the 1980s, and a Minneapolis prodigy called Prince Rogers Nelson. His backing band, the Time, includes Jimmy Jam and Terry Lewis, who eventually left Prince and became writer/producers. While their former leader was effortlessly mixing soul with funk, rock, jazz and pop Jam and Lewis opened their Flyte Tyme studios and explored ways to fit soul and gospel with electro-funk. The funky and soulful 1980s hits they went on to create for Janet Jackson, The S.O.S Band, Alexander O'Neal, Change and others built a bridge between the funk era and the swingbeat/R&B future.

Two new black British acts also sought ways to blend electro with soul melodicism. Carl McIntosh's Loose Ends fused 'Sexual Healing'-type synthetic soul with a tougher hip hop feel, hitting a commercial peak with 'Hangin' On A String' in 1985. This proved to be the harbinger of a sound that will be forever associated with loved-up London at the turn of the 1990s. Jazzie B and his Soul II Soul collective took the Loose Ends sound and doubled it, adding deep hip hop beats, bittersweet optimism and a sense of space borrowed from dub reggae. The 1989 hits 'Keep On Movin' ' and 'Back To Life' effectively reminded America what it was missing by rejecting soul, and inspired R&B's self-consciously retro cousin, nu soul.

A seminal album of the era, What's Going On *addresses many political issues troubling America at the time, and captures the frustration and concern felt by Marvin Gaye and many of his fellow countrymen.*

Contemporary R&B

Although contemporary R&B prefers to align itself with hip hop, the roots of its mainstream practitioners lie firmly in manufactured pop. In a throwback to the Motown era, R&B has become a global phenomenon by combining a producer-led factory formula with a high level of musical innovation.

When Boston boy band New Edition sacked their mentor Maurice Starr in 1984, their subsequent move into a tougher, funkier, hip hop-informed blend of dance pop and balladry set the contemporary R&B train in motion. When Bobby Brown quit the group in 1986 they simply hired replacement Johnny Gill and continued to impress. By 1989, Brown had become the new sound's first superstar and the rest of the band had split. While Gill and Ralph Tresvant enjoyed successful solo careers, Michael Bivins, Ricky Bell and Ronnie Devoe formed Bell Biv Devoe, manufacturing themselves toward further success. Bivins also discovered vocal group Boyz II Men, and the R&B era was brought into being by hugely successful male vocal groups with the above, Jodeci, R. Kelly and Public Announcement all treading a line between graphic teen girl seduction, hip hop attitude and musical sophistication.

The key producer/composer in this wave was Teddy Riley, who coined the term 'New Jack Swing' in an infectious anthem for hip hop crew Wreckx-N-Effect. His melanges of synthetic soul, pop, rap and P-Funk for the likes of Guy and Heavy D made swingbeat a household term.

'It's her aura, her whole personality, her music as well, it definitely touches your heart.'

Romeo of So Solid Crew on Ms Dynamite

But any universal black pop sound needs equal female input to thrive. Enter producers Denzil Foster and Thomas McElroy, who, at the end of the 1980s, put together a girl group who could challenge swing's growing appeal. En Vogue were stylish, sassy and sang with gospel-derived maturity. Pundits played with the term 'New Jill Swing', as equally feisty girl groups such as SWV and TLC began to emerge. All this changed when New Yorker Mary J. Blige teamed up with on-the-make producer Sean 'Puffy' Combs. Combs labelled Blige's debut *What's The 411?* album 'hip hop soul', and Blige's strident vocals and 'ghetto fabulous' style sold millions. Combs, of course, went on to rename himself Puff Daddy and P. Diddy and become the embodiment of the obscenely rich, constantly bragging ghetto superstar.

The ambitious Sean Combs quickly made a name for himself in the music industry and formed his own record label, aptly named Bad Boy. He has courted controversy throughout his career; most famously through his feud with Death Row records.

The New Bohemians

Every cultural action provokes a reaction, and so it was with 1990s R&B. To balance the extravagant, cash-flaunting excesses of the R&B mainstream, a set of artists emerged touting a less style-conscious, more bohemian and organic form of black music. The likes of Maxwell, Ben Harper, Macy Gray, Angie Stone, India Arie and former Fugee Lauryn Hill have all made key records in this vein. But the two crucial artists in what is often termed nu soul are both singular talents from America's southern states.

D'Angelo (originally Michael Archer) from Richmond, Virginia grabbed immediate acclaim with his 1995 debut album *Brown Sugar*, which blended hip hop beats and attitude, classic soul melodies and textures, jazzy technique, and vocals reminiscent of both Al Green and Marvin Gaye. The follow-up in 2000, *Voodoo*, was even more extraordinary, updating the dark, rambling jam feel of Sly & the Family Stone's seminal *There's A Riot Goin' On*.

The female version emerged in 1997 from Atlanta, Georgia. Erykah Badu's debut, *Baduizm*, was both sexual and spiritual, a sparse soundscape of low-tempo funk rhythms, jazzy songcraft and Ms. Badu's smoky, Billie Holiday-esque voice singing lyrics soaked in love, religion and politics. Again, the visual anti-image was strong – shawls and bare legs, headscarf atop a striking, almost regal face. In 2000, *Mama's Gun* added rock to the mix with less success, but she'll undoubtedly return with something equal to that classic first set.

Key Artists

New Edition
Bobby Drown
Mary J. Blige
Ms Dynamite
Guy

The new century sees vocal trio Destiny's Child firmly established as brand leaders in R&B's rise to global popularity, with Beyoncé Knowles & co. fusing sex, money, feminism, vocal virtuosity, cutting-edge production and pure pop fizz into a seamless and irresistible whole. Credible British R&B stars have finally arrived, with Craig David and Ms Dynamite bringing in influences from UK garage and Jamaican reggae respectively. The team of Missy Elliott and Tim 'Timbaland' Mosley continue to mix R&B and rap so thrillingly that it is increasingly difficult to tell where hip hop begins and R&B ends. But, despite the impact of all the artists mentioned, R&B remains a producers' medium, its sound shaped by the likes of Teddy Riley, LA & Babyface, Rodney Jerkins, P. Diddy, Timbaland and the Neptunes, who all have a loyal following regardless of who fronts the video.

With a unique, growling voice and campy 1970s fashion style, Macy Gray has become renowned for her individual, funky sound and stage performances.

BIOGRAPHIES

Foreword: **John Scofield**

John Scofield is considered one of the 'big three' of current jazz guitarists. The possessor of a very distinctive sound and stylistic diversity, Scofield is a masterful jazz improviser whose music generally falls somewhere between post-bop, funk-edged jazz and R&B. He attended Berklee College of Music in Boston. After a debut recording with Gerry Mulligan and Chet Baker, Scofield was a member of the Billy Cobham-George Duke band for two years. In 1977 he recorded with Charles Mingus, and joined the Gary Burton quartet. He began his international career as a bandleader and recording artist in 1978. From 1982–85 Scofield toured and recorded with Miles Davis. His Davis stint placed him firmly in the foreground of jazz consciousness as a player and composer. Since that time he has prominently led his own groups in the international jazz scene and recorded over 30 albums. He is an Adjunct Professor of Music at New York University, a husband and a father of two.

General Editor: **Julia Rolf**

Julia Rolf developed a love of jazz at a young age after hearing Robert Parker's BBC Radio 3 series *Jazz Classics in Digital Stereo*, and has retained a particular interest in the New Orleans and Chicago jazz of the pre-Swing Era. She has worked as an author and editor on a wide range of music books, with an emphasis on jazz and blues titles. Her recent projects include *Bob Dylan: Highway 61 Revisited* and *The Rolling Stones: Beggars Banquet*, both from Flame Tree Publishing's Legendary Sessions series, and *Blues: The Complete Story*.

Authors

Bob Allen (Influences: Country)

Bob Allen is a country music journalist, historian and critic. He is former Nashville editor for, and has been a regular contributor to, *Country Music Magazine*, since 1977. His writing on country music has appeared in *Esquire*, *Rolling Stone*, the *Washington Post*, the *Atlanta Journal*, and the *Baltimore Sun*. Allen is the author of *The Life and Times of a Honky Tonk Legend*, the (unauthorized) biography of singer George Jones, and he has contributed to various historical and reference books on country music in recent years. He resides in Eldersburg, Maryland.

Lloyd Bradley (Influences: Reggae)

Lloyd Bradley toured the USA as a member of ParliamentFunkadelic. As a teenager he was sucked into the nether world of north London sound systems. For the last 20 years he has written about music for *Mojo*, *Q*, the *Guardian*, *NME* and *Blender*, amongst others. He is the author of *Bass Culture: When Reggae was King*, *Reggae: The Story of Jamaican Music* and was associate producer of the BBC2 series of the same name.

Keith Briggs (Influences: Gospel)

Since 1983 Keith Briggs has been the reviews editor of the magazine *Blues and Rhythm: The Gospel Truth*. He has also contributed articles to this and other specialist publications as well as compiling and/or writing the notes for several hundred CDs.

Leila Cobo (Styles: Latin Jazz)

A native of Colombia, Leila Cobo is *Billboard* magazine's Latin/Caribbean bureau chief, and the first woman to hold that post for the magazine. Ms Cobo is considered one of the leading experts in Latin music in the country and is regularly interviewed and consulted by outlets such as CNN, VH1, the BBC, Reuters, the *Los Angeles Times*, the *Washington Post* and *USA Today*.

Cliff Douse (Styles: Hard Bop to Smooth Jazz)

Cliff Douse has written hundreds of articles and columns during the past 10 years for many of the UK's foremost music and computer magazines including *Guitarist*, *Guitar Techniques*, *Total Guitar*, *Computer Music*, *Future Music*, *Rhythm* and *Mac Format*. He is also the author and co-author of several music books published by *IMP*, *Music Sales*, *Music Maker* and *Thunder Bay*. He is currently the editor of *Guitarist Icons* magazine (a quarterly special issue of *Guitarist* magazine) and is working on a number of new books and music software projects.

James Hale (The Seventies)

Based in Ottawa, Canada, James Hale is a feature writer, Critics Poll jury member and a frequent CD reviewer for *Down Beat*. He is also a frequent feature and review contributor to *Coda*, *Planet Jazz* and the *Ottawa Citizen*, and his work has appeared in *Jazziz*, *Pulse!*, *The Jazz Report*, *Modern Drummer*, *Words & Music* and *RhythmMusic*. In 2002 and 2003, he was nominated for a Canadian National Jazz Award as Best Journalist. A member of the Jazz Journalists Association, Hale is managing editor of the organization's website – Jazzhouse.org – and associate editor of their newsletter, *JazzNotes*.

Todd Jenkins (The Sixties)

Todd S. Jenkins is a contributor to *Down Beat*, *All About Jazz*, *Signal To Noise*, the *ZydE-Zine* and *Route 66* magazines. He is the author of *Free Jazz and Free Improvisation: An Encyclopedia* (Greenwood Press), *Eclipse: The Music of Charles Mingus* (Praeger), and an upcoming biography of pianist Jimmy Rowles. A resident of San Bernardino, California, Todd is a member of the American Jazz Symposium and the Jazz Journalists Association.

Howard Mandel (The Contemporary Era)

Howard Mandel is a writer and editor specializing in jazz, blues, new and unusual music. Born in Chicago, now living in New York City, he is a senior contributor to *Down Beat*, produces arts features for National Public Radio, teaches at New York University, is president of the Jazz Journalists Association and edits its website www.Jazzhouse.org. Mandel's *Future Jazz* (Oxford University Press, 1999) ranges from the AACM to John Zorn; he has written for *Musical America*, *The Wire* (UK), *Swing Journal* (Tokyo), *Bravo* (Rio de Janeiro), and many other periodicals.

Kenny Mathieson (The Forties; The Fifties)
Kenny Mathieson lives and works in Strathspey, Scotland. He studied American and English Literature at the University of East Anglia. He has been a freelance writer on various arts-related subjects since 1982, specializing in music, primarily jazz, classical and folk. He contributes to the *Herald*, the *Scotsman*, the *List*, *The Times Educational Supplement Scotland*, *Jazzwise* and other publications. He has contributed to a variety of reference books. He is the author of two books on jazz, *Giant Steps* and *Cookin'* (both Canongate), and edited and co-wrote *Celtic Music – A Listener's Guide* (BackbeatUK). He writes on arts for the *Inverness Courier*, and is the commissioning editor for the HI-Arts online arts journal (www.hi-arts.co.uk).

John McDonough (The Thirties)
John McDonough has been critic and contributing editor at *Down Beat* since 1968, and a contributor on jazz and other cultural topics to the *Wall Street Journal* since 1986. A three-time Grammy nominee for Best Album Notes, he has written biographies on Lester Young, Pee Wee Russell and Coleman Hawkins for Time-Life Books as well as the book accompanying the Grammy winning *The Complete Ella Fitzgerald Song Books* on Verve. McDonough is also editor of *The Encyclopedia of Advertising* (2003) and a long-time contributor to *Advertising Age* and National Public Radio, for which he writes and produces historical pieces in partnership with former CBS anchor Walter Cronkite. He lives near Chicago with his wife and son.

Bill Milkowski (Introduction; The Twenties; The Eighties; Styles: Ragtime to Cool Jazz, Brazilian Jazz; Influences: Blues)
Bill Milkowski is a regular contributor to *Jazz Times*, *Jazziz*, *Bass Player*, *Modern Drummer*, *Guitar Club* (Italy) and *Jazzthing* (Germany) magazines. He was named the Jazz Journalists Association's Writer of the Year for 2004. He is also the author of *JACO: The Extraordinary Life of Jaco Pastorius* (Backbeat Books*)*, *Rockers, Jazzbos & Visionaries* (Billboard Books) *and Swing It! An Annotated History of Jive* (Billboard Books).

Garry Mulholland (Influences: Soul and R&B)
Garry Mulholland is a music writer based in London, and has contributed features and interviews on pop, rock, dance and black music to *NME*, *Select*, the *Guardian*, *The Sunday Times*, the *Independent* and *Time Out*. His first book *This is Uncool: The 500 Greatest Singles Since Punk and Disco* was published by Cassell Illustrated in 2002.

Steve Nallon (Influences: Musicals)
Steve Nallon is a writer, broadcaster, performer and theatre director. His work on musical theatre includes contributions to the magazine *Musical Stages*, the BBC series *Soul Music* and the book for the musical *Like Love*. He is also a contributor to the *New Statesman* and *Screenwriter*. Steve has been a visiting lecturer at the department of Drama and Theatre Arts at the University of Birmingham since 1995, notably in the Broadway musical, Greek theatre, stand-up comedy, screenwriting and film studies. As a theatre director Steve specializes in new writing.

Douglas J. Noble (Influences: Rock)
Douglas J. Noble is a musician, guitar instructor and freelance music journalist based in Edinburgh. He has written books on Jimi Hendrix and Peter Green as well as a guitar tuition book – *The Right Way to Play Guitar* – and has contributed to several books on the electric guitar. He is the music director of *UniVibes*, the international Jimi Hendrix magazine, and is an examiner for Rock School/Trinity College of Music. He has contributed to over a dozen music magazines, interviewed many of the world's top guitarists and is the tablature editor for the *Guitar Magazine*.

Ed Potton (Influences: Soundtracks and Theatre; Popular and Novelty)
Ed Potton works as a writer and editor. A regular contributor of articles on music, film and literature to *The Times*, he has also written for *Elle*, the *Independent on Sunday*, *Muzik* and the BBC, and is co-author of *Into the Woods: the Definitive Story of the Blair Witch Project*. He has been an associate producer for Channel 4 television and a broadcast journalist for BBC radio. He has lectured at the University of Bournemouth and the Chelsea College of Art. Travel, Billy Wilder films and Stevie Wonder's *Songs In The Key Of Life* are among his favourite things. He lives in London.

William Schafer (The Roots; The Teens)
Since gaining a PhD at the University of Minnesota, William Schafer has worked as editor and publications designer for the military and USDA, and taught at Berea College, Kentucky, where he is chair of the English department and head of the humanities program. His many publications include *The Art of Ragtime* (with Johannes Reidel, LSU Press), *Rock Music* (Augsburg Press), *Brass Bands and New Orleans Jazz* (LSU Press) and *Mapping the Godzone* (University of Hawaii Press). William has also contributed to *Contemporary Novelists* (St Martin's Press), *Contemporary Short Stories* (St Martin's Press), *The Encyclopedia of Southern Culture* (University of North Carolina Press) and Grove's dictionaries of American Music and Jazz. He is also a contributing editor of *Mississippi Rag*.

PICTURE CREDITS

Corbis: Jeff Albertson: 155

Lauren Deutsch: 304–5

Mary Evans Picture Library: 17

Foundry Arts: 153; 213; 391; 429; 459; 499; 515

Kobal Collection Ltd: Dispatfilm/Gemma/Tupan: 455

London Features International: 497

Sylvia Pitcher Photo Library
Weston Collection: 23; 45; 381

Redferns Music Picture Library
49; 76; 78–9; 85; 175; 308–9; 421; Bob Baker: 423; Glenn A. Baker Archives: 377; 471; 501; BBC Photo Library: 81; Dave Bennett: 60; Paul Bergen: 259; 341; 367; 445; Keith Bernstein: 319; Pete Cronin: 331; Frank Debaeker: 417; Deltahaze Corporation: 33; 39; 43; 99; 101; Colin Fuller: 243; GAB Archives: 83; GEMS: 335; William Gottleib: 47; 91; 123; 143; 149; 151; 165; 397; 405; 451; William Gottleib/Library of Congress: 55; 170–1; 223(b); Olivia Hemingway: 437; Leonard Herman: 125; 145; 173; 187; 189; 201; 203; 205; 207; 233; Paul Hoeffler: 177; 245; 251; 281; 293; JM International: 517; 519; Max Jones Files: 13; 15; 35; 41; 51; 61; 64; 74–5; 87; 93; 103; 111; 114; 128–9; 141; 214; 383; 387; 389; 393; 399; 457; Elliott Landy: 255; Andrew Lepley: 285; 291; 297; 301; 315; 317; 337; 343; 345; 353; 355; 357; 371; 419; Library of Congress: 21; Marc Marnie: 279; Leon Morris: 303; 503; Michael Ochs Archives: 19; 25; 66–7; 69; 72; 95; 105; 109; 116–7; 119; 130; 131; 135; 139; 147; 157; 163; 178; 181; 185; 191; 193; 195; 197; 211; 216–7; 224–5; 226; 228–9; 231; 235; 237; 241; 249; 264; 268; 270–1; 328–9; 375; 379; 409; 411; 461; 463; 467; 473; 475; 487; 489; 505; 513; David Redfern: 29; 199; 219; 220; 239; 253; 263; 273; 275; 277; 287; 289; 295; 299; 306; 311; 313; 321; 332; 351; 359; 361; 365; 373; 395; 403; 413; 415; 425; 427; 431; 441; 443; 453; 507; David Redfern/USA Post Office: 223(t); Adam Ritchie: 266–7; Ebet Roberts: 326; Rico D'Rozario: 449; Ron Scherl: 27; Philippe Schneider: 447; Nicky J. Sims: 439; Chuck Stewart: 247; 261; Colin Streater: 435; Gai Terrell: 257; 283; Toby Wates: 433; Bob Willoughby: 126; 159; 323; 339; 363; 401

Tony Russell: 465

S.I.N.
David Corio: 483; 509; Anna Meuer: 511

Topham Picturepoint
31; 37; 53; 57; 59; 62–3; 68; 70–1; 89; 97; 107; 115; 120; 132–3; 161; 167; 169; 265; 274; 385; 407; 469; 477; 479; 481; 485; 491; 495; Arena PAL: 182; 209; 227; 325; 369; Jeff Greenberg/The Image Works: 113; The Image Works: 349; Robert Millard/PAL: 493; Michael Schwarz/The Image Works: 347

FURTHER READING

Appel, A., *Jazz Modernism*, Alfred A. Knopf, 2002

Badger, R., *A Life in Ragtime: A Biography of James Reese Europe*, American Philological Association, 1995

Balliett, W., *Jelly Roll, Jabbo and Fats*, Oxford University Press, 1983

Berger, M. and E. and Patrick, J., *Benny Carter, A Life in American Music*, Scarecrow Press, 1982

Blesh, R. and Janis, H., *They All Played Ragtime*, Schirmer, 1974

Brunn, H.O., *The Story of the Original Dixieland Jazz Band*, Louisiana State University Press, 1960

Carr, I., *Miles Davis: The Definitive Biography*, HarperCollins, 1998

Catalano, N., *Clifford Brown: The Life and Art of the Legendary Jazz Trumpeter*, Oxford University Press, 2000

Charters, S.B. and Kunstadt, L., *Jazz: A History of the New York Scene*, Da Capo Press, 1981

Chilton, J., *Sidney Bechet: Wizard of Jazz*, Da Capo Press, 1996

Crease, S.S., *Gil Evans: Out of the Cool*, A Cappella, 2002

Davis, F., *Bebop and Nothingness: Jazz and Pop at the End of the Century*, Schirmer Books, 1996

Deffaa, C., *Traditionalists and Revivalists in Jazz*, Scarecrow Press, 1993

DeVeaux, S., *The Birth of Bebop: A Social and Musical History*, University of California Press, 1997

Ekkehard, J., *Free Jazz*, Da Capo Press, 1981

Firestone, R., *Swing Swing Swing: The Life and Times of Benny Goodman*, W.W. Norton and Co., 1993

Gavin, J., *Deep in a Dream: The Long Night of Chet Baker*, Chatto and Windus, 2002

Gelly, D. (ed), *Masters of Jazz Saxophone*, Balafon Books, 2000

Giddins, G., *Celebrating Bird: The Triumph of Charlie Parker*, Beechtree Books, 1987

Giddins, G., *Visions of Jazz: The First Century*, Oxford University Press, 1998

Gillespie, D. and Fraser, A., *Dizzy: To Be or Not To Bop*, Doubleday, 1979

Gitler, I., *Jazz Masters of the 40s*, Macmillan Press, 1966

Goldberg, J., *Jazz Masters of the 50s*, Macmillan Press, 1965

Gourse, L., *Straight, No Chaser: The Life and Genius of Thelonious Monk*, Schirmer Books, 1997

Jenkins, T.S., *Free Jazz and Free Improvisation: An Encyclopedia*, Greenwood Press, 2004

Kahn, A., *Kind of Blue: The Making of the Miles Davis Masterpiece*, Da Capo Press, 2000

Keepnews, O., *The View From Within: Jazz Writings, 1948–1987*, Oxford University Press, 1987

Kirchner, B. (ed.), *The Oxford Companion to Jazz*, Oxford University Press, 2000

Lees, G., *Leader of the Band: The Life of Woody Herman*, Oxford University Press, 1995

Levinson, P., *Trumpet Blues: The Life of Harry James*, Oxford University Press, 1999

Lincoln Collier, J., *The Making of Jazz: A Comprehensive History*, Houghton Mifflin Company, Boston, 1978

Litweiler, J., *The Freedom Principle: Jazz After 1958*, William Morrow and Co., 1984

Lyons, L., *The 101 Best Jazz Albums*, William Morrow, 1980

Maggin, D., *Stan Getz: A Life in Jazz*, William Morrow, 1996

Mandel, H., *Future Jazz*, Oxford University Press, 1999

Mathieson, K., *Cookin': Hard Bop and Soul Jazz, 1954–65*, Canongate, 2002

Milkowski, B., *Rockers, Jazzbos and Visionaries*, Billboard Books, 1998

Nicholson, S., *Billie Holiday*, Gollancz, 1995

Nicholson, S., *Jazz-Rock: A History*, Schirmer Books, 1998

Nisenson, E., *Open Sky: Sonny Rollins and His World of Improvisation*, St Martin's Press, 2000

Owens, T., *Bebop: The Music and Its Players*, Oxford University Press, 1995

Porter, L., *John Coltrane: His Life and Music*, University of Michigan Press, 1998

Reich, H. and Gaines, W., *Jelly's Blues*, Da Capo Press, 2003

Roberts, J.S., *The Latin Tinge*, Oxford University Press, 1998

Rosenthal, D., *Hard Bop: Jazz and Black Music, 1955–1965*, Oxford University Press, 1992

Russell, R., *Bird Lives!*, Charterhouse, 1972

Santoro, G., *Highway 61 Revisited: The Tangled Roots of American Jazz, Blues, Rock and Country Music*, Oxford University Press, 2004

Santoro, G., *Myself When I Am Real: The Life and Music of Charles Mingus*, Oxford University Press, 2000

Schafer, W.J. and Reidel, J., *The Art of Ragtime*, Louisiana State University Press, 1973

Schuller, G., *Early Jazz*, Oxford University Press, 1986

Schuller, G., *The Swing Era*, Oxford University Press, 1989

Shipton, A., *Groovin' High: The Life of Dizzy Gillespie*, Oxford University Press, 1999

Stowe, D.W., *Swing Changes: Big Band Jazz in New Deal America*, Harvard University Press, 1994

Sudhalter, R.M., *Lost Chords: White Musicians and Their Contributions to Jazz, 1915–1945*, Oxford University Press, 1999

Szwed, J., *Jazz 101: A Complete Guide to Learning and Loving Jazz*, Hyperion, 1999

Tingen, P., *Miles Beyond: The Electric Explorations of Miles Davis, 1967–1991*, Billboard Books, 2001

Waller, M. and Calabrese, A., *Fats Waller*, Schirmer Books, 1997

Woideck, C., *Charlie Parker: His Music and Life*, University of Michigan Press, 1996

Zorn, J. (ed.), *Arcana: Musicians on Music*, Granary Books, 2000

INDEX

Page references in **bold** indicate main articles;
page references in *italics* indicate illustrations.
Page references collated with a hyphen ignore
intervening illustrations.